Binge
Times

Binge Times

Inside Hollywood's
Furious Billion-Dollar Battle
to Take Down Netflix

Dade Hayes and Dawn Chmielewski

WM

WILLIAM MORROW
An Imprint of HarperCollins*Publishers*

BINGE TIMES. Copyright © 2022 by Dade Hayes and Dawn Chmielewski. All rights reserved. Printed in the United States of America. No part of this book may be used or reproduced in any manner whatsoever without written permission except in the case of brief quotations embodied in critical articles and reviews. For information, address HarperCollins Publishers, 195 Broadway, New York, NY 10007.

HarperCollins books may be purchased for educational, business, or sales promotional use. For information, please email the Special Markets Department at SPsales@harpercollins.com.

FIRST EDITION

Designed by Nancy Singer

Library of Congress Cataloging-in-Publication Data has been applied for.

ISBN 978-0-06-298000-7

22 23 24 25 26   LSC   10 9 8 7 6 5 4 3 2 1

DH

To Stella, Margot, and Finley (my core demo), with all my love

DC

To my A-list: Dan, Alex, and Maddie

► Contents

▶ Streamatis Personae

Amazon

Jeff Bezos, founder and executive chairman, former CEO

Andy Jassy, CEO

Mike Hopkins, senior vice president, Prime
Video and Amazon Studios

Jennifer Salke, head of Amazon Studios

Albert Cheng, chief operating officer, co-head of television

Roy Price, former head of global video content and Amazon Studios

Bob Berney, former head of marketing and
distribution, Amazon Studios

Apple

Steve Jobs, late cofounder and CEO

Tim Cook, CEO

Zack Van Amburg, co-head of Apple TV+

Jamie Erlicht, co-head of Apple TV+

Eddy Cue, senior vice president, internet software and services

AT&T/WarnerMedia

Randall Stephenson, former CEO, AT&T

John Stankey, CEO, AT&T; former CEO, WarnerMedia

Jason Kilar, CEO, WarnerMedia

Andy Forssell, executive vice president and general
    manager, WarnerMedia direct-to-consumer

Bob Greenblatt, former chairman, WarnerMedia

Kevin Reilly, former chief content officer, HBO Max

Jeremy Legg, former chief technology officer, WarnerMedia

Richard Plepler, former chairman and CEO, HBO

Comcast/NBCUniversal

Brian Roberts, CEO, Comcast

Steve Burke, former CEO, NBCUniversal

Bonnie Hammer, vice chairman, NBCUniversal

Matt Strauss, chairman, direct-to-consumer and international

Jeff Shell, CEO, NBCUniversal

Netflix

Reed Hastings, cofounder, co-CEO

Marc Randolph, cofounder, former CEO

Ted Sarandos, co-CEO

Cindy Holland, former vice president, content
    acquisition and original series

Bela Bajaria, vice president, content

Scott Stuber, vice president, original films

Neil Hunt, former chief product officer

Patty McCord, former head of HR

Quibi

Jeffrey Katzenberg, founder

Meg Whitman, CEO

Roku

Anthony Wood, founder, CEO

Scott Rosenberg, senior vice president, platform business

The Walt Disney Co.

Michael Eisner, former chairman and CEO

Bob Iger, former CEO and executive chairman

Bob Chapek, CEO

Kareem Daniel, chairman, media and entertainment distribution

Tom Staggs, former chief operating officer

Kevin Mayer, former chairman, direct-to-consumer
   and international

Jimmy Pitaro, chairman, ESPN and sports content

John Skipper, former president, ESPN

Ricky Strauss, former president, content and marketing for Disney+

Albert Cheng, former chief product officer, digital
   media, Disney ABC Television Group

Anne Sweeney, former cochair, Disney Media Networks;
   former president, Disney ABC Television Group

▶ Preface

Variations on a single question pinged across social media, bobbing in a digital sea just as messages in physical bottles once were set adrift.

What are we supposed to do now?!

Society and popular culture were imitating a scene from the film *Inception*, folding inward on themselves, piece by piece, as fear of the spreading coronavirus reached its peak. Schools, courthouses, museums, sports venues, movie theaters, concert halls, restaurants, and bars all closed their doors. Travel bans and border shutdowns took effect. "Social distancing" prevailed, with hugs and high fives shunned and everyone instructed to stand six feet apart. Even the "Happiest Place on Earth," Disneyland, closed its gates to the public for just the fourth time since its 1955 debut. The previous three occasions, after a presidential assassination, a terrorist attack, and an earthquake, were single-day closures. This time, days without visitors stretched into months without an end in sight.

The U.S. followed Italy, China, South Korea, and other countries in forcing most of its population to hunker down for weeks and leave home only when it was necessary. There was no other term for it: this was quarantine. Derived from the Italian phrase *quaranta giorni*, translated as "forty days," quarantine began as a practice in the fourteenth century as Europe confronted a series of deadly plagues. A casualty rate comparable to the Black Death's had not yet accrued in this new pandemic, but people were contending with an invisible, inchoate threat that had upended daily life and unsettled the collective consciousness. What, those social media messages-in-bottles implored, would ever fill our yawning void?

Streaming, it turned out, was one of the few medically sound answers to that question. America, already accustomed to spending hours a day in a screen-filled cocoon, would respond to the crisis by serving itself more and bigger portions of comfort food. Traditional television initially saw the benefit of this response, with broadcast viewership in major cities spiking between 10 and 20 percent in a single week in mid-March as frustrated viewers tracked the contagion and its effects on financial markets and the 2020 election.

The momentary lift provided by the nation's news obsession didn't last—in fact, it exposed the threadbare nature of the viewing options available through traditional TV. Unless you were committed to constantly monitoring local or national news, there was little else to watch. With network programming disrupted by production shutdowns and the freeze on live events—everything from reality and awards shows to *Saturday Night Live* to sports contests—the pay-TV bundle felt more anachronous than ever. A sudden and intense economic recession, which followed a solid ten-year expansion, accelerated the trend of customers' cutting and shaving the cord. Thankfully for traditional cable operators, broadband internet access became more essential a commodity than Purell, and those profit margins remained fat.

Netflix, the leading global streaming service, had long been nagged by Wall Street and the press about when it would finally get in the "regular" TV game and start carrying live sports or news. Co-CEO Ted Sarandos was asked in 2018, when networks were setting ratings records with day-long coverage of the Senate confirmation hearings for Supreme Court justice Brett Kavanaugh, about Netflix's streaming such an event one day. "We're primarily embraced as an entertainment brand," he replied. "That kind of watching you're describing is a lot of things, but it's not terribly entertaining." Appointment viewing, daily programming schedules, advertising, a ninety-day interval between a film's run in theaters and its debut for home audiences—all of the staples of traditional TV and film—were anathema to Netflix. Its shunning of those customs and relentless focus on "delighting" customers had helped it reach a massive scale. This singular focus is something Netflix shares with another interloper, Amazon, which thought of movies and TV shows as a glittery lure to attract customers—much as banks once handed out free toasters for opening an account. "When we win a Golden Globe, it helps us sell more shoes," Amazon founder Jeff Bezos once said in a 2016 interview. "And it does that in a very direct way. Because if you look at Prime members, they buy more on Amazon than non-Prime members, and one of the reasons they do that is once they pay their annual fee, they're looking around to see, 'How can I get more value out of the program?'"

In quarantine, having access to thousands of shows and films on demand seemed like a not-insignificant consolation prize, something that still could inject a welcome element of familiarity into a disorienting time. But the intensity and duration of this binge-viewing period had no precedent. "I'm running out of things to watch being stuck at home," tweeted Jason Blum, producer of films like *Get Out*, *Us*, and the *Purge* franchise. "Any suggestions?" The post elicited more than 1,100 replies and lists were soon flying around the internet with the same ubiquity as recipes and pet pictures.

The pandemic did more than elevate streaming as an inextricable element of modern life. It seemed to almost inject all of us *into* the stream, like platelets flowing through blood in a massive vein. Government bodies convened and teachers delivered lessons online. Companies conducted business via Zoom, circulating advice and even sending equipment to employees. ("Turn on the camera," the *Wall Street Journal* chided its workers.) Houses of worship live-streamed services, christenings, b'nai mitzvahs, and funerals. Zoos and aquariums minted a succession of nonhuman video stars. Yo-Yo Ma played his cello and stand-up comedians delivered their sets to virtual crowds. The Metropolitan Opera streamed vintage performances, and a starry tribute to musical theater legend Stephen Sondheim's ninetieth birthday took on extra poignance because the performers originally slated to share a physical stage all appeared, isolated but joined, onscreen. "Take me to the world," its title entreated, and, for two blissful hours, the performers did.

TV networks featured on-air personalities and aesthetics heavily influenced by the online realm. Guests occupied murkily lit, Skype-like split screens as they weighed in on the news of the day from their home offices. Morning and late-night shows featured household names broadcasting from their living rooms, with nary a hair or makeup crew member in sight. Quarantine TV felt like one long group FaceTime call. *Le stream, c'était nous.* "If you don't like it," late-night host Conan O'Brien mordantly said of the diminished, home-produced version of his TBS late-night show, "there's always Netflix."

THE PANDEMIC HIT ABOUT HALFWAY through our work on this book, which began as a more straightforward look at a business phenomenon that was already rich with drama and consequence. Having spotted Netflix a ten-year head start, major rivals from the tech and startup realm (Apple, Quibi) and traditional media (Disney, WarnerMedia, NBCUniversal) had all decided to make splashy entries into streaming. At a cost of billions, each had targeted the same seven-month span, from November 2019 to May 2020, for their launches. Our aim was to document this unprecedented chase and try to understand how the industry had reached such a consequential juncture. Even though the larger story would resonate long into the future, the massive influx of new money was a singular event. Both of us had covered the competition from our respective front-row seats as daily journalists in New York and Los Angeles, getting inside the machinery of entertainment and technology. We never fully embraced the armchair metaphor that these were "the streaming wars." That rickety expression, inaccurate in its suggestion that there would be one winner and one loser, also became downright tacky with each invocation by doctors and government officials of wartime as a proper way of thinking about the fight against the deadly wages of COVID-19.

Watching and reporting on the strategies and maneuvers of all of the top media and tech entities gave rise to this book. It took root as the two of us collaborated in 2018 on daily (nigh hourly) business and technology stories for Deadline, the entertainment news outlet that originated as Nikki Finke's rule-breaking blog. Both of us had spent years covering Hollywood, Silicon Valley, and Wall Street in equal measure. We chronicled stories with far-reaching consequences, among them the emergence of the internet, boom and bust times interrupted by 9/11 and the global financial crisis, and the devastation of the Sony Pictures hack. But we had never experienced anything like the eruption of streaming, which was rewriting the rules of the entertainment business so quickly that it often gave our daily work an Etch A Sketch quality. Every day we would shake the slate clean and draw companies' new game plans. The volume and ambition were unprecedented. It was clear that we were living in Binge Times.

That sense of evanescence and the hyperaccelerated news cycle made a lot of people wonder how we would keep our account current or tell a story with a definitive ending. The digital transformation that we set out to chronicle, particularly during the seven-month span when new competitors arrived, only intensified once COVID-19 began to sweep across the globe. We resolved to do honor to critic Manny Farber's notion of "termite art," which he defined as a "buglike immersion." We burrowed inside the industrial machinery in an effort to understand its many interlocking components. In exploring the personalities, business motives, technologies, marketing, and financial patterns of this boom period—as well as key parts of the history leading up to it—we would have a chance to document an extraordinary moment. This sweeping, multibillion-dollar influx of streaming investment was a one-time event, and we wanted to gain a deeper understanding than our day-to-day scrambles allow.

To give the book a central narrative, we decided to focus on the five major new challengers to the streaming establishment, all of them with different personalities and corporate DNA. In a compressed period of months, Apple, Disney, HBO parent WarnerMedia, and NBCUniversal would all launch major new subscription streaming offerings. Those four companies had previously either shunned the direct-to-consumer video marketplace or participated in it only by licensing film and TV titles to others. The fifth new player was Quibi, a mobile-only streaming venture led by DreamWorks cofounder Jeffrey Katzenberg and former eBay and Hewlett-Packard chief Meg Whitman. It made its debut in this same seven-month span, powered by $1.75 billion in startup capital. In addition to these five newbies, we also decided to spend time with incumbents like Netflix, Amazon, and Hulu, as well as a number of other streaming stakeholders.

A series of events during a single month in the fall of 2019 vividly illustrated the redrawing of the entertainment map. At Lincoln Center, the New York Film Festival hosted the world premiere of Netflix's *The Irishman*, a big-budget feature film that heralded the streaming sector's upending of the century-old movie business. A month later at the same venue, Apple lifted the curtain on *The Morning Show*, one of the first original series produced for its new subscription streaming service, Apple TV+. The next day, on the Warner Bros. lot in Burbank, AT&T and WarnerMedia executives held an investor day for HBO Max. Also in Burbank, just a few days later (with an encore performance in New York), Disney executives met with the media to offer demos of and field questions about Disney+.

With all of the successive, overlapping action, our story began to take on the collagist feel of a Robert Altman film or a Picasso mural. It would not have one central protagonist or antagonist, but rather an ensemble cast of innovators, operators, dealmakers, and imitators. In trying to document the exploding world of streaming, we would be spotlighting a handful of consequential efforts but only gesture at the sprawling mosaic of streaming as a whole. One reliable estimate in 2019 pegged the number of pay streaming services in the U.S. at 271. Hundreds more free, ad-supported services have also proliferated thanks to internet-connected smart TVs that come with preinstalled streaming apps. Bruce Springsteen, having had his sold-out Broadway show reach a mass global audience via Netflix, was presumably not inclined to pen a sequel to his song about the cable TV wasteland, "57 Channels (And Nothin' On)." But one could easily envision it.

As the pandemic unfolded, the same question that nagged at us was the one that tormented the collective psyche of all cooped-up souls: *How can we possibly adjust to this?* Our story had taken a sharp and unforeseeable third-act turn. Trillions of dollars of corporate market value had been erased in just a few weeks as stock markets plunged. The financial outlook for the entire business world had changed overnight. Investors feared that the medically recommended cure—social distancing, the wheels of commerce forcibly slowed to a crawl—was ruinous to the balance sheet. As sectors like travel, transportation, and hospitality fought for their very survival, the task of marketing streaming platforms and acquiring customers hardly seemed essential.

And yet, the sheer ubiquity of streaming made it even more compelling than when we began. And each character in our drama had its own unique circumstances. For Apple, its nascent Apple TV+ effort was a fascinating venture for a host of reasons. Materially, it amounted to a rounding error, factoring little into the tech giant's weightier deliberations about supply chains and contagion protocols. Quibi, meanwhile, had managed to raise a boatload of initial funding. Its fundamental consumer premise—"quick-bite," short-form video on the go—suddenly seemed less viable with shelter-in-place orders in effect, though TikTok's weedlike surge proved that people stuck at home still want to watch videos on their phones.

Traditional media companies faced a more vexing conundrum. Their streaming services would still require intensive capital investments, in terms of both hiring and digital infrastructure, as well as a willingness to forgo millions in licensing revenue. Now, with the coronavirus established as a long-term challenge, they would have to remain committed to disrupting themselves despite the devastating loss of revenue from movie box offices, TV advertising, sports, and theme parks.

Would streaming be their route to redemption or just a mirage given the high bar set by Netflix and Amazon?

One way to respond would be to deviate from business practices that had guided them for nearly a century, loosening the shackles that made it tougher to compete with Big Tech. NBCUniversal made the first move in that direction. Citing the closure of most U.S. movie theaters, it announced that a handful of its 2020 film releases would be made available at home (including streaming) simultaneously with their abbreviated theatrical runs. The longtime agreement between studios and exhibitors was to honor a roughly ninety-day exclusive period for a film's theatrical run—which industry insiders refer to as the "window" of initial release. "That sound you just heard," observed veteran film distribution executive Steven Friedlander, "is the theatrical windows shattering." Disney and WarnerMedia followed with their own movie experiments, a tantalizing stimulus plan given the number of stir-crazy viewers endlessly searching for something new to watch and the need to keep pace with Netflix. Having initially disrupted television, the streaming leader was now putting its shoulder into reshaping the movie business, hustling a range of films, from modestly budgeted festival darlings to $200 million blockbusters, onto its platform after a cameo appearance in theaters.

Not unlike walking around COVID-altered neighborhoods, where everything seemed recognizable and yet unmistakably *off*, experiencing so much sped-up change never stopped feeling slightly surreal. We found alternate ways to connect with the people navigating the ever-evolving landscape. We attended virtual premieres and online trade shows and conducted scores of interviews via videoconference. It was several steps beyond meta, but it also didn't feel entirely temporary.

In the eerie, restless mood of the moment, a favorite short story— "By the Waters of Babylon" by Stephen Vincent Benét—offered some welcome perspective. The story resonated in a whole new way during our weeks in quarantine, a period we had largely spent thinking, talking, reading, and writing about streaming, with occasional breaks . . . to watch streaming services. The picture of the world outside that we gleaned from our screens had a postapocalyptic feel. Freeways, city centers, and airports were almost completely devoid of people. Fish swam in Venice's revitalized canals as nature reclaimed its place in a long-polluted ecosystem and gondolas went into dry dock. Institutions and traditions had never felt less secure—cafés, handshakes, television. Benét's story describes a landscape in which a nameless tribesman uncovers evidence of a human society destroyed by its own hubris and devotion to technology. Walking through the ruins of Washington, D.C., he describes salvaging pieces of metal from "Dead Places," as the structures decimated by the long-ago Great Burning are known. The tribesman resolves to try to learn and preserve the folkways of the lost civilization. "It is not for the metal alone we go to the Dead Places now—there are the books and the writings," he says. "They are hard to learn. And the magic tools are broken—but we can look at them and wonder. At least, we make a beginning."

Benét wrote the story in 1937 as a meditation on fascists' destruction of the Basque town of Guernica during the Spanish Civil War. Nuclear weapons were not yet a reality, but years of Depression anxiety had taken a toll on the national psyche in between world wars. Streaming would never be this kind of life-or-death matter, of course. But it is nevertheless a profound experience to stand at an existential crossroads, watching long-established customs and models crumble into dust. We had spent years looking at the entertainment world's magic tools, modern civilization's newest artifacts, and wondering what new order would emerge. "Perhaps, in the old days," Benét's narrator warns, "they ate knowledge too fast."

Binge Times

▶ The Reckoning

The sardonic, British-accented voice on the PA system at Radio City Music Hall signaled that this night in New York City would be anything but routine. "Welcome," it declared, "to the beginning of the end."

This world premiere of the final season of fantasy TV series *Game of Thrones* would indeed mark a terminus both literal and symbolic. It would be a send-off to the most-watched show in the forty-seven-year history of the prestige storytelling trailblazer known as HBO. (Viewership over the last run of episodes peaked at 19.3 million, 13.6 million of that on linear TV.) On a deeper level, it would punctuate the contraction of a longtime fixture of the entertainment business. For decades, HBO had been in the vanguard of television's rise to power as a cultural force. It developed TV shows like the Medicis fostered works of art. Now this singular network, this long-invincible hypnotist of the cognoscenti, suddenly found itself under new ownership and beset on every front by streaming rivals and internal strife. That backstory imbued the premiere night's atmosphere with far more angst and uneasiness than the exaltation and elegy of most official send-offs.

Because Radio City seats five thousand people, not everyone in the large crowd was preoccupied by palace intrigue; some instead vibrated pure fan excitement as they waited for the big screen to light up. They had scored one of the toughest tickets in the epicenter of media, filing past a twenty-five-foot-tall promotional throne erected at the center of

Rockefeller Plaza and into the Art Deco auditorium known for hosting the Tony Awards and annual Rockette holiday shows. This was the same venue where HBO's creation *The Sopranos* had swaggered onto the scene in the midst of its glorious run in the 2000s. It was also the place where Hollywood classics like *The Godfather* screened for the first time.

As the countdown to showtime proceeded, even buttoned-down business types in the crowd had trouble containing their glee. "Dragons!!" a gray-suited man hollered as the lights finally went down, presumably savoring a respite from his daily diet of Excel spreadsheets. Dragons—the impressively computer-animated mascots of *Thrones*—were indeed about to be unleashed on this crisp and moonlit night, and for the hour they flew across the one-hundred-foot screen, all would seem copacetic in House HBO.

Of the five thousand in attendance, though, two thousand were HBO employees, and they could tell something was out of sync as soon as the night began. There were flashes of the old Radio City magic—an organist playing live, illuminated by a spotlight, as stars and celebrity *Thrones* fans like Dave Chappelle, Michelle Wolf, and Keegan-Michael Key settled in. But the absence of one person from the limelight could not be overlooked. Richard Plepler, the silver-tongued, perma-tanned executive who had led HBO's image machine as its PR man in the 1990s before climbing to the top job in the 2000s, got multiple mentions during introductory onstage remarks before the screening. But he never took the stage during what was meant to be his moment of glory. All he could do was offer a brief wave and a smile from his seat. The bon vivant known for hosting elegant and starry dinners at his Upper East Side town house had convened an intimate cast-and-crew meal at an Italian restaurant on Central Park South the night before. On the official premiere night, therefore, he skipped the after-party, knowing it was apt to be a decidedly bittersweet affair.

Plepler, by the time of the premiere, had already packed his office and was about to leave the company after twenty-eight years, as HBO's new owner, AT&T, was beginning an epic restructuring process. The century-old telecommunications behemoth had acquired HBO's parent company, Time Warner, for $85 billion and was trying desperately to make the math work. An exodus of talent with collective centuries of experience at the network was well under way as AT&T labored to trim its $181 billion debt load—the largest of any nonbank corporation in America. Among many assets marked for extinction was HBO's longtime New York headquarters building overlooking Bryant Park, a fifteen-story midrise whose influence far exceeded its modest stature. The company, along with sister operations like CNN and Warner Bros., would soon move into a gleaming new home at Hudson Yards, the most ambitious commercial real estate project in New York since Rockefeller Center broke ground in the 1930s. The company's "supertall" skyscraper stands eighteen feet higher than the Empire State Building.

In the post-Plepler era, the guy in the room with the most juice was a fifty-seven-year-old Eagle Scout who grew up in Southern California, the youngest child of an insurance salesman and a housewife: John Stankey. Striding through the Radio City lobby without an entourage, the six-foot-five-inch Stankey attracted no notice but moved with purpose, as was his wont. Soon, his portfolio at AT&T would expand. He would become chief operating officer and presumed CEO-in-waiting at the sprawling organization with a market value of $280 billion. Stankey was a "Bell Head," as many AT&T lifers proudly refer to themselves, invoking the company's roots operating Bell telephone companies. WarnerMedia rank and file had nicknamed him the Cowboy, a nod to AT&T's Dallas base and Stankey's directness. He spoke in a bass-heavy, deliberately paced vocal tone that resembled a more straitlaced version of Patrick Warburton, who played Puddy on *Seinfeld*. Stankey brought a dispassionate, mathematician's sensibility to the executive suite, and even in Hollywood's eclectic annals he ranked high on the list of those least likely to run an entertainment enterprise. Asked to sum up Stankey in a single word, one prominent tech CEO thought for a moment and landed on "linear." He made liberal use of terms like "federated data" and "flywheel" and hardly endeared himself to the creative community by casually referring to the films and TV shows they made as "tonnage."

Stankey's mission was not only to redefine HBO and break down the silos that once made Time Warner a collection of largely autonomous nation-states, but also to take on his greatest nemesis on its own turf. Netflix had eclipsed HBO's cultural cachet, especially among young viewers, and had managed to equal HBO's total number of Emmy Awards in 2018. That was a once-unthinkable feat for a former DVD-by-mail business ridiculed as the "Albanian army" (as in, a force unlikely to pose a serious threat) by former Time Warner CEO Jeff Bewkes. Along with that line, the other oft-repeated maxim was originated by Netflix content chief Ted Sarandos, who said the streaming giant's mission was "to become HBO faster than HBO can become us." For many years, though, it was abundantly clear that HBO and its corporate overseers not only didn't *want* to become Netflix, they considered the concept completely irrelevant. With Stankey in charge, that ambition came right to the surface, but it did not seem to be a comfortable fit.

Standing in the Radio City lobby, the newly minted media titan didn't seem entirely at home but looked relaxed in an unbuttoned blue oxford dress shirt. He ate small handfuls of popcorn from one of the red-and-white-striped boxes being handed out to attendees. Asked what he was most looking forward to about attending the premiere of *Game of Thrones*, he replied straightforwardly, "Seeing the first episode." Sitting next to his 120-inch TV at home, Stankey said, was a stack of 4K Blu-ray discs containing the entire final season, a stash that millions of *Thrones* fans would have battled an army of White Walkers to acquire. But he hadn't watched any of them yet. Sitting down to view scripted programming of any kind felt like a chore, with college football games being the CEO's preferred diversion during rare breaks from the work grind. After Stankey learned in the spring of 2017 he would be running Time Warner, he had committed to getting through three seasons of *Thrones*. In preparation for Season 7 in his first summer in his new role, he decided to watch the next four seasons in two months in order to prepare for the premiere that summer. His plan was to maintain that pace once the final season was under way. "Once I've seen the first one,

I will binge the rest," Stankey said firmly, his eyes scanning the lobby. "But I like the spectacle."

The spectacle at Radio City reflected the upheaval reshaping the broader entertainment industry landscape. It wasn't just AT&T and its new prize, Time Warner. Several other media companies with similar century-old roots had decided to mount serious, multibillion-dollar challenges to Netflix.

NBCUniversal was one of the new contenders, and its executive leadership had started sensing a building arms race as far back as the middle of the 2010s. One executive who attended regular NBCU planning meetings about streaming said it was widely understood that a tipping point had been reached. "We always figured if Disney launches, or Warner launches, or somebody else launches, we can't be too far behind," the person said. "There was a feeling that there'll be a handful of general-entertainment streaming services in the future, but there won't be twenty-five. And if you're too late, you run the risk that you're not part of the handful."

From a financial perspective, Comcast, Disney, and WarnerMedia were the only companies with the financial wherewithal to go direct to consumers with a large-scale offering. Other media companies—ViacomCBS, Discovery, Lionsgate, and AMC Networks—also marshaled significant streaming resources, and some talked of rivaling Netflix, but the reality was they were not yet in the same league. Most U.S. rivals were still at a fraction of that scale and still made their money from traditional sources.

Unlike tech companies, whose investors are willing to tolerate losses (in the case of Amazon, nine years of waiting for the company to turn a full year's profit) in pursuit of future stratospheric growth, media companies are more earthbound. They'd have to continue financing the movies and TV shows that account for the bulk of their revenue and invest in additional programming and technical infrastructure to compete in streaming, while at the same time surrendering revenue from buyers like Netflix. The combination of making a lot of original shows and forgoing licensing fees would result in a net cost of billions of dollars.

Steve Burke, who was CEO of NBCUniversal for eight years,

expressed confidence that the gap between Netflix and everyone else could be narrowed. His reasoning was simple: the streaming leader had never faced true competition before. "I think Netflix is going to have a very interesting five to ten years," he said in 2020, the year he retired from the company. "All of a sudden you've got Disney, AT&T and us all coming at [it] and all three are going to have lower or no-cost options. Netflix will find that the world's going to get a lot more competitive."

The increasing level of competition in the marketplace, and the collision of old and new media, manifested itself in increasingly public and fascinating ways. Apple's premiere for *The Morning Show* also functioned as an elaborate opening ceremony for Apple TV+. The event radiated legacy-broadcasting energy (winkingly? mockingly?) at the same time it heralded a bold new chapter for a tech giant with a market value north of $1 trillion. The company's CEO, Tim Cook, made a rare foray onto the red carpet (technically, the carpet was jet-black), the start of a stretch when he would make his first appearances at awards shows like the Golden Globes. Cook joined the show's lead actors and executive producers, Jennifer Aniston and Reese Witherspoon. For Aniston, whose fame was cemented by her role as Rachel Green on *Friends*—the NBC sitcom that dominated the ratings from 1994 to 2004—the *Morning Show* turn was her first regular post-*Friends* series role. She played Alex Levy, a veteran broadcast TV morning anchor contending with the arrival of Bradley Jackson (Reese Witherspoon) as her unlikely coanchor. Bradley takes the place of the long-tenured Mitch Kessler (Steve Carell, playing a version of Matt Lauer) after he is forced off the show amid multiple sexual harassment allegations. As *The Morning Show* was premiering, Aniston and other cast members from *Friends* were collecting nearly $2.5 million apiece to appear in a reunion special in 2020 on WarnerMedia streaming service HBO Max.

The sprawling black carpet, two hundred feet wide in places, spilled down the main steps of the Lincoln Center plaza nearly to Columbus Avenue. It was lined with fans, photographers, and looky-loos, with plenty of muscle-bound security guards keeping watch as dusk fell. Cast members Carell, Witherspoon, Billy Crudup, Mark Duplass, and Mindy Kaling mixed with dozens of actual morning TV hosts past and present who were invited for the occasion, familiar faces like Joan Lunden, Diane Sawyer, and George Stephanopoulos. A passageway through the plaza was lined with logos for Apple and the show, a rare spasm of corporate branding outside one of America's highest temples of culture. It featured a background styled like the classic TV color bars, the "test pattern" invented in 1951 by engineers at RCA Laboratories at the start of the medium's boom decade of mass adoption.

Jokingly described as "Apple's bar mitzvah" by *Morning Show* executive producer Michael Ellenberg, the premiere encircled the plaza's famous Revson Fountain (which has had cameos in films like *The Producers*, *Ghostbusters*, and *Moonstruck*). The trappings suited the lavish budget of the show, which was estimated by multiple insiders to cost $16 million per episode, making it one of the priciest series ever produced. (Producers insist it was less expensive.) In the background, the Metropolitan Opera and its massive Marc Chagall tapestries were dark due to a scheduled Monday night off. The quiet on one end of the plaza enabled jazz standards to boom out of speakers on another. Above, on the terrace of David Geffen Hall, 1,500 guests in cocktail attire sipped Veuve Clicquot from flutes as a jazz combo played.

Apple's display of old-fashioned star power and pageantry sent a jolt of energy into the early-autumn night. But there was also widespread curiosity about what exactly Apple's effort would amount to once it was actually on the screen. Steve Jobs had spoken tantalizingly about having "finally cracked" television in his remarks a decade earlier to biographer Walter Isaacson, but the company behind such market-defining products as the iPod, iPhone, and iPad never pulled the trigger. Years of speculation finally ended as Apple committed about $2 billion to its streaming foray, which featured a select portfolio of films, specials, and series. Several dealmakers, though they had had fruitful negotiations with the cash-flush tech behemoth, described a picture of disarray inside a company more versed in the mechanics of sleek product design than the art of storytelling. Apple's reach was global—putting the streaming service in 106 countries and on millions of screens on day one—but its brand and its $225.8 billion-a-year hardware business were too valuable to allow an "anything goes" approach to Apple TV+ programming. Because of its worldwide reach and the close alignment of the programming with devices, the idea of releasing truly groundbreaking, edgy series like *The Sopranos* or *Breaking Bad* was unlikely. Religion, drugs, sex—all were regarded warily by the company. (Netflix had occasionally run into the same complications, yanking an episode of its topical weekly series *Patriot Act* because host Hasan Minhaj criticized the Saudi crown prince Mohammed bin Salman.) The same company known for 1990s ad campaigns urging people to "think different" and celebrate renegades was also the one that launched Apple Music in 2015 with censored, "clean" versions of explicit songs like N.W.A's hip-hop classic "Fuck Tha Police" and Dr. Dre's "Let Me Ride."

The creators of *For All Mankind*, an alternate history of space exploration in the 1960s, clashed with Apple executives over the amount of smoking in the show, according to a person familiar with the production process. The conflict arose even though cigarettes are as essential to the aesthetic of Cold War–era Mission Control as buzz cuts and horn-rimmed glasses. In the end, the smoke remained, but the company had acquired a reputation that was the notes-heavy opposite of the laissez-faire approach that drew many filmmakers and TV creators to Netflix. "They're trying to be uncontroversial in a way that, I think, inspires blandness," observed a seasoned Hollywood dealmaker who has done a considerable amount of business with Apple. "There's a lot of talent that has been concerned about that. I've had people make choices to not go with Apple based on that."

Jamie Erlicht, co-head of Apple TV+ along with his former Sony Television colleague Zack Van Amburg, didn't sugarcoat the strenuous effort to make *The Morning Show*, which Aniston dubbed Apple's "flagship" series. "Nothing about this show has been what I would describe as easy," Erlicht said. "But the great ones never are." Unlike other services, Apple would launch without any library product, so it had to create a brand out of whole cloth. This bespoke approach to content looked meager when compared with Disney's rival service, which leveraged its animation vault and the Marvel and *Star Wars* catalogs. WarnerMedia and NBCUniversal similarly leaned on their libraries, though all players understood the streaming maxim: new original programming was the path to acquiring customers, while a strong library helped retain them.

The Morning Show not only lacked library support, but it started out as a more straightforward drama set in the milieu of TV morning news and had to engineer a complete revamp under intense deadline pressure. Its source material was CNN media reporter Brian Stelter's book *Top of the Morning*, which chronicled the competition between hugely lucrative news shows *Today* and *Good Morning America*. That personality-rich environment presented fertile and fun possibilities, but soon Apple fired original creator Jay Carson, Hillary Clinton's onetime press secretary, and sought a dramatic change of direction. By early 2018, morning news was no longer the domain of happy talk or gossip or talent striving that dominated Stelter's narrative. It had become a battleground in the #MeToo movement. When *Today*'s Matt Lauer and *CBS This Morning*'s Charlie Rose both had their careers destroyed by sexual misconduct allegations, it forced wholesale changes to *The Morning Show*. It would need to locate a deeper register, a more gimlet-eyed handling of gender relations in a big media company's news organization. The series was reconceived to center on Carell's character and the fallout of his removal from the anchor's chair, with episodes being shot as Harvey Weinstein's criminal trial was set to begin in New York. It was an exercise in constant rewriting. "Sometimes I was on the floor crying, but for the most part, I just kept going," executive producer and showrunner Kerry Ehrin recalled. "By the end of that year, it was a lot of stress."

Erlicht recounted trekking with Van Amburg two years earlier to the Century City headquarters of powerful talent agency CAA to hear a pitch for the show. It was just the third day on the job for the former Sony executives. Even though, "right away, [they] knew this was *the one*," he noted that first, the duo had to master logistics like securing an offer letter and payment in a company that was completely new to the TV game. Even once the lay of their new corporate land became more clear, three to four months of negotiations ensued.

In Apple's telling, Aniston and Witherspoon embraced the chance to be the tech giant's launch partners. "Before anybody believed in us, before we started anything, before we knew what we were going to call it, they believed in Apple," said Eddy Cue, Apple's senior vice president of internet software and services (and Erlicht and Van Amburg's boss). While the show had initially been pitched to several different networks, it came down to a bidding war between Netflix and Apple. Both companies made "incredibly aggressive" offers, according to a person familiar with the negotiations. Ultimately, the chance for the creative team to be pioneers carried the day.

Once the first two episodes of *The Morning Show* began to screen at Lincoln Center, it was clear that the spending had been worth it—in many different ways. The production values and direction by Carson's replacement, Mimi Leder (known for features like *On the Basis of Sex* and cinematic TV series like HBO's *The Leftovers*), were top-shelf. But also, from an Apple promotional perspective, the show offered endless teases. Characters fondle iPhones in almost every scene. They set predawn alarms, fire off texts, glance at push notifications. The branded connectedness became so ubiquitous in the pilot episode that the audience chuckled at times. Mostly, though, they seemed to stay on board, though critics not part of the Veuve Clicquot gala premiere seemed much less persuaded. As with the other eight shows in Apple's launch slate, reviews for *The Morning Show* were decidedly mixed.

Cory Ellison, the reptilian yet somehow charismatic network president played by Billy Crudup, drew a hearty laugh from the industry crowd with a speech midway through the pilot. "It's kind of funny how the entire world of broadcast could just fall off a cliff in a few years," he says. "Like, 'Boom! Bang! Lights out.' Unless we reinvent it. We're all going to get bought out by tech unless something changes."

THE ARRIVAL OF NETFLIX'S *THE IRISHMAN* featured a palpable dimension beyond the cross-section of cultural, financial elites and A-list stars attending the premiere. Simply put, it had real stakes. Netflix's backing of the film—and its plan to hustle it from the festival circuit to a brief run in a few theaters and then to streaming around the world within just two months—gave the night a frisson of anticipation verging on disorientation.

Even in the age of streaming, the general approach to releasing prestige films had remained trapped in a twentieth-century mindset. They would wind their way around the world, collecting an award here or a critic's praise there, racking up box-office dollars before finally reaching video on demand and then, a year or more later, streaming on a subscription service. *Parasite*, which captured the Best Picture Oscar in February 2020, first emerged as a world premiere at the Cannes Film Festival the previous May and then played in festivals and overseas theaters before beginning its U.S. commercial run in mid-October. *The Irishman* debut in New York accomplished its primary goal of putting the Martin Scorsese–directed film on the Oscar map with style. On a broader level, though, it sent a clear signal that the assumptions that had prevailed in entertainment no longer applied. Fresh from turning television upside down, Netflix had moved on to revamping the clubby, century-old business of motion pictures. Depending on where you stood in the entertainment hierarchy, that reality was either galling, energizing, or perhaps a bit of both.

An inner dining room at Central Park's Tavern on the Green tested the fire marshal limit as *Irishman* partygoers piled in after screenings let out at nearby Lincoln Center. Revelers did not seem to be deterred by the late start to the party at about midnight, a result of the film's three-and-a-half-hour running time. Conversations among those traveling the half mile to the park on foot had one main thrust: the masters of the modern gangster picture had done it again. Despite the advancing age of the film's stars—Robert De Niro, Al Pacino, Harvey Keitel, and Joe Pesci—their energy never flagged as they joined Scorsese to greet scores of well-wishers. Spike Lee, John Turturro, Maggie Gyllenhaal, and the visual artist JR were among hundreds paying their respects. Netflix film chief Scott Stuber, a six-foot-four former high school and college baseball player from California's San Fernando Valley, strode toward the VIP-filled back room, informing a colleague, "We're going to go where De Niro is." The brown-haired, square-jawed Stuber had abundant experience with gravitating toward talent. He got his start as an intern in the marketing department of Universal Pictures, soaking up lessons from Lew Wasserman during the famed mogul's twilight years and eventually rising to become president of the studio. His arrival at Netflix in 2017 is generally considered a marker for when the company got serious about the original movie business.

As Stuber entered the restaurant's inner sanctum, Leonardo DiCaprio, who has acted in five Scorsese films, found himself caught in the crush. He pulled his girlfriend, Camila Morrone, by the hand behind him toward the exit. Helped by a phalanx of bodyguards, the couple fled through the kitchen in an escape worthy of *La Dolce Vita*. The horde was intense enough that Netflix content chief Ted Sarandos joked to director Noah Baumbach, after squeezing through to a less populated adjoining room, "I'd better watch my wallet!"

He wasn't entirely kidding. Netflix's wallet had become the fattest in media history, and that alone helped explain the night's electric charge. Like Stuber, Sarandos had grown up a film geek in the Southwestern U.S. (Phoenix, in Sarandos's case). He spent the late 1980s and 1990s managing video stores and rising through the executive ranks of a major video chain in the Western U.S. His expertise suited the ambitions of Netflix, which had started out as a DVD-by-mail outfit and a haven for cinephiles discovering the potent combination of film and the internet. By 2019, the streaming giant had racked up some 167 million subscribers in 190 countries worldwide. It spent several times more than its rivals on content—as much as $15 billion in 2019, up from $4.6 billion in 2015—and planned to keep on upping the ante. Unlike any other contender in the streaming race, its 8,600 employees were focused on a primary objective: attracting and retaining subscribers. No advertisers. No theme parks. No linear channels. Nothing to distract the company from beaming programming to viewers through a sole, precision-tooled app.

Disruption had always been part of Netflix's DNA. One of the bullet points in its "culture deck," addressed to current and future employees, deploys the imperative tense: "You thrive on change." On the TV side, the company had fired a major volley in 2013 by simultaneously releasing all ten episodes of its political thriller *House of Cards*, ushering in the concept of binge watching. Animation, kids' fare, reality shows—all genres have since entered the crosshairs of Netflix. Its average view time exceeded two hours per subscriber, but its total addressable market (TAM) was still vast. Cofounder Reed Hastings noted that it accounted for only 10 percent of total global viewing of video on TV sets. Its subscriber level kept rising around the world, even if the U.S. pace had slowed. As overall viewership of Netflix had continued to grow, the number of U.S. pay-TV households had dropped 15 percent since 2015, with the losses accelerating over time. Netflix also exerted unusual pull with the creative community, waging all-out campaigns for Emmys, Oscars, and Golden Globes and reaching parity with traditional media companies in terms of nominations. The rise of a single monolithic company unsettled plenty of Hollywood veterans, not to mention theater owners, cable and satellite TV distributors, and other legacy stakeholders. Still, a lot of talent was drawn to Netflix in the way they always had tended to flock to deep-pocketed backers, who often throw the most opulent parties.

Netflix started streaming films and TV shows over the internet in 2007, a decade after opening its doors as a business sending customers DVDs through the mail in red envelopes. The company's rule-breaking ways earned loyalty from customers impressed by its tech-minded approach to delivering entertainment. Netflix started out by stocking its unlimited shelf space with what seemed like every DVD ever made, attracting the most passionate film buffs. As it transitioned online, Netflix licensed programming from the very media companies now intent on competing with it. Its executives wrote massive checks, sometimes into the hundreds of millions of dollars, for the rights to well-worn staples like Disney's Pixar movies or sitcom classics like *Friends* and *The Office*.

Especially in its early phase, before it was making its own original content or championing films like *The Irishman*, it wasn't always *what* Netflix offered, but *how* it offered it. Subscribers didn't need to wait months to watch studio-quality films from their living rooms. They didn't have to sit through ads or wait a week for each new series installment to light up the screen. They also could watch an entire series in one go, consuming all ten episodes in a single shot, egged on by prompts embedded in the user interface. The system invited viewers to skip a show's opening credits (so long, theme songs) or advance to the next episode as easily as taking another tablet of Pez candy from the dispenser, with the touch of a button. Cable and satellite providers didn't offer these sorts of frictionless features to viewers looking to catch up with programming on demand, leaving the pay-TV players years behind the curve.

Innovation, however, tends to elicit suspicion or even outright hostility from industry gatekeepers. The Cannes Film Festival had banished Netflix from its preeminent global film showcase and marketplace in 2018, on the grounds that streaming with a filigree of presence in actual theaters is anathema to true cinema. "The intransigence of their own model is now the opposite of ours," Cannes artistic director Thierry Frémaux explained. Even by the middle of 2021, a time when theatrical and streaming releases were mingling more freely than ever, Cannes maintained the ban on Netflix. Publicly and privately, many industry influencers supported the stance. Steven Spielberg declared that features backed by streaming companies were, in his words, "TV movies" and therefore should not be Oscar-eligible. Major U.S. exhibition chains like AMC and Regal held talks with Netflix in pursuit of a compromise deal, some way of bending the rule that had long stipulated a three-month exclusive window in theaters for most films. (Years of pressure from studios had compressed the typical window on studio films to seventy-four days.) The parties "got pretty close," according to one participant, "but things fell apart" when the theater chains wouldn't agree to a shorter window. Stuber and his team had identified forty-two days—roughly half the length of the standard window—as the point after which box office tends to decay. Sure, there are always slow-building success stories, but major releases almost always burn out after six weeks.

The New York Film Festival, by contrast with Cannes, warmly welcomed Netflix and other streaming titles even though it was staged by the Film Society of Lincoln Center on hallowed fine-art ground. In addition to *The Irishman*, Netflix would also bring *Marriage Story*, Baumbach's incisive divorce drama, and Mati Diop's supernatural, Senegal-set *Atlantics* to the fifty-seventh annual edition of the New York festival.

For Scorsese, seventy-eight, hitching his wagon to a streaming giant—a counterintuitive move given his bona fides as a film preservationist and avatar of traditional cinema—was a practical decision. The director had initially pitched the movie, a passion project long nurtured with De Niro, to Paramount Pictures, where he had an overall deal and made movies like *Silence*, *Shutter Island*, and *Hugo*. But the director couldn't win support for the film's $160 million budget within the traditional system. The hefty budget included funds for cutting-edge "de-aging" effects that would enable the same cast members to play characters across decades. Other studios soon passed, one by one. *The Irishman*—putting aside the romance of Scorsese's making his first film with Pacino and his ninth with De Niro, and luring Pesci out of retirement—was precisely the kind of film that Hollywood spent the 2010s ardently avoiding. It was a pricey, carefully paced period drama with no franchise potential or merchandise tie-ins. Even if it somehow ran the gauntlet of awards season and swept the Oscars, it still looked like a break-even proposition at best.

"We found the people who would back it, and that was Netflix," Scorsese explained on opening night. "No one else would give us what we needed to make the film. They didn't have much interest, really." Sarandos and Stuber, he added, were "creatively attuned to us and there was no interference at any time." Jane Rosenthal, De Niro's longtime producing partner, came to value her experience with Netflix—she's made two other projects there, *When They See Us* and *This Is a Robbery*—but said it required some adjustment. "You start to speak a different language," she recalled. "We'd sit in marketing meetings and I would say, 'What's the one-sheet?'" In traditional movie marketing, the one-sheet is the poster art and the central image defining the campaign—think of the shark rising toward the female swimmer in *Jaws*. At Netflix, "they'll keep changing those tiles" to emphasize different elements of a film or show depending on subscriber demographics and habits. "How it shows up in your queue is different than how it shows up in someone else's," Rosenthal said.

Producers like Rosenthal also found themselves in a unique position in terms of monitoring their works' performance. No more overnight Nielsen ratings—instead, producers and talent were supplied with Netflix's self-reported viewership numbers at two intervals: ten days and twenty-eight days after a show started streaming. The external data included familiar insights in terms of the gender and age of the audience, as well as more modern gauges, such as the average duration of viewing. For films like *The Irishman*, though, gone was one of the preeminent rituals of Hollywood: the opening-weekend box-office tally. In its place was viewership as of the first month—an eternity for a business accustomed to projecting a movie's lifetime financial performance based on the number of people lining up for a Friday matinée.

Knowing he was inviting criticism by aligning with a force of disruption, Scorsese took care not to blow the trumpets of the streaming revolution as he promoted his film. Even so, he accurately described *The Irishman* as "an interesting hybrid." Its very existence, he observed, would prompt a conversation about "how you balance between what a film is and what is viewed at home or in a theater, and in a theater or not in a theater at all, only at festivals." When *The Irishman* made it to Netflix streaming on Thanksgiving, viewers soon debated why it was a single feature instead of a multipart series. A Twitter conversation broke out with users recommending exact time codes where it could be broken into four manageable forty-five-minute chunks. Even compared with his undergraduate days at NYU in the New Wave/New Hollywood 1960s, Scorsese observed, "We're in an extraordinary time of change."

PART I

Netflix Sets the Bar

CHAPTER 1

▶ The Discovery of Television Among the Bees

As an independent filmmaker, David Blair had presented his movies at plenty of festivals and college campuses, where the screening ritual was well established. Audiences would wait expectantly for the room to darken before his images would fill the giant screen.

On this April day in 1993, as Blair entered the General Motors building in Manhattan, he knew this screening would have a completely different feel. The audience would watch on their computers as his experimental new work, *Wax, or the Discovery of Television Among the Bees*, became the first feature-length film ever streamed online.

A group of people gathered in an office that looked as if it once housed a giant, room-filling computer, sipping drinks from plastic cups. They greeted Blair, who held a VHS cassette of his film. The walls of the room were lined with exposed insulation that looked, to Blair's eye, "like a cheap Russian space suit." A lone piece of furniture dominated the room: a table holding a VHS tape player and a high-end Silicon Graphics machine connected via a T-1 dedicated telephone line to the internet's multicast backbone (or MBone), which was used to transmit real-time video and audio. The streaming experiment would easily outdo the most

daring office activity at the time, according to one Sun Microsystems engineer: watching someone brew coffee. This demonstration would require
all the computing firepower the group could muster. Only four years earlier, British scientist Tim Berners-Lee had conceived of a way for scientists
in universities and research institutions to share information via a network
of computers known as the World Wide Web.

Blair had struggled to get distribution for his film, which he wrote
and directed. It centered on a maker of weapons guidance systems named
Jacob Maker, who falls under the control of his bees. The insects turn
out to be agents of dead souls who insert a crystal television in his head,
using Maker as a guided missile of sorts to attack Iraqi commandos in the
desert.

The filmmaker touted his project on an electronic mailing list known
as Phrack, which was devoted to phone hacking. That caught the attention of a noted computer scientist, Dave Farber, who shared the details
with members of his "Interesting People" email list.

Soon enough, the buzz among the technorati reached the ears of the
founders of a new magazine celebrating digital culture called *Wired*. In its
review of the film, the magazine hailed it as "one of the hottest pieces of
'electronic cinema.'" Blair received an invitation to *Wired's* launch party,
where he encountered "slightly larger, more dangerous fish"—two of
whom followed up with a proposition, which he eagerly accepted, to "play
[his] movie on the internet." Soon, the provincial world of independent
film would have unprecedented reach.

The technology demonstration, by all accounts, was a clumsy engineering endeavor. Blair popped the film into the VCR and fed it into the
computer, which pushed the video out onto the internet. A team of Sun
Microsystems engineers in Mountain View tuned in the flickering image
on their massive computer workstations midway through its digital premiere.

Thomas Kessler, then engineering manager at Sun, was on the receiving end of the transmission, which in those days was known as a multicast.
The stream represented the culmination of research in video compression

done at Stanford University, the University of Southern California, and the Lawrence Berkeley National Laboratory, distributed via the internet. Most internet traffic, at that point, was devoted to research and government business. But telecommunications companies like WorldCom and AT&T were interested in creating a more robust network for business applications. "That particular movie—that was the first effort to go completely global," recalls Kessler. "This guy came along . . . He was doing it as a bit of a publicity play. It was kind of a cult movie. He wanted to get a little coverage. We were looking for interesting things to experiment with so we said, 'OK.'"

The picture was blurry, in Kessler's recollection. It was delivered at a sluggish fifteen frames per second, about half the standard broadcast rate, with sound "like a bad phone call." Nevertheless, that moment, two decades before the widespread adoption of streaming, marked the birth of digital video. Blair found his moment in history's spotlight oddly anticlimactic. "Here was a room with no seats and a VHS machine," he said. "This is like the lowest resolution—and nobody's watching. They carefully put it in, pressed the button on the keyboard, and it just went."

Even if it wasn't an obvious triumph, the screening was historic. More than that, it connected with a long line of visionary attempts to make pictures move through machines. The public's fascination with moving images on a screen can be traced back almost two hundred years and largely parallels the rise of industrialization. As Jeff Kisseloff relates in his indispensable oral history of television, *The Box*, the first efforts date to the 1820s. "These early marvels had equally marvelous names," he writes, like the fantascope, the phenakistoscope, and the zoetrope. "They were made by imprinting drawings around the edges of a disc. When the disc spun and was seen through a viewer, the pictures appeared to be in continuous motion."

After the astonishing invention of the telephone after the Civil War, a feat credited to AT&T cofounder Alexander Graham Bell, spellbound Americans started to anticipate that images would one day mingle with voices. An 1879 spread in *Punch* magazine showed a fanciful rendering by George du Maurier of a fictional but entirely plausible device beaming moving pictures onto a living room wall. His fanciful pencil drawings showed a family communicating from their home with tennis players taking a break from their match. French artist and writer Albert Robida in that same era—well before the advent of vaudeville, motion pictures, radio, or television—created a futuristic vision of a device similar to du Maurier's. He named it the *téléphonoscope*.

A contemporary of Jules Verne who is considered one of the progenitors of the genre of science fiction, Robida wrote and illustrated a range of technology-obsessed stories. One of his most enduring novels, *Le Vingtième Siècle* (*The Twentieth Century*), postulated in 1883 a multimedia environment that would take at least a century to become reality. Robida uncannily anticipated devices and consumer habits that lie at the heart of today's connected, streaming world. He imagined six hundred thousand subscribers paying for live news, tawdry serials akin to modern reality shows, and an array of other enticements. The *téléphonoscope* screen would take up the entire wall of a room and serve as the nerve center for a pipeline of personalized, on-demand programs from around the world. It would display footage of a war in China, soap operas, musical follies, opera and ballet from European capitals, retail goods for sale, and remote-classroom lessons. (How *very* 2020.)

RealNetworks founder Rob Glaser remembers crowding around a computer screen with board members of the Electronic Frontier Foundation in Austin, Texas, one day during the spring of 1993 and glimpsing the future. "You've got to see this Mosaic thing," said Dave Farber, who was a foundation member, as he launched the first modern web browser. Up until that point, the internet had been a collection of flickering letters, numbers, and characters. Mosaic displayed images, inspiring Glaser to go one step further and give the mute collection of words and pictures a voice. He used stock proceeds from his decade at Microsoft and money raised from investors like Lotus founder Mitch Kapor to finance a startup to deliver voice across the web, "because at the bit rates we're talking about here, doing polyphonic audio in a way that would be at all aesthetically pleasing would seem a challenge," Glaser said. His company launched the RealAudio Player in April 1995 with a broadcast of National Public Radio's morning and evening news programs *Morning Edition* and *All Things Considered* and updates from ABC News. Internet speeds and compression were continually improving, making it possible to stream music and video.

Around the same time, Mark Cuban was sitting in a California Pizza Kitchen in Dallas, having lunch with his friend and business partner Todd Wagner, chewing over an idea of transmitting live sports to people's pagers. "I didn't think that it was feasible to broadcast to pagers," said Cuban. "So we abandoned that idea quickly and I discussed with Todd that I could try to figure out a way to use this brand-new thing called the internet to listen to our alma mater Indiana University's sports." Anything would be better than putting a radio next to a speakerphone in Bloomington so he could listen to the games in Dallas. The duo launched AudioNet.com from the second bedroom in Cuban's home, selling a local AM radio station on the notion "that the internet could be as big a disruptive force to radio as cable was to TV." They hooked up a $30 VCR to the radio station's audio board and every eight hours, when the tape was full, brought it to Cuban's house, encoded it, and put it on a server to stream. By the time it went public in 1998, in a record-setting IPO, the rechristened Broadcast.com was carrying live events, including the Super Bowl. Its sale to Yahoo for $5.7 billion, at the peak of dot-com mania in 1999, would make the company's provocative cofounder with a Texas-sized swagger a billionaire. Netflix, founded in 1997, would soon be able to lay the foundation for its global business on these early technologies, as would internet e-commerce pioneer Amazon.com and democratizing video platform YouTube. "We made streaming mainstream," said Cuban. "We made it something that millions of people used every day. It was a special time."

Once this early proof of streaming's potential existed in the marketplace, it didn't take long for one Hollywood producer to develop a vision for how it could move entertainment forward.

Jonathan Taplin began his career in show business as a tour manager for Bob Dylan and the Band. In a few short years, he transitioned to film, producing Martin Scorsese's breakthrough feature, *Mean Streets*. Over the next two decades, his creative portfolio would expand to include twenty-six hours of television documentaries and a dozen feature films (including Scorsese's *The Last Waltz*, which captured the Band's farewell performance in San Francisco). As a film producer, Taplin was well aware of the challenges of theatrical exhibition—especially for makers of documentaries or auteur dramas who had to vie for screens with blockbusters like *Titanic*, *Jurassic Park*, and *Men in Black*. The advent of the megaplex jammed as many as thirty screens into the same venue, doubling the number of U.S. screens over the course of a decade. But even though the 1990s were a fertile time in the indie business after the success of *Sex, Lies, and Videotape* spurred a succession of breakout hits, top Hollywood titles hogged most of the screens. Taplin recognized that technology had provided an opportunity to revolutionize movie distribution with on-demand digital video.

An early demonstration of video delivered via a phone line at the CableLabs research facility in Louisville, Colorado, convinced Taplin it could be done. The video was choppy, as he later recalled, but big enough to fill a television. "That was just like a light went off in my head," says Taplin, who wanted to offer consumers a more expansive array of video rental options than could typically be found lining the back wall of the Blockbuster video store on a Friday night. "I thought, 'This is a horrible experience, and yet, people want to see movies. They want what they want, when they want it.' That was our theory."

In June 1996, he launched Intertainer, developing a consumer interface and conducting tests of delivering movies via the internet to computers. Microsoft offered the venture access to its software tools and Windows Media Player, having failed to win over any of the studios with that proposition. Taplin raised almost $100 million from Microsoft and other corporate heavyweights like Sony, Intel, and Comcast to build a service that could stream entertainment to TV sets and computers.

Intertainer amassed the largest online movie library of its kind and started to gather momentum as high-speed internet access reached an increasing number of homes. Taplin struck catalog deals with most of the major Hollywood studios—not only the one owned by its investor Sony Pictures, but also Warner Bros., Universal Pictures, Lionsgate, and MGM. Paramount Pictures chief Jonathan Dolgen was a belligerent holdout, expressing a fear and loathing of technology's disruptive power.

"He said, 'I'm not putting my movies on any wire, anywhere,'" remembers Taplin. One of Dolgen's assistants reassured him with an account that may well have exaggerated the media executive's hostility toward the digital future: "You got off easy. Last week, the guys from TiVo came in here and gave us a demonstration. When it was all over, they said, 'Well, can we do some kind of a deal?' . . . Dolgen took the TiVo box and threw it out the [window of the] second-story building." While he may not have been a tech utopian, Dolgen had a practical reason to preserve the status quo. Paramount's corporate parent, Viacom, also owned Blockbuster.

Intertainer's premature death, in 2002, could be traced to the studios' decision to pull back all the rights and control internet distribution themselves, through a Sony-led venture called Moviefly (and later renamed Movielink). "In one week, we went from having about eight thousand movies on the service to having about eight," Taplin said. "So, I had no choice but to shut it down."

Taplin sued Sony Pictures, Universal Studios, and AOL Time Warner (then parent of Warner Bros. and New Line Cinema), claiming the studios stole his idea and reneged on agreements to provide Intertainer their movies. After a three-year court battle, the case was resolved with a settlement in the tens of millions. But it was a pyrrhic victory for Taplin, who effectively ended his film career when he chose to take on the studios. He started a new chapter in academia, teaching at the University of Southern California and writing and speaking about technology and media.

With the backing of studios, Movielink got out ahead of even Netflix, which transitioned to streaming in 2007 after an initial decade mailing discs to subscribers. Ira Rubenstein began work in 1999 on a prototype for Movielink, conceived of as a movie download service intended to help Sony Pictures and other studios combat the gathering threat of internet piracy. It would afford consumers a certain degree of flexibility—they could rent a movie or burn a copy of a movie and loan it to a friend (who would need to jump through the extra hoop of obtaining the digital "keys" to unlock the file). But it would come with technological locks to thwart unauthorized copying.

Rubenstein met with executives at Paramount Pictures, Universal Studios, and 20th Century Fox to build support for a legitimate online movie service. He concluded each presentation with a demonstration that underscored the urgency of the threat. "By the way, your movie's already on the 'net," Rubenstein recalled telling angst-ridden studio executives, who would use his computer to screen a pirated copy of a film that was currently showing in theaters.

Movielink capitalized on a rare moment when the studios' interests aligned—or, perhaps more accurately, coalesced in a shared paranoia that the movie industry would suffer the same fate as the music business. After moving too slowly in developing an alternative to peer-to-peer file-sharing sites like Napster, the music industry was seeing its revenue fall off a cliff. Having peaked at $14.6 billion in 1999, it would drop to about $7 billion in 2015, according to the Recording Industry Association of America. The prevailing feeling in the rest of entertainment was, "There but for the grace of God go we." Movielink at least offered a tangible, proactive path that would help the studios to avoid getting Napster-ed.

Metro-Goldwyn-Mayer Studios, Paramount, Universal Studios, and Warner Bros. all joined the venture. Soon, their interests diverged. Paramount insisted on disguising the download file to frustrate piracy, a technical demand that delayed the service's launch. Studio attorneys insisted on limiting the rental period to twenty-four hours—dramatically less than the seven-day rentals at Blockbuster—to comply with language in contracts with HBO that restricted the terms of pay-per-view offers. The studios refused to discount the rental or sale price, for fear of cannibalizing DVD sales or cutting into profit margins.

"I stopped going to the board meetings because it was too painful watching someone kill my baby," Rubenstein said.

Movielink launched in 2002 with online movie rentals, but it struggled to gain traction with its stale selection of titles offered thirty to sixty days after their availability on DVD. By 2006, it began selling digital movie downloads on the same day as the home video release—a milestone in the industry's embrace of digital distribution that nonetheless failed to lift the service. A year later, it was sold to Blockbuster, as the movie-rental giant saw Netflix, Apple, Amazon.com, and Walmart all moving to online distribution.

Blockbuster, of course, would go the way of the videocassette itself. The once-dominant force in the movie-rental market lost out to fleet-footed technological rivals, filing for bankruptcy in 2010. The last of the company-owned stores closed by 2014. Along with Netflix, Amazon, and Apple's iTunes, the video streaming space was also populated by niche digital purveyors like GreenCine and Jaman. As a category, these services would surpass DVD and Blu-ray sales in the U.S. for the first time in 2016.

After squandering early chances to innovate, the mandarins of media closed out the 2010s rushing headlong after futurist Albert Robida into the living room, no longer in need of convincing that Binge Times had arrived. The simplicity and promise of Robida's vision, which the writer described as the "supreme culmination" of prior innovations, called to them across the decades. Sure, the majors would still distribute movies to movie theaters, even after a pandemic, and would look to stock their own streaming services with films even after turning away from promising offerings like Movielink and Intertainer. The most striking of Robida's many remarkable prophecies about streaming was the appeal of its most distinctive trait: efficiency.

"The device consists of a simple crystal screen, flush with the wall or set up as a mirror over the fireplace," Robida mused, with eerie foresight, about his creation. "No need for the theater lover to leave his home: he simply sits in front of the screen, chooses the theater, establishes the communication, and the show begins at once."

CHAPTER 2

▶ Hollywood's New Center of Gravity

The story of Hollywood is, in many ways, the story of arrivistes. The first movie studios were founded a century ago by a group of mostly Jewish immigrants whose boundless ambition belied their modest initial means. They landed in Southern California after hardscrabble, long-distance journeys, building a fantasy factory from a patch of desert scrubland. "They were living in a mud hole," playwright Arthur Miller once said, "but here the dreams were absolutely feasible. If you could think it, you could do it. It was magic. And they filled the movies with that magic."

Conjurers though they were, those early architects of entertainment were still regarded as new money. Jack Warner, cofounder of Warner Bros., personified this emergent class, converting his Spanish-style mansion in Beverly Hills into an ersatz-antebellum echo of Thomas Jefferson's Monticello. He put a bowling alley in its basement and built a nine-hole golf course on its grounds. In the manner of William Randolph Hearst's estate up the coast, the house was stocked with purloined amenities, including a Versailles parquet floor found in France.

The decorator of Warner's pleasure palace was a onetime actor named Billy Haines. After managing the unusual feat of being a leading man in golden age Hollywood while living openly with a male companion, he eventually saw his acting career snuffed out by MGM's Louis B. Mayer. The studio boss insisted that Haines find a wife, as was the practice for many other gay actors at the time. Thankfully, Haines discovered other career options. He soon opened an antiques and interior design store and became one of the originators of the aesthetic known as Hollywood Regency. Along with designing homes, he loaned his personal art collection to film productions and worked with clients like Joan Crawford, George Cukor, and Ronald Reagan.

Ryan Murphy, known for creating TV shows like *The People vs. O.J. Simpson*, *Nip/Tuck*, and *American Horror Story*, made Haines one of the characters in his 2020 alt-history Netflix melodrama *Hollywood*. The series was shot on various L.A. locations and soundstages, but it came fully to life thanks to the efforts of workers in a building at 5808 Sunset Boulevard, the de facto U.S. headquarters of Netflix. Nicknamed "Icon," the modern, fourteen-story, glass-and-steel structure appears worlds away from the opulent, colorful designs that appealed to Haines and his elite clients. Its sleek white facade emphasizes the uniform shape of its windows. Stare at it for long enough and it starts to resemble the Netflix home screen, with its scrolling array of rectangular movie and TV tiles.

In a town that knows establishing shots, Hollywood studios recognize the importance of signaling the part they play in the industry's long-running drama through the physical space they inhabit. Paramount Pictures' ornate, wrought-iron entry gate, with its elaborate filigree, evokes the studio's roots in an earlier film era. (The ironwork, according to legend, was added after fans of Rudolph Valentino overwhelmed security and climbed over the unfortified entrance.) Disney's main corporate headquarters building, designed by Michael Graves, puckishly nods at the company's animation heritage. It features seven nineteen-foot bas-relief dwarves from the studio's first feature-length animated film, *Snow White and the Seven Dwarfs*, propping up the roofline.

Icon's aesthetic is thoroughly twenty-first century, but it shares the energy of the places Haines defined in 1940s Hollywood in one important

respect: it is the new center of show-business gravity, the physical manifestation of the images streaming on screens. As Thom Andersen noted in
his essayistic documentary film *Los Angeles Plays Itself*, "Hollywood isn't
just a place, it's also a metonym for the motion picture industry." Netflix,
similarly, is emerging as a metonym for all of streaming, given the outsized
import of what goes on within Icon's sleek walls.

The building sits in the middle of a neighborhood hard by the Hollywood Freeway, a section of town that has been gentrifying in fits and starts.
It is five short blocks from "Gower Gulch," a cluster of fabled soundstages
where *I Love Lucy* and Columbia Pictures once held sway. Jack Warner's
studio shot *The Jazz Singer*, the first talking picture, there in 1927. A
mile and a half away is the Egyptian Theatre, the golden age movie palace where the first movie premiere, for *Robin Hood* with Douglas Fair-
banks, was held in 1922. Not long after moving into Icon, Netflix took
over operating the Egyptian in an arrangement with the not-for-profit
American Cinematheque, and started using it for screenings and events.
A similar investment by Netflix saved New York's Paris Theater next to
the Plaza Hotel. The lease deals fueled rumors, repeatedly denied by the
company, that it could simply start buying up distressed movie theaters if
exhibitors resisted booking Netflix films. That scenario was championed
by cinephiles in the spring of 2021 when Hollywood's famed Cinerama
Dome and ArcLight Cinemas announced they were closing due to the
pandemic. "Netflix, you know what to do," tweeted journalist Yashar Ali.

Show-business glamour isn't the first thing that comes to mind
during a trip through the area surrounding Icon. Tinged with grit, it
has witnessed more than a century of boom-and-bust cycles. A Denny's
restaurant two blocks down Sunset is a favorite of panhandlers. Day la-
borers pack the parking lot of Home Depot just on the other side of the
freeway. In 2019, before the COVID-19 pandemic forced a widespread
rethink of office spaces in many business sectors, Netflix announced a
major expansion to a building across the street. That new structure is
to be called "Epic." The company also has leased several floors of office
space in "Cue," another nearby building.

It is hard to predict the future of the U.S. workplace, though Netflix founder and co-CEO Reed Hastings has called remote work during COVID-19 a "pure negative" and only part-facetiously vowed to summon employees back to the office "twelve hours after a vaccine is approved." Regardless of how many workers are inside, Netflix's offices convey its core brand values. In 2016, speaking at a Hollywood Chamber of Commerce event, content chief Ted Sarandos said of Icon, "A building like this is a statement of who you are, what you believe, and what you want to do." The aesthetics of Netflix's newest office spaces have been overseen by San Francisco–based architecture and design firm Gensler. The firm has worked with a range of clients, including tech firms like Facebook, Airbnb, and Salesforce. The activities of employees are not incidental to the way the buildings look and operate. In a description of Netflix's main office in Japan, Gensler said it "playfully incorporated functions and spaces that allude to the company's rich selection of streaming internet content, allowing staff to immerse themselves in various scenes, just as customers do with Netflix's ubiquitous programming."

In the main lobby of Icon, it is easy for visitors to get immersed. Even if some aspects of the space were rethought during the pandemic (goodbye, free organic snacks), the lobby still merits the label given it by the *New York Times*: "Hollywood's Town Hall." A-list guests like Leonardo DiCaprio, David Letterman, Beyoncé, and Brad Pitt are spotted daily. On one recent weekday morning, Sylvester Stallone and his entourage stood in a semicircle, some of them sipping espressos prepared by the on-site barista. Overlooked by an eighty-by-twelve-foot screen playing trailers and clips (a full screening room is just on the other side of the wall), the space is the successor to longtime meeting grounds like Chateau Marmont, Tower Bar, and Soho House. Unlike those public spaces, though, Icon offers a "lobby experience" (in its designers' description), wrapped in the bosom of a single company. The headquarters of CAA and Endeavor, or studio lots in various eras, may come close in terms of juice. But the fact that such a volume of shows and movies, and so much talent, passes through the tech company's meticulously engineered machine makes this space a subject of abiding fascination. Few can resist the chance to take a meeting at Netflix.

People enter the main door of Icon—unless they are top-level VIPs like Barack Obama, who access it via an underground tunnel—next to a large glass display case. BAFTA, Golden Globe, Oscar, and Emmy statuettes are clustered together on the shelves of the case, facing outward. A "living wall" features more than 3,500 plant species. Sculptures commemorating the company's top titles rotate through, and the screen is often customized depending on who is making an appearance. (Director Alfonso Cuarón, for example, might look up as he walks in to see his 2018 Netflix film *Roma* playing on the big screen.)

If Icon symbolizes the company's ascendance during the 2010s, its early years were significantly more down-to-earth and scrappy. Before founding Netflix, Reed Hastings was CEO of a software company called Pure Atria, which bought a firm called Integrity QA, where Marc Randolph was a cofounder. Randolph then headed marketing at Pure Atria, which soon was sold in one of the flurries of tech deals during the 1990s boom. Hastings stood to leave the company with a rich payday once the deal cleared regulatory review, and Randolph was also on his way out. While waiting a few months for the merger to close, the two still drew a paycheck and showed up every day to Pure Atria's office in Sunnyvale, working on various projects. With venture capital flowing and the bull market surging, Randolph had the itch to get a new startup off the ground. Hastings was increasingly focused on education reform but planned to keep his "toe in the water" as an investor or advisor. Hastings and Randolph both lived in Santa Cruz, so they soon developed a habit of carpooling on Highway 17 up and over the Santa Cruz Mountains, spitballing ideas along the way.

As Randolph observed, Silicon Valley loves a good origin story, a tale of inspiration or keen insight that distills the essence of a company. The best-loved of these creation stories involve disruptive change that holds the promise of rich rewards. Consider the alcohol-soaked genesis of Uber, an idea StumbleUpon founder Garrett Camp began incubating after he and his friends spent $800 to hire a private driver on New Year's Eve. Or the *voilà* moment when Airbnb founders Brian Chesky and Joe Gebbia turned their loft into a bed-and-breakfast—renting out air mattresses at $80 a guest—as a way to cover their exorbitant San Francisco rent.

Netflix's saga starts, at least according to popular legend, with a moon shot. Cofounder Hastings describes getting socked with a $40 late fee on *Apollo 13* at Blockbuster and wondering, "What if there were no late fees?" But the streaming giant's origin story is more complicated than this convenient narrative, which neatly distilled the service's initial consumer proposition of renting DVDs without worrying about return dates or late fees. The idea was hardly a bolt from the blue, says cofounder Randolph, but a concept arrived at over countless brainstorming sessions with Hastings as they logged miles together.

From behind the wheel of his beat-up Volvo, or as a passenger in Hastings's immaculate Toyota, Randolph pitched various ideas for a startup that would sell personalized surfboards, dog food, and shampoo via the internet. The coolly analytical Hastings rejected each as unworkable. Finally, they landed on an idea with real potential: movies on video. VHS tapes proved too bulky to ship (and, at $75 to $80 a cassette, costly), but soon after the original inspiration struck, Hastings read about the introduction of the compact-disc-sized DVD in 1997. The discs were more affordably priced and slender enough to travel by post. But would the DVDs survive intact if shipped through the mail? They bought a used Patsy Cline greatest hits compilation from a record store, stuffed the disc into a greeting card envelope, slapped on a thirty-two-cent stamp, and mailed it to Hastings's home. It arrived two days later, intact—proof of concept.

With $1.9 million in startup capital provided by Hastings, Randolph, and a group of angel investors, the company hired a dozen people. In its first six months, its primary focus was building a simple e-commerce website to facilitate disc sales and rentals. "At the time, in

1998, there were not that many titles and there was almost no place that they were available," said Randolph. "So we decided we could do the one-stop shop." The first Netflix office was a former bank branch in an office park in Scotts Valley, one of the towns they would drive through on Highway 17. It had "smelly green carpet," Randolph recalled—the same color as the money the company planned to make, he and his colleagues liked to joke. Its initial supply of DVDs was kept in the former bank's old vault. Because the cash-strapped company was moving too fast to fuss over office furniture, "people were bringing in beach chairs" to work in, Randolph remembered. When Netflix formally opened its doors on April 14, 1998, the first 150 orders landed all at once and crashed Netflix's servers. The startup struggled during its first year in business. "At that time, we weren't worrying about how we were going to fend off Blockbuster. We weren't worrying about the future of streaming," Randolph said. "We were worrying about this little website we built."

Netflix wasn't making any money. It was selling plenty of DVDs, but its costs were high. DVDs were expensive. Shipping them was expensive. It was expensive giving them away by the thousands in promotions. At a meeting with Amazon's Jeff Bezos, to discuss a possible sale, one thing became clear: Netflix would soon be competing with the e-commerce giant, which had ambitions to sell commodities other than books. "That drove one of the first really difficult decisions for an early company," Randolph said. "Which is: Do you stick with the business which is ninety-five percent of your revenue, but is eventually going to go out of business, or do you bet everything on the business which is not working, but, if you can get it to work, could potentially be a big success?"

Netflix took the risk. Randolph says the team explored "hundreds" of approaches over the next year and a half before landing on a rental system that the earliest Netflix customers would recognize, paying a fixed monthly subscription fee for up to three movies at a time. The discs would arrive by mail in red envelopes, like so many gifts on Chinese New Year. The open-ended rental model offered consumers greater convenience, even as it solved a more practical problem for Netflix.

"We had this warehouse, which at the time had several hundred thousand DVDs in it, and Reed and I began riffing, 'It's kind of a shame that we have all these DVDs sitting here in a warehouse doing no good. I wonder if there was some way to store them in our customers' houses?" said Randolph. "Can we let them keep the DVDs? Can they just hold on to them as long as they want? And when they want another one, they'll just mail it back and we'll replace it. There'll be no due dates and no late fees."

The service Netflix introduced in 1999 changed the struggling startup's fortunes, attracting 239,000 subscribers, winning loyalty from those who appreciated not only its novel approach to DVD rentals but also its recommendation engine and the community of cinephiles gathered around its website. At the time, prior to the arrival of social media, chat rooms and message boards were the primary means of expression. Netflix subscribers could build "queues" of desired rental titles and trade reviews with other subscribers. Compared with Blockbuster, whose khaki-and-blue-shirt staff uniforms and regimented aisles were directly inspired by mass brands like McDonald's, Netflix emphasized the individual. It encouraged customers to rate each movie, reflecting those ratings on its site. It was also beginning to gather data from each subscriber that would become a revolutionary tool.

Netflix's subscribers weren't the only ones who were enthusiastic. Silicon Valley investors had pumped $100 million into the startup, allowing it to grow to more than 350 employees. As the dot-com boom approached its frenzied apex, bankers sniffing another initial public-stock offering in the air began "circling [Netflix] like vultures with briefcases." When the tech bubble burst in March 2000, the easy money dried up. The company was on track to lose $57 million when Hastings and Randolph traveled to Dallas, Texas, in early 2000, with an exit plan in mind: to convince Blockbuster CEO John Antioco to buy the startup for $50 million and let Netflix build its online presence. The head of the

$6 billion home entertainment giant turned them down flat. The rebuff came as little surprise. "What did we possibly have to offer that they couldn't do more effectively themselves?" Hastings reflected in his 2020 book, *No Rules Rules*.

Netflix soon hit a wall, forcing Hastings to lay off one-third of the company's workforce, winnowing the staff to its highest performers— the "keepers"—in a wrenching period that crystallized a key element of the company's performance culture. "This was my road to Damascus experience, a turning point in my understanding of the role of talent density in organizations," Hastings wrote. The holidays delivered the struggling service an unexpected gift: DVD players were popular purchases, fueling a surge in DVD-by-mail subscriptions. That set the stage for the company to go public in 2002, raising $82.5 million on the strength of a subscriber number that now seems quaint: six hundred thousand.

As Netflix grew, Hastings recruited key executives, including Ted Sarandos, the gregarious executive who'd served as regional director at one of the largest video distributors in the United States, East Texas Distributing, and who later helped the five-hundred-store Video City/ West Coast Video retail chain migrate from VHS tapes to DVDs. The two men couldn't be more different. Sarandos grew up in a poor neighborhood in Phoenix, Arizona, the fourth of five children. Sarandos's paternal grandfather emigrated to the U.S. from the Greek island of Samos, changing his surname to Sarandos when he arrived as a teenager. His mother liked to keep the TV on all day while his father worked as an electrician. Both were high school dropouts. "My parents were very young, so I was raised by wolves," he liked to joke. Needing only about five hours of sleep a night, Sarandos grew up drinking thirstily from the cup of popular culture. New Hollywood films helped define his childhood, among them *The Godfather*, *Mean Streets*, and *Dog Day Afternoon*. (His spacious office, decades later, would feature 1970s totems like *Godfather* posters and a large silhouetted window decal of Norman Lear's head that would literally project the *All in the Family* creator's image onto his workspace at certain times of the day.) As a teenager, Sarandos got his parents to drop him off in downtown Phoenix to watch the filming of Clint Eastwood thriller *The Gauntlet*. "It was the hottest day in Arizona history," he said. "I sat out all day and watched them shoot, and my tennis shoes literally melted on the street, it was so hot. It was just to get a glimpse of this magic that was happening. . . . I got close to the gods that day." Later, working for his high school newspaper and dreaming of a journalism career, he interviewed Ed Asner (then starring on TV as irascible newsroom leader Lou Grant). He soon realized he sparked more to Asner's show-business stories than to the craft of journalism.

While attending Glendale Community College, Sarandos began hanging out at Arizona Video Cassettes West, where he became a regular, and cajoled the store owner to hire him. The store wasn't too busy, so he'd drive his Ford F-150 pickup there and spend his days watching videos. Eventually, he viewed its entire collection of VHS tapes, developing an encyclopedic knowledge of film that would serve him well later in life, as Netflix's head of content and eventually its co-CEO. Sarandos recalled how people would seek him out for recommendations, an experience that helped him appreciate the remarkable diversity of people's tastes. He dropped out of college to manage the video store chain where he had previously worked. This segment of the retail industry was taking off in the 1980s as VCRs became mainstream. Working at a series of chains that were smaller rivals to Blockbuster, he hit on DVDs as a growth area while helping lead Video City and West Coast Video, two midlevel chains that merged. Many of its stores were in medium-sized markets near U.S. military bases, where many families had disposable incomes and a zeal for the latest in electronics.

Sarandos struck a deal with Hollywood studios, who gave the stores an inventory of discs for free and then shared in rental revenue. He remembered first encountering Netflix via a card it had inserted into DVD player packaging, inviting customers to sign up and get ten free rentals.

Joe Amodei, a film producer and executive who befriended Sarandos in the 1980s during his time working at Turner Broadcasting, recalls their shared taste in music and movies. Sarandos worshipped musical icons like Frank Sinatra, Tony Bennett, and Bruce Springsteen and emulated their all-American irrepressibility. Compactly built, with wide-set eyes and dark, wavy hair, Sarandos always had a surplus of energy. When he met Amodei, Sarandos was a video wholesaler, far from the bright lights of show business, but he approached the task with uncommon brio. "He would shotgun calls to stores around the country, pitching my movies," Amodei says. "It was like he had made these movies himself, he was so passionate. We bonded almost immediately."

Hastings, by contrast, was a child of privilege. His maternal great-grandfather, Alfred Lee Loomis, was a Yale-and-Harvard-educated Wall Street tycoon who made a fortune financing electric utilities. He liquidated his holdings ahead of the 1929 stock market crash and lived through the Depression in high style, according to *Forbes*, backing a yachting syndicate that competed in the America's Cup and acquiring much of Hilton Head Island, South Carolina, for use as a personal playground. He then turned his attention to science, bankrolling an experimental physics lab in Tuxedo Park that attracted such luminaries as Albert Einstein, Enrico Fermi, and Ernest Lawrence. Reed Hastings grew up in an affluent suburb of Boston with well-educated parents—his mother was a Wellesley grad, his father magna cum laude at Harvard. Hastings attended private schools, then surprised the family by choosing Bowdoin College in Maine, which was a selective and rigorous school but outside of the Ivy League. He spent two years in the Peace Corps in Swaziland, teaching math to high school students, before returning to the U.S. to study artificial intelligence at Stanford.

The two executives would develop a successful left-brain/right-brain collaboration spanning more than twenty years at Netflix. Hastings held things down in the company's Los Gatos technology nerve center and corporate base, while Sarandos fostered a creative hub in Los Angeles. Sarandos, who was living in the Southern California coastal enclave of Palos Verdes when Netflix hired him, persuaded Hastings to let him stay put. He felt it was a more natural way to establish ties with the creative community than being based at the company's Silicon Valley home in Los Gatos. "It turned out to be a good strategic bet," Sarandos later recalled. "You can respect the tech culture in the entertainment community, and the entertainment community can respect the tech culture. But they hardly ever get together, mostly because it's just a tribal thing. Most of Hollywood was convinced that the tech guys would come down and clumsily write big checks and would be all gone pretty soon." Unlike the new arrivals from up north, he added, Hollywood executives felt, "'We'll be here like we have been the last one hundred years doing this. We've seen this come and go, come and go.' And then the tech guys were convinced that all the studio guys were stupid and they were doing everything wrong. It wasn't a great culture to work together. But because [Sarandos] was [in L.A.] and started building out the team there," Netflix got traction. Ultimately, Sarandos concluded, "It's a relationship business."

The original Netflix team working with Sarandos fit into part of a floor in a low-rise office building in Beverly Hills. In those DVD-centric days, it would rotate posters of top sellers on and off the walls of the main conference room, a primitive version of the self-promotion at Icon.

As it charted a course beyond the might-have-been Blockbuster exit, Netflix had become an exponentially larger organization than its early incarnation in the green-carpeted former bank branch. (It ended 2020 with 9,400 employees.) The first recruits had all been known to the founders—including those who followed Hastings from his first startup. As the company grew, Hastings worked to preserve the culture of innovation and risk-taking that thrives in early-stage organizations but can become stifled as businesses expand and institute cumbersome processes. "Normally, companies organize around efficiency and error reduction, but that leads to rigidity," he said. "We're a creative company. It's better to organize around flexibility and manage right on the edge of chaos." He and his management team created a document laying out the company's values and an approach to work that differed drastically from that of traditional media companies. The result was a document— initially a slide deck created by Hastings in PowerPoint—that has come to be known as a contemporary Magna Carta in business and tech circles. It was the Netflix Culture Deck.

"We want to entertain the world. If we succeed, there is more laughter, more empathy, and more joy," the document begins. "To get there, we have an amazing and unusual employee culture." Former longtime HR head Patty McCord was among several executives who collaborated on the elaborate mission statement. Since Hastings decided to post it publicly online, the deck has been viewed nearly twenty million times.

Netflix would seek out "rock stars," pay them generously, and grant them wide autonomy. This would assure a fleetness in decision-making that would allow Netflix to outmaneuver its more staid corporate rivals. But with freedom comes accountability. One of the central beliefs is radical honesty. Coworkers "up, down and across" the company give one another candid feedback frequently, and without regard to hierarchy. One former executive described the constant feedback as creating a culture of fear—"Everybody is chipping away at each other at every moment, because you're rewarded." When someone makes a mistake, they talk about what they've learned publicly in a practice called "sunshining," a way to encourage employees to accept failure as an outcome of risk-taking.

Even compensation is subject to transparency. About five hundred employees at the director level and above know the salaries of everyone at the company. A "360 review" policy enables workers to submit performance reviews of others, again regardless of level. Results of the company's activities in many areas are also tracked and made public. "Memos on each title's performance, on every strategy decision, on every competitor, and on every product feature test are open for all employees to read," the deck points out. Employees enjoy a high degree of independence and autonomy, being entrusted to set their schedules and make decisions. In its entertainment operations, rather than the single boardroom-style green-light committee that often clogs the pipelines of traditional studios, Netflix gives dozens of employees that authority. Hastings credits the company's success, and its ability to navigate through massive transitions, to its maverick culture.

The emphasis on transparency can produce agonizing spectacles. Netflix's former head of corporate communications, Jonathan Friedland, who is White, used the n-word twice in meetings—once while attempting to provocatively underscore a point about offensive language in stand-up comedy specials, for which he later apologized, the *Wall Street Journal* reported. He used the term a second time while speaking with two Black human resources employees who were trying to help him come to terms with the offense. Hastings sent a letter to employees, publicly explaining the reasons for Friedland's firing, saying using the word shows "unacceptably low racial awareness and sensitivity, and is not in line with our values as a company."

For those who fail Netflix's "keeper test"—the term for what happens when a manager fires a good employee to get a great one—the company says it offers generous severance. "We've always said it's a team, not a family," says Hastings. Netflix alums often are snapped up by new employers, given the halo around the company. But many employees express concern that "radical transparency" is just another phrase for "office politics." Terms sprinkled throughout the Culture Deck like "highly aligned, loosely coupled" and "north star" feel like a language members of a secret society might use to reinforce an "us versus them" narrative. "You're using those words in how you do business," said one former executive. "In your emails. In the way you talk to your colleagues. It's using that language and those words in order for you to understand one another."

Tahirah Gooden, manager of original studio films, came to Netflix from more traditional companies like New Regency and Lava Bear Films. "I don't think you ever understand the Netflix culture, as many times as you read through the culture memo, until you get here. It's really quite refreshing once you understand the ins and outs of it. There are definitely some adjustments you have to make," she said in a 2019 appearance on the in-house podcast *We Are Netflix*. In her previous jobs, providing "less information until you've gotten the job done is probably safer for you," she added. "At Netflix, overcommunication was the way to go." Despite feeling she had made a successful adjustment, Gooden said receiving feedback is difficult. "You immediately go to, 'Oh my God, I'm messing up. I'm doing something wrong.' Instead, I have to reframe it as, 'They're just trying to help me succeed.'"

Hastings isn't shy about applying the keeper test. In 2017, he fired Neil Hunt, a close friend who served as Netflix's chief product officer for almost twenty years, the principal architect of the company's famous algorithm. "I would not have chosen that moment to move on," Hunt said in an interview. The executive, who earned the nickname "brain-on-a-stick" because he's six foot four, rail thin, and razor sharp, became CEO of a health tech startup. Another target of the keeper test was one of its creators, Patty McCord. In 2011, the company was weathering a rocky period after a doomed announcement of a plan to spin off its DVD business into a new company called Qwikster. Netflix's stock price plunged, and Hastings decided to evaluate the entire executive team to determine who should remain. McCord was let go. "It made me sad," she conceded later, though she felt gratified by Hastings's embracing the concept she had instilled from Netflix's founding. A belief in the Culture Deck far outlasted her tenure at the company. In 2018, it served as the centerpiece of her book, *Powerful: Building a Culture of Freedom and Responsibility*. "The fundamental lesson we learned at Netflix about success in business today is this: the elaborate, cumbersome system for managing people that was developed over the course of the 20th century is just not up to the challenges companies face in the 21st," she wrote.

CHAPTER 3

◉ Netflix Lives Up to Its Name

What to watch? Netflix has been solving this fundamental consumer riddle since its earliest days peddling DVDs. Its relentless focus on delivering what people want to watch, and its multilayered approach to understanding individual consumer preferences, is something that sets it apart from its Hollywood studio rivals. The traditional focus of entertainment companies has been convincing consumers to tune in at a certain hour or to show up in theaters on a particular weekend. Netflix saw its role as that of matchmaker, not carnival barker. The company launched its first recommendation engine, Cinematch, in February 2000 to help subscribers navigate a library of five thousand movie titles that was too unwieldy to browse. Six years later, it held a closely watched contest to boost the accuracy of its recommendations by 10 percent. Netflix dangled a $1 million prize, though the ultimate lure for nerds was access to a data set of over 100 million ratings on 17,700 movies from 480,189 customers. A development team led by AT&T research engineers calling themselves BellKor's Pragmatic Chaos claimed the prize in 2009, though Netflix implemented a stripped-down, less computationally demanding version of their algorithm for predicting consumer tastes. The bigger boon was the halo it created for Netflix in the technical community as a place that tackled serious computing challenges.

"Our ability to attract star talent was the best outcome of the whole thing," recalls former chief product officer Neil Hunt. "The algorithm was great, but more important was the fact that we were able to hire dozens of experts in machine learning on recommendations, and hundreds of people in a broader field, to engage and contribute and really sort of upgrade the skills and the competence."

Netflix's approach to recommendations evolved as the business shifted from one centered on DVDs, which drew inferences from customer ratings, to streaming, which provides direct, real-time insights into what movies or TV shows its customers sample and which they binge in copious amounts, one after the other. And the talent it attracted in its waning mail-order days would give it the technical prowess to pioneer a revolution in entertainment. Hastings, a Stanford-educated computer scientist and mathematician who speaks in the measured tones of a college professor, seems to have been preparing for this moment since the company's founding. One early investor and board member, Richard Barton, recalls challenging Netflix's DVD rental model over dinner with Hastings in early 2000, echoing the conventional wisdom in Silicon Valley that the upstart would be either bulldozed by Blockbuster or rendered obsolete by the internet.

"I said, 'Reed, it's obvious the form factor of the DVD is going to be dead. It's obviously just temporal. And that's it. Your company is going to hit a wall and it'll be over,'" Barton said. "He said, 'Rich, I didn't call it "DVDs-by-mail-flix," I called it *Net*flix.' . . . He's one of these people who have this rare ability to take the very long view and understand the really big trends. We don't know what all the decisions will be along the way but we know the destination."

For Hastings and his technical team, it was a simple matter of applying Moore's law, the theory, developed by Intel cofounder Gordon Moore, that computing power will double every two years. So, too, will internet speeds, says Hunt. With the turn of the millennium, broadband internet access began to sweep the country, expanding from just 1 percent of U.S. households in 2000 to 51 percent by 2007. "It was not rocket science to say we need to deliver by internet," Hunt said. "The question was whether we were going to trickle the discs down overnight, or we were going to try to stream them in real time."

Netflix spent a year prototyping a service that mirrored its mail-order DVD business. Subscribers would go online to order a movie and the service would "trickle down" the bits overnight, when bandwidth was plentiful, and store it on a disc in the home. Those plans got shelved when the burgeoning popularity of YouTube demonstrated that consumers preferred the instant gratification of streaming. Delivering on the promise of streaming would require delicate diplomacy. Netflix had arrived on the scene as the ultimate disruptor, but it also craved acceptance. With one foot in Silicon Valley and the other in Hollywood, it set about trying to bridge the gap. Studio executives, who had watched in horror as internet piracy ravaged the music business, were extraordinarily sensitive to the risks of online delivery. The content owners initially set requirements that were either technically impossible, too expensive to implement, or too intrusive on customers—such as one demand that consumers scan their driver's licenses to prove they lived in a part of the world that was covered by Netflix's distribution agreement, Hunt recalls. "A piece of that fell on my shoulders, on the technical side," said Hunt. "But a good deal of it fell on the team that was doing the content procurement, purchasing, licensing deals, to draw the lines in: 'We'll do this. We will not do that.'"

The Watch Now service that Netflix launched in January 2007 was far from perfect. The internet was pushed to the limit, so it was hard to deliver a quality picture, Hunt said. And the viewing was restricted to computers running Microsoft's Windows Media Player. But waiting for the technology to mature simply wasn't an option. "One of the challenges of some kinds of technical leaps is that the technology initially doesn't work well enough to satisfy the mainstream customer," Hunt said. "But if you don't jump on top of it and ride the wave as technology gets better—twice as good every two years—you're likely to let somebody else steal your business away by appealing to a different set of customers for whom it does work. Once the wave sweeps through your mainstream customers, it's over."

Hastings told investors that Netflix planned to straddle both worlds, physical and digital, focusing on aggressively growing its profitable DVD subscription business even as it launched its streaming service. The lucrative rental business would sustain the company until Netflix could overcome the barriers that prevented consumers from fully embracing streaming—namely, a limited selection of content and the lack of a technology to deliver movies and TV shows to the living room TV.

Netflix wasn't alone in its vision of an on-demand future. Amazon had been charting the dramatic rise in DVD purchases and began assembling a team in 2004 to capitalize on the inevitable pivot to online delivery. One of its first hires was Roy Price, who grew up steeped in Hollywood tradition, to lead the effort. Price's maternal grandfather, writer and producer Roy Huggins, endured being blacklisted and forced to testify before the House Un-American Activities Committee, and went on to create two enduring film and television franchises, *The Rockford Files* and *The Fugitive*. His father, Frank Price, developed a string of hit television shows in the seventies as head of Universal Television, including *The Six Million Dollar Man*, *The Incredible Hulk*, and *Battlestar Galactica*, then went on to lead Columbia Pictures and Universal Pictures. Price's mother, Katherine Crawford, starred in such Hollywood films as *Riding with Death* and *A Walk in Spring Rain*, and the television miniseries *Gemini Man*.

"When I arrived, there was a goal and opportunity but no detailed plan," Price said. "So we started from scratch." He began triangulating what kind of service Amazon could offer that would be interesting to customers, technologically feasible, and palatable to the studios, whose reactions to internet distribution ran the gamut, from intrigued to "hell no." He remembers the team's sharing a cramped conference room, heavy with the smell of perspiration and littered with spent Diet Coke cans, as they worked toward launch. The resulting download site, called Unbox, was announced on September 7, 2006, just days ahead of Apple's own scene-stealing announcement that it would sell downloads of Disney, Pixar, and Miramax films and popular ABC TV shows through its iTunes store.

Netflix sought to differentiate itself from its well-heeled competitors by offering streaming as a perquisite for DVD subscribers, effectively free, whereas rivals charged consumers anywhere from $2 to $3 to rent movies or $15 to buy them.

The initial streaming offer was slender: about one thousand movies and television shows, representing a fraction of the more than seventy thousand DVDs in Netflix's collection.

A team of eight people worked on streaming in those early days, a skunkworks initiative that one executive described as "a little bump on the side of what was this DVD-by-mail rental business." As the executive remembered it, "We were this sort of a science project kind of thing that was going on. We literally would have our streaming meetings in one medium-sized conference room, and that was the entire team that was working on it."

In the days before Netflix took the internet video leap, Hastings would occasionally meet with another Silicon Valley disruptor, Anthony Wood, whose pioneering digital video recorder, ReplayTV, offered an appealing alternative to network programming schedules by enabling time-shifted TV viewing but landed in legal hot water when it began promoting a thirty-second commercial-skipping feature. Netflix invested a modest sum in Wood's next venture, Roku, and, in exchange, the sage would regularly drop by the Los Gatos offices to, in his words, "pontificate on the future of streaming."

Wood's next big idea was a device that would deliver internet video to the dominant screen in the home, the television, a theory he continually pressed on Hastings. One day, a Netflix recruiter approached Wood about joining the company to oversee development of the first version of its streaming service, which initially delivered movies to the PC. Wood agreed on the condition that he could keep his job as CEO of Roku and continue developing his passion project, a streaming device. Code-named Project Griffin, reportedly named for Tim Robbins's character from the film *The Player* (though Wood could not recall the derivation of the name), the team set to work on the Netflix Player. At the same time, it initiated licensing talks with Samsung, LG, and Microsoft about incorporating the streaming service into internet-connected TVs and game consoles.

The device came within months of its December 2007 launch when Hastings pulled the plug, fearing that manufacturing its own hardware would complicate Netflix's relationship with Apple. Netflix spun out the hardware operation into Roku, which launched the player under its own name. As Netflix's Los Gatos coding brigade worked out the kinks of the service's streaming technology, Sarandos began looking to fill the content pipeline. In October 2008, he struck a three-year, $90 million deal with Starz for the streaming rights to Disney and Sony movies. It represented a significant bet for a company that had just crossed $1 billion in revenue.

"At the time, they thought they were spending a lot of money for Starz. Ted will tell the story, and Reed will tell the story; they argued about whether that was too much money," recalls former Starz CEO Chris Albrecht. A onetime stand-up comedian, Albrecht helped usher in television's turn-of-the-century golden age as the head of HBO, where he green-lit some of its most acclaimed series, including *The Sopranos*, *Sex and the City*, *Six Feet Under*, *Entourage*, *Band of Brothers*, and *The Wire*.

Hastings and Sarandos wouldn't have to wait to find out whether the pricey new programming they'd brought in would resonate with customers.

Netflix added nearly three million subscribers in 2009, growth it attributed, in part, to streaming. Once it added new ways for viewers to watch movies and TV shows from the couch in their living rooms, via internet-connected game consoles like the Sony PlayStation 3, Microsoft Xbox, and Nintendo Wii, and devices like Apple TV, subscriptions skyrocketed 63 percent. Growth continued apace, as Netflix deepened its streaming library with films from Paramount, Metro-Goldwyn-Mayer Studios, and Lions Gate Entertainment Corporation, courtesy of a five-year, $1 billion deal with premium cable channel Epix.

The budding streaming service grew at Hollywood's expense. Hastings and company deftly exploited the studios' compensation structure, which paid rich bonuses when executives hit their financial targets. Netflix flashed enough cash to exploit this short-term focus on profits. Some studio executives would brag about picking the novice's pockets. The true toll of these deals would only be apparent years later, as Netflix achieved a seemingly insurmountable lead over the hidebound entertainment establishment.

"They got access to everything, everything that Starz was paying hundreds of millions of dollars for," says Albrecht, who joined the premium cable network after the fateful 2008 deal with Netflix, which he refused to renew. "It created a great windfall for Netflix and it created a huge problem for Starz, because all of the [pay-TV] operators were outraged that Starz was selling their stuff for pennies—what the other guys were paying dollars for." Underestimating Netflix was an industry default. Lauren Zalaznick—whose decade-plus run as a senior executive at NBCUniversal put networks like Bravo on the cultural map—recalled internal discussions systematically removing disruptors from consideration. "The debate around who was competitive with us," she recalled, "was so compartmentalized that this thing called Netflix was thought of as something else. It did not register."

Streaming began to command more and more of Netflix's cash and engineering resources, though it was offered as a "freebie" for existing DVD subscribers, remembers Hunt, who left Netflix in 2017 and joined a medical startup, Curai, which uses machine learning to help patients provide the right information to their doctors. Netflix needed to find a way to charge for streaming.

The race to embrace Netflix's streaming destiny set in motion the biggest mistake in the company's history—the decision in 2011 to separate the company's DVD rental business into a separate service called

Qwikster. Critics trashed the idea, and Hastings himself became the object of ridicule by *Saturday Night Live*, which parodied his awkwardly lo-fi YouTube video apologizing for the misstep. The debacle cost Netflix millions of subscribers and pummeled the company's stock, which dropped more than 75 percent. Hastings tearfully apologized for damaging the company at a weekend management retreat months later, though executives say a pall remained over the company for a year. "The strategy was right, it was just implemented too quickly without listening to the customer, the consumer, and knowing their pressure points," said Steve Swasey, who was a communications executive at Netflix during the Qwikster affair.

Fortunately for Netflix, the dominant media giants were a few years away from embracing the future Hastings and his team were already creating. That gave the company time to smooth over the missteps. Disney even rode to a humbled Netflix's rescue with a 2012 deal that gave the streaming service access to new Disney, Pixar, Marvel, and *Star Wars* films starting in 2016, and library titles even sooner. The core of what Disney would launch with Disney+ years later would be offered to Netflix subscribers, and the titles would quickly become some of the service's most popular.

As Starz CEO, Albrecht said he personally appealed to Disney's Bob Iger to renew its licensing deal with the pay-TV network. But the Netflix pact had thrown a wrench into things. He warned Iger, in an email he declined to share, that Disney was making a giant mistake by enabling a disruptor. "God knows everybody made that mistake. Everyone took the money—they took the short money," Albrecht said. "What they thought was, 'When bonus time comes at the end of the year I will have met or exceeded my target max, and therefore I will max out my bonus.'"

The deal fattened the Burbank entertainment giant's bottom line. One analyst estimated it would deliver as much as $450 million in revenue in 2017 alone. But it was a bigger boon to Netflix, which added seventy-six million subscribers and billions in market valuation. Its stock rose from $12.38 a share when the deal was announced to $178.36 in August 2017, when Iger said he would pull the studio's movies from Netflix to launch its own direct-to-consumer business.

"Some people might have seen Reed as a wolf in sheep's clothing, but he had a head start. He had data and he knew the value of premium content that sat in the libraries of partners who would one day be competitors," says Yahoo CEO Jim Lanzone, a longtime internet entrepreneur and former chief digital officer of CBS who led development of its streaming service, CBS All Access. "What some people called 'overpaying' for the content at that time, Netflix knew very well what it was worth and what they were building towards."

For years, the club of studio executives in control scoffed at Netflix as a competitive threat. "It's a little bit like, is the Albanian army going to take over the world?" Time Warner chief executive Jeff Bewkes said in a 2010 interview. "I don't think so." The line eventually became one of the all-time "Dewey Defeats Truman" misreadings of the media landscape and consumer inclination.

By the time Hollywood started to get wise, Netflix was financing its own original series.

Sarandos and Cindy Holland together transformed Netflix into one of the industry's most prolific producers of television. "And a lot of that culture, I think, is a hybrid of Ted's showmanship and Cindy's beautifully modulated creativity," producer Ryan Murphy once told *New York* magazine. Holland grew up "a nerdy little kid" in a small town near Omaha, Nebraska, surrounded by cornfields and nurturing big ambitions. The family didn't have cable TV, so she immersed herself in books (Kurt Vonnegut's *Cat's Cradle* and *Slaughterhouse-Five* were favorites). When her parents—a father who was an army helicopter pilot and Rhodes scholar who practiced law, and a stay-at-home mom—assured Holland and her sister they could do anything they put their minds to, she took them at their word. She studied political science at Stanford University and delved into competitive water-skiing for a year after graduation.

Holland's path to Hollywood began as a manuscript reader for Paramount Pictures in New York, which combined her love of reading and movies. "I could read really quickly and turn around coverage overnight," she said. Within a few months, though, it became clear that if she wanted to work in the film business, she would have to relocate to Los Angeles, so she headed west with the names of a couple of more literary-minded producers tucked in her pocket. She joined Paula Weinstein's Spring Creek production company and stayed as it merged with Barry Levinson's Baltimore Pictures to form Baltimore/Spring Creek Productions. She spent the next four and a half years on the Warner Bros. studio lot working on mainstream studio projects but found herself drawn to independent and art house films and documentaries and foreign films that struggled to find an audience.

"I was frustrated. After seeing directing samples from these incredible filmmakers, documentarians and narrative filmmakers who were trying to break into the big movie business—these works weren't being seen anywhere," Holland said. Recognizing that pursuing a career as an independent producer would be fraught with challenges, she accepted a position working for Mutual Film Company with two accomplished producers/financiers, Gary Levinsohn and Mark Gordon, who had built a network of partners to finance and distribute films around the world. The dot-com boom signaled a sea change for Holland, who believed the internet could solve the distribution problems for the types of films she loved. She joined a startup called Kozmo, which promised one-hour deliveries of DVDs (among other impulse items). She began negotiating direct deals with the studios' home video divisions for a supply of VHS and DVD titles for home delivery. The only other company doing that was a West Coast startup called Netflix. Kozmo crashed and burned. Netflix, well, didn't. Sarandos recruited his former rival, Holland, who was initially leery of joining another pre-IPO startup running out of cash. But she was impressed enough with Hastings and the team he surrounded himself with to take the leap. She found herself aligned with Sarandos, who shared her passion for outside-the-mainstream fare.

As vice president of content acquisition, Holland oversaw U.S. licensing and helped build Netflix's film and TV library, first on DVD and then for its streaming service. A call came in 2012 from Media Rights Capital to gauge her interest in an original series that forever changed the streaming service's trajectory—*House of Cards*. Netflix had dabbled briefly in acquiring independent films through a division called Red Envelope Entertainment, and its demise was a personal frustration for Sarandos. He and Hastings agreed they should instead focus on amassing as much content as possible to attract the broadest group of subscribers. Original programming was intended to come into the picture down the line.

House of Cards represented a singular opportunity. The political thriller starred Kevin Spacey, the Academy Award–winning actor whose reputation later plummeted amid sexual assault allegations. He played Frank Underwood, a ruthlessly ambitious South Carolina congressman. The series marked director David Fincher's television debut following an acclaimed film career, whose eclectic body of work included *Se7en*, *Fight Club*, *Zodiac*, and *The Social Network*. Holland was familiar with the original British series on which this new drama was based and was impressed with the script from playwright Beau Willimon (which she had to read in a room in MRC's offices), who brought a gimlet-eyed insider's perspective to the Washington political scene, having worked on the Senate campaigns of Chuck Schumer and Hillary Clinton and the presidential bids of Democrats Bill Bradley and Howard Dean.

"I went back and told Ted, 'If we're going to do original content, we have to do this,'" recalled Holland, saying the talent associated with the project would provide quality control. "David Fincher has never made a bad movie. At the time, Kevin Spacey was 'Kevin Spacey of Oscar-winning fame,' and it would be his first TV project."

Sarandos knew, from reviewing years of DVD rental data and streaming reports, that this combination of talent would draw a big audience, larger than one might assume for a political drama. If Netflix was going to venture into original programming, it needed a big, ambitious test to see if it could compete with Hollywood's elite. Holland and Sarandos made an offer that Fincher and company simply couldn't refuse: $100 million for twenty-six episodes over two seasons. "We're going to have to go into the room and they have a thousand reasons to say no," Sarandos said. "We have to give them at least one reason to say yes."

Sarandos said he later reviewed the deal points with Hastings, whose gobsmacked response was: "Why would you do that?! That's a lot of money." Sarandos framed the gambit as a classic risk-reward proposition: "If it doesn't work, we will have overpaid for one show, which we're always at risk of doing, and if it does work, we could fundamentally change the direction of the business."

The February 1, 2013, debut of *House of Cards* marked a watershed moment for Netflix. Reviewers fawned over the series, casting it as a platform-defining show in the mold of HBO's *The Sopranos*. Overnight, Netflix redefined internet content, which heretofore had been synonymous with skateboarding fails, music videos, and cheap, low-quality fare. Netflix's offer broke with the orthodoxy of network development cycles—which required a pilot be produced to demonstrate the concept could be effectively realized before a full-season order was placed. It also flouted the time-honored tradition of releasing one television episode a week.

Netflix dropped the entire first season of *House of Cards*, all thirteen episodes, in one binge-worthy pile. Everything else on Netflix was available all at once, on demand, Sarandos reasoned. Why make an exception for a single show? Doing otherwise would fly in the face of the service's philosophy of putting consumers in control of when and how they watched. Besides, the data backed them up—when subscribers watched TV series on Netflix, it was like the old Lay's potato chip commercial. No one ever ate just one. The week Netflix announced the all-at-once release strategy for *House of Cards*, one prominent network executive called Sarandos, incredulous, and asked, "Ted, do you know how television works?" But Sarandos couldn't have cared less about honoring the industry's traditions or preserving its business models. The disruptor's singular focus was making its subscribers happy, and network executives themselves would ultimately be forced to adapt.

Lilyhammer marked the company's inaugural foray into originals. The series starred musician-turned-actor Steven Van Zandt as former gangster Frank "the Fixer" Tagliano, who enters the federal witness protection program, trading the gritty streets of New York for the fjords of Norway. The character was deliberately modeled after Silvio Dante, the mob consigliere Van Zandt played for eight years on *The Sopranos*. Netflix acquired U.S. rights to *Lilyhammer*, which was produced by Norwegian broadcaster NRK and Germany-based Red Arrow Studios International, after the first season was fully produced. Its budget had not been *Sopranos*-esque. Instead of the on-set trailers that are staples on most film and TV productions, this show had to rely on the generosity of local residents who agreed to host cast and crew members in their houses. Van Zandt knew he was in new territory, fronting an internet-distributed series. "All of my business people said, 'Are you crazy? You just came off of the greatest show in history, and now you're going to go to Norway? Who knows how good this show's going to be,'" Van Zandt said.

Sarandos, a lifelong fan of Van Zandt's work as the bandanna-clad guitarist in Bruce Springsteen's E Street Band, spoke with the star before closing the acquisition deal. He mentioned the plan to release every episode in one fell swoop. "He goes, 'Wait a minute, wait a minute, we just spent nine months of our lives making this show, and you're just going to dump it out all at once?!' And I go, 'Yeah, just like an album,'" Sarandos remembered with a chuckle.

Despite a lukewarm reception from critics in 2012, Netflix was able to use *Lilyhammer*'s debut to get attention for its foray into binge-release originals. A red-carpet launch event in Tribeca attracted Springsteen and other bandmates, as well as Tony Bennett and *Sopranos* actors like Vincent Pastore and Tony Sirico. The show went on to run for three seasons. Holland said *Lilyhammer* would serve another, unpublicized purpose:

it was a trial balloon to determine whether Netflix could successfully stream a piece of content across multiple territories and languages at once.

Each new series garnered progressively more prestige and subscribers. Prison comedy *Orange Is the New Black* quickly became a twin hit with *House of Cards*. Holland had read Piper Kerman's memoir about her year in prison and met with *Weeds* creator Jenji Kohan, whose studio, Lionsgate, had optioned the rights, to hear her describe how she would make it into a series. "We were taken with the vision," said Holland, herself a member of the LGBT community who had spoken to the nation's television critics in 2018 about growing up and rarely seeing herself reflected onscreen. "This is a good way to explore women and incarceration, issues of identity, issues of race and subverting people's expectations of these people and what their stories are, who they are as fully dimensionalized beings. I can't tell you I knew it would be a global sensation. I knew I loved it."

Behind these two brand-defining hits came a gritty drama about the life of Colombian drug lord Pablo Escobar, *Narcos*; the opulently mounted historical drama *The Crown*; and the bracingly retro science fiction thriller *Stranger Things*.

The decision to make *House of Cards* reshaped the company and the industry, and it also continues to resonate quite literally on the Netflix platform itself. Each original Netflix show starts with a mnemonic (also called an audio signature) based on the "double knock" of Frank Underwood at the end of the show's second season. The sound has become so inextricably associated with watching Netflix that the company decided to name a major 2021 promotional event Tudum. "You know it when you hear it," a press release explained.

After taking on the establishment by making its own shows, the next act for Netflix would be to challenge the industry's incumbents in virtually every corner of the world. Hastings laid bare those ambitions as he took the stage in January 2016 to deliver the keynote at the Consumer Electronics Show in Las Vegas. The company had already notched an impressive list of television milestones before the lanky, goateed executive appeared in the spotlight. It was the first to offer a full season's worth of episodes at once, inaugurating the era of binge viewing. It was the first to debut shows across the globe on the same day, so viewers from Argentina to Finland could enjoy the same stories at the same exact moment. It had replaced the network programming schedule with its on-demand world fueled by personal choice.

As the flags of the world's nations appeared in a video backdrop, Hastings declared that the service had just gone live in 130 countries, including India, Nigeria, Poland, Russia, Saudi Arabia, Singapore, and Turkey. "Right now, you are witnessing the birth of a global TV network," said Hastings, his voice rising with enthusiasm as he spoke. "Whether in Sydney or Saint Petersburg, Singapore or Seoul, Santiago or Saskatoon, you now can be part of the internet TV revolution. No more waiting. No more watching on a schedule that's not your own. No frustration. Just Netflix."

PART II

War Drums

CHAPTER 4

▶ The Red Wedding

The *Game of Thrones* production team spent fifty-five nights shooting outdoors in Ireland, enduring subfreezing temperatures, snow and rain, and wading through mud and sheep droppings, to create a battle sequence involving the Army of the Dead. It was among the most ambitious continuous battle sequences ever filmed. Peter Dinklage, who played Tyrion Lannister, called it "brutal" and said it made the fan-favorite "Battle of the Bastards" scene from the show's sixth season "look like a theme park." That extensive production effort is one reason why the show cost about $15 million per episode to make.

Given the show's budget and the once-high-rolling style of a network known for its elaborate Emmy and Golden Globe bashes and year-round tastemaker gatherings, the party after the *Thrones* premiere felt like a letdown. It wasn't the price tag—at $2 million, it was the most expensive event the company had ever hosted, but a lot of that was due to the onerous cost of New York City logistics and union wages. Certainly, the millions hadn't bought a posh venue. The party for one thousand guests was held at the Ziegfeld Ballroom, an antiseptic event hall built on the ruins of one of moviedom's most famous palaces, the Ziegfeld Theatre on West Fifty-Fourth Street. The Ziegfeld, which had been the site of *Close Encounters of the Third Kind*'s premiere and a succession of other events, replaced a Broadway theater erected in 1927. The original venue had hosted the Emmy Awards and, for a decade, TV's *Perry*

Como Show. Emotional nights had later unfolded in the grand, single-screen movie house, such as the 2006 world premiere of *United 93*, the docudrama about the doomed September 11 flight. It had screened for a Tribeca Film Festival opening-night audience that included family members of the doomed flight's victims. Dozens of them wailed en masse during the film's harrowing final reel.

Decades removed from such emotion, Sterno cans kept bins of brown-sauced appetizers warm as screens on the walls played video footage of flickering flames on a loop. Servers working the event wore bright red T-shirts bearing the show's logo. Generous-spirited *Thrones* fans might have interpreted the splashes of color as a nod to House Lannister from the show. Mostly, though, it just looked garish—a word seldom associated with HBO.

Previous HBO affairs at Radio City had been followed by lavish takeovers of the restaurant levels downstairs at Rockefeller Center. Thousands of guests would pick fresh shellfish off four-foot towers of shaved ice as mixologists made them perfect Manhattans with artisan cherries. Now the perfunctory scene seemed like something found on a cruise ship.

Just six weeks before the premiere, AT&T had finally escaped the long shadow of the U.S. Department of Justice. The department's antitrust division had waged a suspiciously dogged effort to block the company's acquisition of Time Warner, which had first been proposed in October 2016. An appeals court in February 2019 had unanimously rejected the DOJ's appeal of a June 2018 federal court ruling that allowed the merger to proceed. Even though AT&T–Time Warner was a "vertical" deal—combining disparate distribution and content operations with little overlap, unlike "horizontal" mashups of similar assets—antitrust regulators decided to file suit in the fall of 2017. The basis of the legal complaint was that the merger would harm both consumers and competitors. By owning DirecTV and other cable and internet distribution outlets, as well as major programming entities like HBO, Warner Bros., and Turner Broadcasting, the government argued, AT&T

could manipulate pricing and saddle both rivals and customers with higher fees.

President Donald Trump's very public loathing of CNN, a key Time Warner asset, clearly played a role in the decision by Trump appointee Makan Delrahim, the DOJ's antitrust chief, to try to block the deal in court. The lawsuit came a full year after the merger was first proposed and after a host of other regulatory agencies around the world had given it their blessing. When the case went to trial, it became the first vertical merger to be challenged by U.S. regulators in more than forty years. U.S. District Court judge Richard J. Leon denied a request by AT&T's legal team to unearth documents that could have established a clear Trump tie, and the White House adamantly denied putting any thumbs on the scale. Press reports since the trial, including a piece by *New Yorker* political writer Jane Mayer, have cited Washington and administration sources asserting that Trump had ordered the DOJ to wage war on the deal.

There was also this awkward piece of circumstantial evidence: When Disney spent $71.3 billion to acquire most of Rupert Murdoch's 21st Century Fox in 2018, Trump made a congratulatory phone call to Murdoch and publicly praised the transaction. That massive deal, which netted the Murdoch family billions, also gave Disney half of the theatrical movie market, control of Hulu, and other advantages of scale, and resulted in thousands of layoffs. That was a warmer reception than AT&T and Time Warner received two years earlier, when candidate Trump blasted the proposed merger as "a deal we will not approve in my administration because it's too much concentration of power in the hands of too few."

As the six-week antitrust trial unfolded in federal court in Washington, John Stankey—who had been appointed as head of the Time Warner portfolio in 2017 despite lacking any entertainment experience—attended the court proceedings in person every day. There was little for him to do, seated in the gallery of the cavernous, windowless courtroom as witnesses testified before Judge Leon, who would decide the case without the involvement of a jury. As Stankey; his boss, AT&T CEO Randall

Stephenson; and other top executives like Time Warner CEO Jeff Bewkes took the stand, drama came only sporadically. At times, the interactions between lawyers, witnesses, and the judge could be difficult to hear across the courtroom's expanse, and Judge Leon often opted to turn on a white-noise machine to protect sensitive details. Daniel Petrocelli, the flamboyant, white-haired attorney who had successfully sued O. J. Simpson in civil court, was leading AT&T's legal defense and appeared to have a distinct edge over the discursive and bookish DOJ prosecutors. In June 2018, several weeks after the trial ended, Leon issued his ruling, siding overwhelmingly with AT&T, shredding the government's lead witness, and cautioning the plaintiff not to pursue an "unjust" appeal. The DOJ surprised many observers by ignoring that advice and filing an appeal. It would pursue the legal claim until February 2019, when a three-judge federal appellate panel delivered a unanimous rejection. Instead of trying to take its quest to the U.S. Supreme Court, the government finally relented.

As the trial dragged on, Stankey and the Time Warner troops were quietly but avidly moving forward with their plans under the assumption that Judge Leon would give his blessing. Stankey had much more in mind for WarnerMedia than a new corporate identity and logo—he was orchestrating a series of wholesale changes to a company whose main divisions had largely prospered for several decades. In the streaming era, Stankey believed, the whole enterprise needed to be reconceived. Gone would be the silos that separated the company's three main business units—Turner (home of CNN and other cable networks, like TNT and TBS), Warner Bros., and HBO.

To achieve $2.5 billion in cost savings from the deal, operations like distribution, marketing, and affiliate relations could be centralized, the thinking went. At the same time as this dramatic consolidation—which meant losing an array of seasoned executive talent—the company would make a bold move in a different direction. It would wean itself from the lucrative licensing deals it had struck for years with major streaming services, primarily Netflix. With its pay-TV networks in an irreversible decline of subscribers, it would look to acquire video customers directly, over the internet. Instead of reaping hundreds of millions of dollars from selling off shows like *Friends* to Netflix or HBO's slate to Amazon as Time Warner (like its media peers) had long done, WarnerMedia would instead look to hold back content for deployment on a subscription streaming service of its own.

When it came to naming the new service, several brands under the corporate tent were considered, including several variations involving "Warner Bros." Consultants were hired and focus groups convened, and the resulting research pointed to Warner Bros. as the name that resonated most with consumers. It wasn't on the same level of recognition as Disney, certainly, but the blue-and-white "WB" shield was known from the start of Bugs Bunny cartoons and nearly a century of other work. Bob Greenblatt, a well-traveled TV producer and executive who was installed in March 2019 as entertainment chairman at WarnerMedia, had a different idea. The new operation, he argued, should draft off the success and cachet of HBO. Internal debates pitted Greenblatt and other proponents of using HBO in the name against those who felt certain it would risk diluting the brand. Those in favor included, fortuitously for Greenblatt, key members of the AT&T management team, who considered HBO a valuable asset but not an untouchable one. For example, AT&T executives boggled many minds at WarnerMedia by repeatedly questioning why HBO wasn't running ads. HBO Max, as the new offering would be known, would include the regular HBO portfolio that cable and satellite customers get, plus new original shows, as well as Warner Bros. film and TV mainstays, from *Casablanca* to *Friends*. For those who had spent decades building it up, HBO equaled prestige and distinction. It did not mean reruns of *The Big Bang Theory*.

The sharp left turn from wholesaling—making its service available to pay-TV operators, who then sold it to consumers, as HBO had been doing for nearly fifty years—to direct retail raised a host of thorny questions. None of them could have been anticipated when the network first lit up half a century earlier.

Home Box Office, which went on the air in 1972, had a somewhat unlikely founder in Charles Dolan, paterfamilias of one of New York's most prominent media dynasties—if also perhaps the city's least popular. From its roots in Sterling Manhattan Cable, which later evolved into Cablevision, the Dolan empire eventually grew to include Madison Square Garden and its anchor tenants, the New York Knicks and Rangers basketball and hockey teams. Charles Dolan's son James began overseeing the clubs in 1999, ushering in a period of drift—and no championships—for both franchises. MSG, which promotes itself as "the world's most famous arena," began the 2020s with fans often raising an angry chant directed at Dolan: "Sell the team!"

It is said that innovation starts with a problem in need of a solution. In the case of HBO, the problem was the vexing task of pulling in clean TV signals through New York City's concrete canyons in the 1960s. As one of the earliest investors in cable television—along with other key figures like Ted Turner, John Malone, and Comcast's Ralph Roberts—Dolan decided to run coaxial cables under the streets to deliver *Bonanza*, *Laugh-In*, and the evening news. It would be the first underground network built in the U.S. As Sterling's ad campaign put it: "New York needs help: As TV sets get better, reception gets worse."

Like most things in New York, the project carried a steep cost. Maneuvering heavy equipment underground, around subway tunnels, sewer lines, and basements, required Sterling and its partner, Time Life, to run up significant debt. Dolan needed to find ways to fund his ambitious buildout and keep his company afloat. On a cruise to Europe with his family, the executive had an epiphany. In addition to bringing customers clean, reliable signals of twelve broadcast networks, he would give them an extra incentive to be a Sterling subscriber. He would offer them an entirely new TV experience, for a small monthly fee— effectively a subsidy for laying all that cable. Before long, the idea had a business plan and a working name: the Green Channel. It was later renamed Home Box Office to convey the novel excitement of experiencing top-shelf entertainment from the comfort of the living room. Dolan said the network's assortment of offerings, from sports to movies to live events, all presented without commercial interruption, would make it "the Macy's of television."

The first programs to air on HBO were a feature film (*Sometimes a Great Notion*) and live coverage of a polka festival in Wilkes-Barre, Pennsylvania (the geographical limit of the network's signal before satellite technology took it much farther). The initial shows were hardly milestones, but their mere existence heralded a revolution. Instead of receiving television programming via rabbit ears and putting up with advertising as the trade-off for free broadcast fare, viewers now had the option of paying for a commercial-free signal. This was television's "Mr. Watson, come here" moment—the birth of the bundle. After HBO gained traction, first-wave networks like Nickelodeon, CNN, and MTV would soon follow in the late 1970s and early 1980s, as primitive cable systems and set-top boxes proliferated across the country.

For all of his operational savvy, Dolan, a college dropout from Cleveland who got his start making sports newsreels and industrial films, was never a programming visionary. He saw HBO as a means to an end. After it was up and running, he sold his share to Time Inc. in 1973, which would nurture the pioneering cable network through mergers with Warner Bros. in 1989 and Turner Broadcasting in 1995. HBO found its voice in its early years with edgy comedy specials, R-rated studio movies (a precious commodity, especially in the pre-VCR days), and original satirical fare like *Not Necessarily the News*. Its programming steadily grew deeper and more varied, reflected by a gallery of executives and talent personifying a singular business approach. One former HBO executive whose tenure began in the early 1980s remembered the company's being populated by "the best and the brightest. When you were there, you felt you had just been accepted at Harvard. That was the feeling." The network, the person added, "was new and young and hot, filled with all these scrappy, really smart kids. It was an ambitious, driven group of people."

Operating by a completely different set of rules than traditional network TV—which had to please advertisers and censors and avoid any whiff of controversy—the upstart HBO took a series of big swings. The result was a run of shows few networks have ever matched (albeit with dramatically less shelf space to fill and more financial resources to play with, competitors often pointed out). *The Sopranos. The Wire. Girls. The Larry Sanders Show. Deadwood. Sex and the City. Six Feet Under. Curb Your Enthusiasm.* Comedy specials from George Carlin, Chris Rock, and Robin Williams at their respective peaks. Immersive, cinematic miniseries like *Band of Brothers* and *Angels in America.* Documentary series like *Taxicab Confessions* and *Real Sports*, plus feature documentary films like *Capturing the Friedmans.*

HBO redefined television—that square box long known for Walter Cronkite and Ed Sullivan—by embracing creative risk-taking. It didn't get embarrassed when Marnie masturbated in a public restroom in the third episode of *Girls.* It didn't flinch (after some internal hand-wringing) when *Sopranos* antihero Tony Soprano garroted a mob snitch during a college tour with his daughter just five episodes in. It didn't apologize when *Game of Thrones* character Ramsay, the sadistic bastard son of the Lord of the Dreadfort, tore off Sansa's wedding gown and raped her, with her screams of agony reverberating well beyond the end of the scene, in an episode that drew howls from critics. In its earliest years, it set the template by smirking defiantly as Carlin launched into a monologue about the seven words you can never say on television— "shit," "piss," "fuck," "cunt," "cocksucker," "motherfucker," and "tits"— right there on Milton Berle's square box. HBO from its earliest days forged a brand that stood out by offering to immerse viewers in an *ethos*, a screw-you embrace of ambiguity, scandal, and the dissonant notes previously associated with films and novels. The network's famed slogan, born in the mid-1990s—"It's not TV. It's HBO."—was a sharp line of ad copy that had the added advantage of being largely true.

As it racked up scores of Emmys and hoarded prestige, HBO struggled mightily to reckon with a nascent technology whose own rise to omnipresence paralleled that of the company: the internet. While a similar charge could be leveled at most traditional media companies, the starts and stops and long periods of complacency would leave deep marks on the company's culture, creating an additional challenge when the urgency of streaming took hold.

In 2020, HBO Max arrived on the market months after rival streaming launches like Disney+, Apple TV+, and Peacock. Five years earlier, however, HBO had been the leader, not a laggard, in launching HBO Now, a direct-to-consumer streaming version of its pay-TV network. HBO Now allowed anyone with an internet connection to watch the network's most buzzy shows, departing from four-plus decades of being offered exclusively as an add-on to a pay-TV subscription, a model that had enriched both the network and cable operators as the offering's popularity rose.

There was one big catch, however. Because cable and satellite operators were unsettled by the notion that consumers could finally get HBO without going through them, they insisted that the "most favored nation" clause in their contracts be honored. HBO Now would therefore cost $14.99 a month, the same price as it was through the traditional bundle. Showtime and Starz, rival premium networks, had opted to discount their streaming extensions, which created friction with many of their distribution partners. HBO's newer offering also lacked any new wrinkles compared with linear HBO—again, for fear that the pay-TV operators who had nursed HBO since its infancy would see it as a competitive threat. As a result, HBO Now has been an also-ran, compared with other established streaming services, accumulating a lackluster eight million subscribers by the end of 2019.

In many ways, the streaming version of HBO was the entertainment equivalent of universal health care legislation that finally made it through Congress in watered-down form. It followed more than a decade of active exploration of digital alternatives at HBO and Time Warner, which infamously bore the official name AOL Time Warner from 2001 to 2003. The disastrous merger with America Online was one of the biggest debacles in U.S. corporate history, but it somehow managed not to torpedo Time Warner. In that period, the entertainment side of the house was firing on all cylinders, releasing films like the *Harry Potter* and *Lord of the Rings* franchises and a string of TV hits produced by Warner Bros. Television and HBO. The booming DVD business brought in additional gushers of new revenue. Initial attempts by AOL executives to foster synergy didn't go beyond a brief migration to AOL's email server.

Even inside "old" Time Warner, disconnects that would be hard to imagine at, say, Disney were routine. One division, instead of complementing another's efforts, would simply shrug. When *Harry Potter and the Sorcerer's Stone*, the first film adaptation by Warner Bros. from the mega-selling book series, landed in 2001, *Entertainment Weekly* critic Lisa Schwarzbaum gave it a grade of B and wrote that it had "many charms, but few surprises." By far the most unfortunate aftereffect of the merger's meltdown was that it made the company look askance at technology. The "innovator's dilemma" described throughout this book is perhaps nowhere more evident than at AOL Time Warner in the 2000s.

Jonathan Miller, chairman and CEO of AOL from 2002 to 2006, recalled bringing several potential acquisitions and joint venture proposals to the Time Warner board and to Jeff Bewkes and Dick Parsons, then president and CEO, respectively. Green-lighting many of them would likely have set the company—and the media and tech industries—on a dramatically different course. Miller met with Chad Hurley, one of the cofounders of YouTube, at the bar of San Francisco's Four Seasons Hotel at the end of 2005, the year the online video site launched. After Hurley described a hockey-stick pattern of growth for uploaded videos on the site, Miller scrambled into action, gauging the price range (roughly $550 million) and preparing an offer. In January 2006, Miller pitched the purchase to the board of Time Warner. "They told us to take a hike," Miller remembered. "So obsessed" with making a deal happen, despite the reputation of YouTube as a repository of illegally obtained clips owned by media companies, he approached the board again a few months later. "At that point, everyone was thinking about suing You-

Tube. I said, 'Don't sue it, just buy it. We could put top-level content on it. . . . That'll win.'" The answer was still no. Google would end up paying $1.65 billion to acquire YouTube later in 2006.

Separately, in July 2006, Facebook was being shopped around with a $1 billion price tag by founder Mark Zuckerberg and his business partners. Yahoo held talks but balked at the price. Miller told Zuckerberg he could offer $1.1 billion. The founder expressed disdain for AOL but said he would do a deal for $1.4 billion. "So I went to Jeff [Bewkes] and said, 'You're not going to like this. It's not making money. It's speculative. But it could be the future.'" To make the financials work, and avoid costing Time Warner "a penny," Miller told Bewkes, Time Warner could sell off MapQuest and some of its other digital properties. AOL, despite the misfire of the merger, was still delivering billions in revenue to Time Warner. "'I just need the float,'" Miller remembered telling Bewkes. "'This is a shot. We should take the shot.' His answer was, 'If you think you should sell MapQuest, sell MapQuest.'" As to the bigger prize: "The answer was no."

Today, of course, Facebook has nearly two billion active daily users, owns Instagram and WhatsApp, and brings in more than $85 billion in annual revenue. YouTube estimates that five hundred hours of video content are uploaded to its platform every minute, with viewers watching more than one billion hours of video per day. In July 2021, Google reported that its video platform had raked in a record $7 billion in ad revenue in a single quarter.

Another missed opportunity was Hulu, which started with backing from News Corp (where Miller would lead digital operations after cutting ties with Time Warner) and NBCUniversal. Only years after seeing Hulu become a powerhouse did Time Warner buy a 10 percent stake (which was subsequently sold by AT&T).

Perhaps the most stunning swing-and-miss of all was the chance to buy Netflix. Albrecht said one business development executive proposed snapping up the DVD-by-mail company in 2007, as it began streaming. The idea stagnated.

The marquee acquisition during the Bewkes years became an alba-tross around his neck: the purchase of social networking company Bebo for $850 million. When it crashed and burned almost immediately, he conceded that the company "may have overpaid." As to making a play for Netflix, though, he remained defiant: "We *have* a Netflix; we have HBO," he insisted in 2014.

In those same risk-averse years, executives at HBO did succeed at assembling a digital service called MyHBO, a name that drew inspira-tion from the social media supernova that was MySpace. Later dubbed HBO Go, the streaming version of the network required a pay-TV sub-scription. Time Warner on a corporate level also held extensive discus-sions about an online service that would aggregate content from Warner Bros., HBO, and Turner Broadcasting—essentially a primitive version of HBO Max. The latter would end up being regarded as too risky to the company's legacy business model.

Albrecht, HBO's former chairman and chief executive, recalled bringing in a former digital executive from Warner Bros., Jim Moloshok, to try to crack the code. The reaction from the rank and file was at best indifferent. "I said at a meeting once to a bunch of my associates, 'Jim Moloshok does not have to apologize for the creation of the internet. It's not his fault that we're in this conversation, guys,'" Albrecht said. Inter-nal discussions reflected a deep rift between those who felt the company had to make a leap beyond the traditional TV bundle and those who adamantly believed that it was a foolish digression. Opponents pointed to follies like MySpace, which Rupert Murdoch's News Corp acquired for $580 million in 2005. (It would shrivel to a fraction of that size after being overtaken by social networking rival Facebook, and eventually be sold off for $35 million.) "There was one side of the table that I was ask-ing to bring us into the future," Albrecht, who left the network in 2007 after being charged with assaulting his then-girlfriend, but rebounded and landed leadership roles at Starz and Legendary Entertainment, said, "and another side of the table that was saying, 'That future's going to destroy us too soon. We've got a great business, don't fuck it up.'" The executive shook his head. "Maintaining the status quo is the enemy of innovation."

JOHN STANKEY MAY HAVE BEEN A Bell Head, but he wasn't so ensconced in the clubby confines of telecom that he didn't see tech giants as his direct competitors. The hypothetical scenario of his being in charge when deals for Facebook, YouTube, and Netflix crossed the transom is worth pondering. His sense of urgency about Big Tech did not express itself in a very congenial way after the Time Warner deal closed, however. Stankey was in rare form during a town hall for employees in the summer of 2018, seated across from HBO boss Richard Plepler. In a postmerger get-together with all of the comity of a block party populated by Jets and Sharks, Stankey repeatedly took the air out of the room with his blunt-force comments. First, he said the merger process would be grueling and tantamount to "childbirth" (a comparison, he allowed, that his wife detested his making). Specifically for HBO, the boss stressed to Plepler and his troops, it needed to respond to the ways modern TV viewing had been fundamentally changed by mobile devices and digital technology. HBO needed to attract devoted viewers on more than just Sunday nights. "It's not hours a week, and it's not hours a month," he warned. "We need hours a *day*." Those watching the town hall via livestream found it far more awkward than those gathered in the intimate auditorium, where Plepler fought bravely to retain his game face. "The body language was just horrific," one longtime executive said, cringing at the memory. "When you saw that locked-off two-shot of them facing each other and the back and forth, you just knew it was bad."

In an interview months later, Stankey didn't dwell on body language but reaffirmed the importance of his message. "In a scaled environment, where it's no longer good enough to have a relationship with twenty-five percent of the market, or twenty-five percent market share of pay-TV," he said, "you need to have a relationship with virtually all customers out there if you're going to compete with the Googles of the world or the Amazons of the world and the Apples of the world." This drive to scale up, though, was coming at a time when senior executives were leaving the ship by the dozens, with the consolidation putsch following an anxious wait for the government's lawsuit to play out.

Stankey ultimately acknowledged the level of anxiety that had seeped into WarnerMedia's workplace culture. In such a fraught environment, he reflected, his ramrod absence of subtlety often made the situation worse. Some employees "maybe [didn't] have the greatest things to say about" him, he conceded, and said, "I try to include them and work with them in a constructive fashion. By and large, on most days, I think I accomplish that. But I'm not perfect, and we all can do better from time to time."

If Stankey threw a lot of inside fastballs, AT&T CEO Randall Stephenson, in baseball terms, was more of an off-speed pitcher, delivering curveballs to the investment community and employees. His pronouncements to Wall Street on quarterly earnings calls or at conferences or in media appearances often came as news to the troops. "When he said we would have live sports and news on HBO Max," one Warner-Media executive said in 2019, "no one knew that was happening before he said it."

Despite his folksy manner and Oklahoma drawl, Stephenson memorably rattled his charges in 2018 by suggesting a dialectic for HBO and its staunchest competitor. "I think of Netflix kind of as the Walmart of SVOD [or, subscription video on demand]," he said, whereas "HBO is kind of Tiffany. It's a very premium, high-end brand for premium content." (A high-level HBO executive, still stewing about the comparison weeks later, demanded, "What's Walmart's market cap, like, five hundred billion dollars? Is that supposed to be a *bad* thing?!") Bob Greenblatt didn't wait long before firing a similar shot. Days after being installed as entertainment chairman at WarnerMedia, he told NBC News that Netflix "doesn't have a brand. It's just a place you go to get anything—it's like *Encyclopaedia Britannica*. That's a great business model when you're trying to reach as many people on the planet as you can."

Netflix founder and CEO Reed Hastings, for his part, shrugged off any suggestion of a rivalry. "We compete more with (and lose to) *Fortnite* than HBO," Hastings wrote in a letter to investors in January 2019.

Hastings's dismissive taking of the high road must have been all the more galling to those who vividly recalled how HBO was positioned when Netflix was just gearing up to begin streaming its first original series, *Lilyhammer*, in 2012. Bewkes scoffed at the upstart, insisting that Netflix was "a two-hundred-pound chimp, not an eight-hundred-pound gorilla," just one rival among many. "HBO could have *been* Netflix," Wall Street analyst Michael Nathanson said years later. "But it hasn't seemed like its owners have had the stomach for it." Employees who were at the company in this period paint a picture of hubris. Streaming offerings HBO Go and Now "had four walls," as one former executive put it. Their user experience was circumscribed and designed to be less dynamic than the traditional TV one. It didn't let viewers skip the credits or watch an entire season at once, unlike the precision-tooled, algorithmic Netflix interface, which thousands of engineers had designed to "delight" customers. When was the last time anyone had been genuinely delighted by cable TV?

In mounting its assault on HBO, the Albanian army invaded familiar terrain. It wooed comedians like Amy Schumer, Dave Chappelle, and Jerry Seinfeld with breathtakingly large checks. It locked up television's most prolific showrunners—*Grey's Anatomy*'s Shonda Rhimes, *American Horror Story*'s Ryan Murphy, and *Black-ish* creator Kenya Barris—with nine-figure deals and signed Barack and Michelle Obama to a production deal. When Ron Howard's adaptation of J. D. Vance's bestselling memoir *Hillbilly Elegy* was shopped to buyers, Netflix offered $45 million, more than double the highest bid of any competitor, including HBO.

Netflix has poured billions into making, acquiring, and marketing its programming, including originals like *The Crown* and *Stranger Things* and films like *The Irishman*. In addition to the money, it also leaves talent alone, for better and for worse—echoing the commercial-free, anything-goes sandbox provided by HBO to George Carlin, *Sopranos* creator David Chase, and dozens more. Green-light authority is also far more dispersed than at pay-TV networks. (Small wonder it managed to blast out seven hundred original series on its platform in 2018.)

Traditional networks also smother productions in notes. Maclain and Chapman Way got a "very cold" reaction from a number of distributors when shopping their six-part documentary series, *Wild Wild Country*, about an India-based cult's incursion into rural Oregon. "A lot of people were looking for a name, a recognizable celebrity," Maclain Way recalled. One such skeptic was HBO, one of whose executives said they would consider buying the show, but only if someone famous would narrate the series. Enter Netflix. Without a narrator, *Wild Wild Country* drew an adoring critical response, won a prime-time Emmy Award, and (albeit in the absence of any empirical data) appeared to be one of the most popular original shows ever to stream.

THE LACK OF CONTINUITY WOULD END up being a theme during the final season of *Game of Thrones*. A Starbucks cup mistakenly left behind by one of the actors was somehow overlooked by the crew and network and made it into a finished scene. An HBO statement acknowledged the mistake, and many fans saw the quality-control lapse as further proof that the show had failed to stick the landing. While it attracted a massive audience, scale came at a cost. While Plepler had nurtured *Game of Thrones*, ordering costly reshoots and placing a risky, old-fashioned bet based on creative instincts, the series had devolved into a corporate symbol, managed accordingly. AT&T used footage of dragons from the show in a video promoting the Time Warner deal to employees. The final season had a healthy marketing budget of $20 million, a large chunk of which went to a sixty-second co-branded Super Bowl commercial with Bud Light. The co-branded spot raised eyebrows but went over well with mass audiences. By the time NCAA March Madness arrived, broadcasts of the basketball tournament on TBS were peppered with on-air promos. AT&T stores sold *Thrones*-themed cell phone cases. Company Twitter accounts joined the fray, tweeting things like, "Send a raven - they're on to the #Elite8. #MarchMadness." The tournament's Final Four in Minneapolis featured a *Thrones*-themed shot contest, with replica props from the show on display. AT&T promised its augmented-reality technology would "bring game attendees into the *Game of Thrones* realm on the stadium's video screen above center court."

The reality at Ziegfeld Ballroom could have used some augmentation. Partygoers retreated to their separate camps and did little mingling. Cast members, including breakout stars like Kit Harington and Emilia Clarke and better-known Hollywood names like Jason Momoa and Peter Dinklage, seemed by far the most ebullient, celebrating the show's remarkable path. For the rest of the stakeholders, the mood was uncertain, verging on despondent. Asked how he was holding up, one surviving HBO executive shrugged and said, "I don't know if I'm okay. Ask me in a few months." Where most studio bosses would have been glad-handing and love-your-work-let's-do-lunch–ing, Stankey stood in a cluster of Dallas-based executives from AT&T. "People have been asking if they would have to start paying for their own drinks," the new boss said, scoffing at the notion that AT&T would cut corners. Greenblatt, the urbane television veteran who had joined WarnerMedia weeks earlier as its entertainment chairman, stood with his own small group of loyalists, surveying the scene. "Without Richard there, the party just didn't seem to have much connective tissue," one former HBO executive observed. "That's what he always brought."

David Benioff, the co-creator of *Game of Thrones*, had warmly thanked Plepler onstage at Radio City. Before the screening, Benioff and producing partner D. B. Weiss paid tribute to not only the creative collaboration but to a way of doing business that seemed to be going extinct under AT&T. "We'd like to thank everyone else in the *Game of Thrones* family," the showrunner said. "The experience that we have all had together, out in the rain and the snow and the mud and the sun, it's safe to say that none of us will ever have an experience like this again. It's safe to say that it's possible *no one* will ever have an experience like this again."

CHAPTER 5

▶ "The Status Quo, We Knew, Was Not Sustainable"

In the official, corporate-sanctified narrative of the Walt Disney Company, its drive to invest in its technology capabilities began nearly a generation ago, long before streaming became de rigueur. In this account, two signature deals made with Apple's Steve Jobs indicated the company's bold new direction under Bob Iger, the affable, camera-ready former TV weatherman who rose through the ranks at Capital Cities/ABC to become Disney's CEO in 2005. The first culture-shifting move, within two weeks of Iger's taking over as head of the company, enabled customers to buy popular ABC television shows to watch on their new video iPods, and the second was the $7.4 billion acquisition months later of Pixar, the computer animation pioneer led by Jobs.

"It was an interesting time," Iger mused about the 2000s in his memoir, *The Ride of a Lifetime*, "and marked what I saw as the beginning of the end of the traditional media as we knew it. Of great interest to me was the fact that almost every traditional media company, while trying to figure out its place in this changing world, was operating out of fear rather than courage, stubbornly trying to build a bulwark to protect old models that couldn't possibly survive the sea change that was under way."

The record of the twenty-first century, however, tells a far more complicated story about the timing and extent of Disney's digital wake-up call. It would squander $1.6 billion on acquisitions as it chased fads—from social networks to social gaming to viral video—that mattered little to its core business. It launched a short-lived "digital locker" service designed to prop up flagging sales of DVDs years after millions of Netflix consumers had demonstrated they preferred to pay per month to stream rather than invest larger sums to own Disney movies. As with the music industry, piracy would play an irresistible role in forcing change.

Former Disney-ABC Television Group president Anne Sweeney recalls buoyantly striding into a Monday morning staff meeting on May 23, 2005, eager to share the overnight ratings for the season finale of ABC's hit series *Desperate Housewives*. The sudsy prime-time drama, which explored the dark undercurrents of seemingly idyllic suburbia, had become a cultural phenomenon whose final episode attracted thirty million viewers. But before Sweeney could share the good news from Wisteria Lane, ABC's chief technical officer, Vince Roberts, asked to have the floor. He quietly placed a disc into a DVD player in the fifth-floor conference room and pressed play, and the images of Eva Longoria, Teri Hatcher, and Felicity Huffman flickered across the television screen.

"I said, 'Vince, that's the finale.' And he said, 'Yes, and it was available online for download fifteen minutes after it went off the air,'" Sweeney recounted years later. "Boy, talk about a killjoy . . . It totally gutted what we thought we understood about the size of our audience. Our audience was much bigger and we weren't getting paid for it—and there wasn't any legitimate way we could say to advertisers, 'Hey, we actually had ten million more viewers.'"

A few months later, Jobs would propose a solution to the television industry's online piracy woes—as he had done years earlier, when he met with executives of the free-falling music industry. The Pixar CEO flew to Burbank to offer a personal demonstration of the video iPod. Sweeney recalls Iger arranging a phone conversation with Jobs, in which the lead of the most secretive company in Silicon Valley dangled a tantalizing proposition: "I'd like to show you what we're working on."

Jobs met the ABC network chief in a conference room of the Team Disney executive office building, where he cracked open his laptop to show a version of the iTunes store that featured a giant image of *Lost*. He talked her through the process of downloading the show, then handed her a device that looked like Apple's popular music player, with a 1.8-inch video screen, and she watched an episode of the plane-crash survival drama. "It didn't occur to me until he left. I thought, 'Wait a minute, how did he get an episode of *Lost*?'" Sweeney says, though the answer was obvious. "Well, come on, everybody else was downloading it."

Disney and Apple quickly struck a deal and, in a stealthy logistics operation worthy of an episode of *Narcos*, used the company plane to transport master recordings of ABC's *Lost*, *Desperate Housewives*, *Night Stalker*, and two Disney Channel shows to Apple's headquarters in Cupertino. The chief of engineering hand-delivered the packages, wrapped in brown paper, into a locked room for uploading onto iTunes.

The partnership remained shrouded in secrecy until October 12, 2005, when Apple held a product unveiling at the opulent California Theatre, a restored 1927 movie house in San Jose. Iger appeared onstage and shook hands with Jobs in the first public demonstration of a thaw in Disney's frigid relationship with Pixar's controlling shareholder. Sweeney, who watched from the audience, said the iTunes deal marked the network's first step toward battling piracy. But the affiliates didn't see it that way. "That afternoon, we flew back to Burbank and my phone exploded," Sweeney recalled. "Many of our broadcast affiliates called and were very upset by the announcement. Major advertisers called as well. Not upset but wanting to let us know that they wanted to be a part of whatever we did next."

Having one foot in the future and one foot in the past made it difficult to maintain balance. From the dawn of digital through the modern streaming era, Disney has been a calculated risk-taker, mindful at every turn of its legacy and the billions of dollars being generated by traditional businesses.

The content deal with Apple was a building block in Iger's efforts to repair Disney's frayed relationship with Pixar's chief executive and controlling shareholder, which had grown toxic under Iger's predecessor, Michael Eisner. Disney's audacious deal to acquire the studio behind such animated blockbusters as *Toy Story* and *Finding Nemo* had benefits that extended beyond the movie theaters, merchandise sales, and theme parks: Iger gained one of technology's leading futurists as an advisor, confidant, and board member. Jobs's innate appreciation of the importance of brand, and his uncompromising emphasis on quality, touched every corner of Disney, from its billion-dollar overhaul of Disney's California Adventure theme park to its expansion of its cruise line. He believed that a golden age of content was coming, and that technology would deliver movies and television shows directly into the hands (and pockets) of consumers. This future vision would inform Iger's thinking—emboldening the chief executive to make brash digital forays that at times placed Disney at odds with the rest of the entertainment establishment, like rushing its content onto the latest Apple devices, which rivals grumbled threatened established business models. It helped that Iger was an unabashed tech enthusiast who loved to talk about the gadgets in his home, says ABC's former chief product officer, Albert Cheng, who spearheaded development of the network's online media player and its iPad app.

"He would tell me about all the stuff, and so he has a genuine interest in technology," said Cheng, who is now co-head of television at Amazon Studios. "So, when he became CEO . . . that gave us license to go further. I felt that set the tone for, like, 'The CEO has given permission. So let's do it.'"

A provocative article published in 2004 by *Wired* editor Chris Anderson got Iger and his senior management team thinking about the future. In "The Long Tail," Anderson predicted the internet would radically transform the entertainment economy by creating a frictionless, no-barriers-to-entry platform where niche content would find its audience and flourish. Iger asked corporate strategist Kevin Mayer to examine what this coming democratization of content might mean for Disney as a purveyor of mass-market movies and television shows.

That resulted in a forward-looking document called "Disney 2015," which CFO Tom Staggs and Mayer presented during a board retreat at Walt Disney World in Orlando, Florida. It predicted an end to mediocre content, which had thrived in a world where consumers were looking for something to fill their time at nine P.M. on a Wednesday night but had few choices beyond passively clicking through the electronic program guide on their TVs. Soon, consumers would be armed with infinite choices and informed by a nearly instant feedback loop from friends and tastemakers, texting their reactions to the movie or television show they'd just watched.

The best way for Disney to thrive in the coming period of seismic change would be to focus on producing fewer, higher-quality films and building strong franchises that would serve as a beacon to attract consumers awash in a sea of options. It was a seminal document that won the support of Disney's directors and served as a framework for Iger's transformation of the venerable media company. It guided two of the biggest acquisitions in the company's history: Marvel and Lucasfilm.

In a span of six years, Disney assembled an enviable roster of enduring characters hardy enough to survive the transition to an on-demand world—from comic book heroes like Iron Man, Captain America, and Black Panther to *Star Wars'* Luke Skywalker, Darth Vader, and Princess Leia to *Toy Story's* Buzz and Woody. But the Burbank entertainment giant needed to proceed cautiously toward the digital future and demonstrate the value of its $15.4 billion spending spree to a skeptical Wall Street in the here and now, through blockbuster box-office performances. Its digital efforts, like the Disney-owned ABC network's decision in 2006 to begin streaming popular shows like *Desperate Housewives* and *Lost* online, with ads, a day after they aired on TV nodded to changing consumer habits while being "respectful and helping to evolve" the network's relationship with broadcast and cable affiliates.

"The status quo, we knew, was not sustainable," Sweeney said.

A key inflection point for Disney and the rest of the media business came in 2008. The economy had collapsed into a moribund state not seen since the Great Depression. Money-pinched consumers, aware of their new options thanks to the rise of digital technology, began weighing the unthinkable: canceling their cable TV service. Viewers frustrated by two-year contracts, hidden fees, and objectively poor customer service were beginning to turn away from pay TV in favor of alternatives like Netflix, YouTube, and Hulu.

To stem the tide, the television industry unveiled an initiative by the gee-whiz name of TV Everywhere. Spearheaded by two of the nation's largest cable companies, Comcast and Time Warner, it was an attempt to retain viewers who were already starting to contemplate cutting the cord. The history and industry dynamics of TV Everywhere are knotty and somewhat tedious to untangle. But they are essential to understanding the way media companies approached their desperate leap into streaming a decade later, and the self-inflicted nature of so many of their wounds.

TV Everywhere lets consumers watch TV shows on any internet-connected device, as long as they "authenticate" their pay-TV subscriptions by entering a login ID and password. Time Warner CEO Jeff Bewkes sought to downplay the looming threat of cord-cutting in 2009 as he led the charge for the effort. "Consumers vote every single month with their pocketbook," he said. "They don't have to subscribe to cable. They don't have to pay for these services, yet they do. The number of people paying for subscription television has gone up and up and up every single quarter that we've been in the business."

Disney, even as it pointed to its alliance with Apple and its drive to innovate, found itself facing a massive internal struggle. Leaving old profit centers behind is "easier said than done," Iger would reflect much later, readily conceding his struggles with the innovator's dilemma. "As is the case with a lot of legacy businesses, you have a big, profitable business to continue to protect and to mine for its profitability. There's a lot of responsibility associated with that, with shareholders and customers and employees and the board of directors, to deliver as much profit as possible from the businesses you're in. It's not an easy thing to pivot to a new business that is not only not going to be as profitable right away, but will be directly disruptive to the businesses you're in."

Believing that consumers would always buy what they were selling, proponents of TV Everywhere even urged pay-TV distributors to tack on an additional fee for letting customers watch programming on phones, laptops, and tablets. But that provoked howls of complaint from consumer advocates and proved unworkable, since a competing service, Hulu, initially offered free streaming of prime-time network TV shows to desktop computers.

The Olympic Games offered a prominent showcase for TV Everywhere. Comcast, the leading U.S. cable provider and owner of longtime Olympic broadcaster NBCUniversal, estimated that 1.5 million subscribers used the technology to stream portions of the 2012 London games. But the experience was hardly medal-worthy, especially for millions of viewers in love with the iPod and the iPhone, which promised to beam a galaxy of content to their hands. The frustrating, multistep authentication process of TV Everywhere fueled negative consumer perceptions of cable companies' legendarily abysmal relationships with customers. After airing their complaints on social media, chat boards, and blogs, they created spoof software that enabled access to the BBC's UK-only streams of the Olympics.

For legacy TV programmers and distributors, protecting their content was the top priority. Too much was on the line for the stream to ever feel completely fluid and open. "I spent my first five years [at ABC] on the cable side, negotiating hideous internet distribution restrictions on our cable networks," said Cheng, with obvious disdain. The entire pay-TV bundle, one of the biggest zero-to-billions success stories in the history of American business and one that had been carefully nurtured over many decades, would now be at risk. Piracy, hacking, password-sharing, and other headache-inducing breaches, all unknown to the old linear-TV days, would now loom as constant threats. Like the major record labels infamously gobsmacked by the rip-mix-burn era, TV's gatekeepers opted to extend their offerings online—but only up to a point. The clearest indication of this reticence was the default feature of TV Everywhere apps that automatically logged users out after a few days. Unlike the far more seamless experience of Netflix, whose engineers ensured that it retained login information and never forced customers to sign back in, TV Everywhere apps erected the digital equivalent of high border walls topped with barbed wire.

The friction didn't end there. Because most of the bundle remained ad supported, entirely new advertising models needed to be created for streaming. Programmers wanted to be sure they would be fairly compensated by advertisers for ads online—which wasn't the case in the early years of YouTube. In asking advertisers to pay up, though, networks had to ask clients paying X for a linear ad to pay X+1 to also get the same placement in streaming. Since many clients didn't yet feel a great urgency for so-called multiplatform campaigns, large gaps opened up in the inventory, which was built in the traditional manner of linear ad blocks, which were inelastic in terms of running time. On the traditional airwaves, if a four-minute "pod" of ad time didn't sell to blue-chip advertisers, networks would never opt to shrink the length of the pod, but instead would offer the ad time to less prestigious advertisers. This tried-and-true practice is how fringe cable networks end up airing so many clumsy pitches for reverse mortgages and mesothelioma lawyers.

In the streaming arena, those rigidly enforced ad blocks grew even more conspicuous if the sales teams were unable to persuade Procter & Gamble or Microsoft to pony up for TV Everywhere. Veteran media analyst Rich Greenfield, then working for BTIG, released a report in 2014 documenting the "viewer-unfriendly" experience of watching *The Last Ship*, a drama that aired on the TNT network and its TV Everywhere app. Both platforms were overseen by Time Warner's Bewkes, the leading TV Everywhere evangelist. A numbing twenty minutes of unskippable ads had to be viewed on the streaming platform to access forty-five minutes of actual show time, Greenfield and his team found. Not only were there a lot of ads clustered together, but the unused inventory resulted in many ads being repeated. Three Chevy ads ran in a single break, for example, and the same Verizon ad appeared four times throughout the episode. "Online video should be so much more compelling of a user experience, not the same (or even worse) than traditional television," the analyst grumbled.

If the history of American television shows us anything, however, it is the remarkable ability of the medium to prosper despite a glut of advertising, which sacrifices viewer satisfaction for the bottom line. In other countries, the economic model centers on a license paid annually by consumers, who then get to enjoy largely commercial-free programming. In the U.S., from the airing of the first TV ads in the 1940s, the prevailing concept was that the set could be plugged in for free, but the trade-off for "free" programming was having to endure ads.

But wait, there's more: Beyond commercial clutter, distribution rights would also bedevil TV Everywhere. Many of the shows the networks wanted to stream to paying cable and satellite subscribers were encumbered by layers of licensing issues. Some had already been licensed to Hulu, Amazon, or Netflix, creating a tangle of contracts that would need to be updated or replaced. In many other cases, the original contracts did not contemplate the landscape of streaming, leaving open many possible legal interpretations. All of these bottlenecks delayed the rollout of TV Everywhere and also created an uneven programming lineup and an inherent promotional obstacle.

Even inside the industry, there was not universal agreement about the level of urgency of the need to connect with consumers beyond linear broadcasting. "TV is an application and applications ride on all sorts of devices," argued Joe Ambeault, Verizon's director of product management for media and entertainment, in 2011. In a dog-eat-dog marketplace, he added, "If you're not on the screen, your competitor will scoop the customer up." Not everyone was on that page, however. Many legacy executives fretted about their streams not being counted accurately by Nielsen, the dominant third-party measurement firm, and therefore losing revenue. Also, the fact that pay-TV distributors emerged as the most aggressive proponents of the new offering automatically made programmers suspicious, as the two camps have long done business with operators as Hatfield-McCoy frenemies. "The distributors want content for free as added value," said Denise Denson, EVP of content distribution and marketing for Viacom Media Networks, as TV Everywhere emerged. "But I don't think consumers understand what it is," she said. In other words, it was not seen as "critical" to a pay-TV package.

Disney at first had some reservations about TV Everywhere. Iger articulated the company's position during a keynote speech at the 2009 National Cable Television Association conference. "Preventing people from watching any shows online unless they subscribe to some multichannel service could be viewed as both anti-consumer and anti-technology, and would be something we would find difficult to embrace," he said. The remarks burnished his tech-curious reputation as CEO, but at the same time, Iger understood his audience and the need to avoid rocking the boat too much in such an uncertain economic climate. "Let me state the obvious: cable television is vitally important to our company," Iger said, drawing applause from the industry crowd. "It provides us with a crucial connection with consumers. And it is a critical creative engine that drives value across a number of our businesses and across markets and territories around the world."

By 2013, Disney had decided to set aside any misgivings and embraced the TV Everywhere effort, creating an expanded portfolio of apps for ESPN, the Disney Channel, and other networks. "We are extremely supportive of authentication and believe this is just the beginning of a trend that we will be seeing not just for ESPN, but for multiple Disney-owned so-called cable television properties," Iger said.

Like other media companies, Disney was continuing to sell off its movies and TV shows to Netflix and other platforms even as it began making content available on its own gated streaming platforms. It was not a difficult call, given that licensing to third parties generated several billion dollars in found money, easing the pain of the declining market for DVDs—which began to erode, not coincidentally, in 2007, after Amazon, Netflix, and Hulu started offering movies and TV shows on demand. In 2012, Disney and Netflix struck a long-term licensing deal that brought Disney $300 million a year. The goodwill would last for several more years. Asked in 2015 about the companies' relationship during a quarterly earnings call with Wall Street analysts, Iger described Netflix as "more friend than foe. They've become an aggressive customer of ours."

They were also rewiring the brains of TV viewers, especially the younger ones, to experience programming in a different way. Show after show would do moderate ratings on linear TV, only to rocket to the top of the Netflix charts when it started streaming months later. AMC shows like *Mad Men* and *Breaking Bad* were among the beneficiaries of Netflix's broader circulation—with viewership growing over time instead of dwindling with each successive season. Netflix even gave its UK and Ireland customers access to *Breaking Bad*'s final-season episodes the day after they aired in the U.S. The Netflix experience had become a media activity quite removed from the channel surfing and appointment viewing of traditional TV. Accordingly, evidence was mounting that plenty of viewers were content to "wait for Netflix." Rather than rushing to watch the show when it hit the airwaves, even if they could stream it via a TV Everywhere app, they would enjoy the ad-free version later, with the advantage of being able to binge-watch entire seasons. (Most pay-TV systems compounded the issue by failing to "stack" full seasons in their video-on-demand libraries, a misguided attempt to push fractious viewers toward the linear time slot.) Disney-owned ABC had several cases of this kind of viewer pattern on its network, including with one of its mainstay shows, *Grey's Anatomy*, the first show it had licensed to any streaming outlet apart from Hulu. "It's incredibly bingeable," ABC's head of research, Andy Kubitz, said of the series' appeal on Netflix. "People just want to curl up with a blanket and a bowl of popcorn and watch *Grey's*."

The risk inherent in eating fruit from the Netflix lotus tree became glaringly apparent in 2013. By then, pay-TV subscriptions had peaked, posting the first full-year decline in history, falling by more than a quarter of a million to 100.8 million subscribers. The bundle then entered years of secular decline, dropping to 81 million by the end of 2020. With broadband internet proliferating, increasing numbers of consumers availed themselves of other options. In addition to stand-alone services like Netflix, Hulu, and Amazon, "skinny bundle" services like Dish Network's Sling TV and Sony's PlayStation Vue offered new internet-delivered packages. They offered a few dozen channels at modest subscription prices of $20 to $30 a month and no annual contract. After four decades of bundled prosperity, TV gatekeepers suddenly found themselves under unprecedented assault.

Angst about the pay-TV bundle, the media industry's golden goose, overshadowed what should have been a crowning moment for Disney as the preeminent power in entertainment. In December 2015, the company took over Hollywood Boulevard, swathing a quarter-mile stretch in red carpet and putting six thousand guests in three separate theaters for the world premiere of *Star Wars, Episode VII: The Force Awakens*. The first *Star Wars* feature in ten years was also the first since Disney's acquisition of Lucasfilm. More than the return of Luke Skywalker and Han Solo, though, many attendees wanted to ask Bob Iger about the trajectory of cable TV subscribers, especially regarding ESPN, which had lost seven million subscribers in two years. "Is that a reason to panic? Absolutely not," Iger said evenly on the company's quarterly earnings call a few weeks before the premiere. "People still love television, they still love ESPN and they love live sports." Investors didn't seem so sure. Disney stock, hit by a couple of downgrades, declined nearly 10 percent in December, even as *The Force Awakens* set records en route to a potent global box-office gross of nearly $1.6 billion.

Iger and other members of the Disney management team have painted a picture of speed and all-in brinkmanship once they committed to streaming directly to the consumer. In his memoir, Iger recalls his "too-candid" remarks to Wall Street in August 2015, in which he professed a degree of indifference to the downturn in pay-TV subscribers. In his telling, he had sensed, almost Obi-Wan Kenobi–like, that streaming was the future. One former executive said it wasn't like the company was simply able to flip a switch. "Truth be told, our focus has been around this assembling and nurturing of the franchises, getting creative centers really working, et cetera," the executive said. "If you look back at Disney's licensing strategy, like everybody else, we were a little slow to say, 'Hold on a second, we got to really make this hard pivot towards direct-to-consumer.'"

Another complication for Disney was the company's decidedly mixed track record with regard to technology through most of its ninety-seven-year history. Like others in the media sector, the company had to reckon with the arrival of the internet as a major force in the 1990s. After looking at several options (including a potential merger with AOL), Disney embarked on a major initiative that set an unfortunate precedent for its tech efforts: the creation of the Go Network. The web portal was a joint venture with early search engine Infoseek, which Disney ended up acquiring in its entirety after declining to pursue another emerging search leader, Yahoo. (Kevin Mayer, an MIT-educated engineer and Harvard MBA, had recommended a Yahoo deal instead from his perch as the company's chief technology strategist.) Tom Staggs, also a member of the strategy team and who would become CFO and the chief operating officer in a sixteen-year run, had worked out a deal in principle with Yahoo in which Disney would pay $180 million for a 10 to 15 percent stake in the company. Yahoo, in exchange, would be able to draw visitors thanks to Disney's portfolio of household-name brands. Michael Eisner, who was CEO at the time, scotched the deal, scoffing, "Why do this with anyone else? We'll do this ourselves." For emphasis, according to James B. Stewart's book *DisneyWar*, he called the strategy team "wimps" and demanded they develop a plan for Disney to plot its own course. The Go Network was the solution.

Go quickly ran into a succession of problems, with dysfunction in the spread-out offices in several cities, trademark issues with its traffic-light logo, and visitor metrics too weak to get any advertisers excited. A damaging blow came in 1999, when one of Go's senior executives, Patrick Naughton, was arrested for possessing child pornography and soliciting sex online with a thirteen-year-old girl. (The executive was convicted of crossing state lines with intent to have sex with a minor but escaped jail time because he developed technology to help the FBI catch pedophiles online. Naughton, who'd shown up at the Santa Monica Pier for a rendezvous, asserted the "fantasy defense," arguing he believed he was to meet with an adult.)

Steve Bornstein, an accomplished ESPN executive, was persuaded to take the reins of the Go Network, but he never believed in its potential. His first recommendation to Eisner was to shut down the portal, which employed two thousand people in nine countries, and instead focus on the potency of individual brands like ABC News, Disney, and ESPN. Eisner, allergic to admitting defeat, felt Bornstein needed to be more of a visionary. "You're running a railroad when planes are flying overhead," he complained to Bornstein. Internal squabbles over Go's direction dragged on for months, until finally Disney pulled the plug in 2001, taking a $790 million write-down.

Other railroad derailments would follow. Playdom, a hot social gaming startup that Disney acquired in 2010 for $763 million, became a casualty of the company's decision, six years later, to shut down its gaming division. Club Penguin, an online social network for kids that Disney bought for $351 million in 2007, eventually faded in popularity, like a playground version of MySpace. Fusion, a joint venture between ABC and Univision, blended digital platforms with the ill-timed launch of a new linear cable TV network targeting Latino millennials in 2013. The Spanish-language broadcaster bought out Disney's stake three years later. Maker Studios, a multichannel network acquired in 2014 for $675 million, posted blockbuster early-stage growth but was quickly dragged down by the adverse economics of YouTube, which takes half of all ad revenue generated by creators.

In Bob Iger's version of events, Disney saw around corners and decided to render the innovator's dilemma moot by willingly disrupting
itself. But the feats of properly integrating tech operations and successfully adopting the approach of a tech company are extremely difficult
for any organization outside of Silicon Valley. Heading into its pivot to
streaming in the 2010s, Disney was a best-in-class media operation. Its
code-cracking film studio had an industry-leading share of the global
box office thanks to a pipeline stocked with Marvel, Pixar, and Lucasfilm titles. In pay TV, while ESPN penetration was declining, its grip
on high-value sports rights enabled it to keep charging cable operators
ungodly sums (more than $8 per subscriber, compared with pennies
charged by most networks). "We had a bunch of businesses that were
highly profitable, and their profits were derived from the old infrastructure. And that's the kind of thing that makes it more difficult to embrace the change," a former top Disney executive told us. With profits at
ESPN outdoing those from theme parks, turning the battleship would
take enormous will and determination over a long period.

Organizationally, dozens of executives operating businesses were
compensated based not on their appetite for long-term risk or their yen
for adventure but by the quarterly numbers. They had no financial incentive to reinvent anything, only to maximize the existing infrastructure. Their years of toil and struggle placed them in positions of some
authority, but deals for Playdom and Maker "were too small to change
the DNA of the company," the former executive noted. "And the DNA
of the company did not contain the code that allowed you to build and
nurture those kinds of businesses." Despite that genetic defect, Disney
in 2016 got to an advanced stage of merger talks with Twitter. It did
not end up moving forward with the acquisition, though, after Iger
determined a deal would be "corrosive to [Disney's] brand," as he later
recalled.

But the future kept intruding on business as usual at Disney. Andy
Bird, the lanky, urbane Brit who shaped the company's global strategy
for a quarter century, recalls the cognitive dissonance of attending back-

to-back staff meetings where, in one, ESPN's John Skipper talked about committing billions of dollars for the rights to carry professional sports on its lucrative cable network, while the studio subsequently touted the potential windfall of shifting its library away from the premium cable service Starz to upstart Netflix. It was enough to induce vertigo. Bird was convinced video would inevitably follow the same trajectory as music, with consumers preferring to pay for access to content instead of ownership. The executive, whom Iger deputized to shake up the company's Burbank-centric culture to create a truly global media company, proposed diving into the stream.

"Bob was great in terms of going, 'Well, if you think that passionately about it, then come up with a plan,'" said Bird.

That was the genesis of a family-focused offering in the UK called DisneyLife, which brought together a trove of content—animated movies from *Bambi* to Pixar's *Toy Story*, blockbuster films like the *Pirates of the Caribbean* franchise, a catalog of five thousand songs, and digitized versions of Disney books. Bird's team devoted countless hours to renegotiating distribution contracts and clawing back nonexclusive rights to Disney's movies and TV shows from the region's dominant broadcaster, Sky. The service, developed by an in-house team, debuted in the fall of 2015 for a monthly fee of £9.99.

"We could have chosen a smaller market and flown under the radar, but I thought that more than anything, this gave us an opportunity to learn a lot and get some learnings that we may not have got in a more minor market," recalled Bird. "It came with risk. You're putting your head above the parapet, but I thought that was a risk worth taking, so we decided to launch it there."

DisneyLife was a dud. The homegrown technology was buggy, especially for customers using Android phones. The price was too high. And the marketing campaign shockingly fell short. The leadership in London treated the launch like a movie premiere and ran commercials on TV. They failed to figure out how best to reach streaming consumers or mine the theme park's intelligence for insights into what would appeal to Disney's most devoted fans. Rather than shutter the service, Iger supported Bird's recommendation to keep the service going as "this real-time, large-scale focus group."

The lessons of DisneyLife would inform Kevin Mayer's decision to look beyond Burbank for a technical team to support the company's on-demand ambitions, to the streaming arm of Major League Baseball. MLB Advanced Media ran a range of digital operations, but it became best known for its streaming unit, which it eventually spun off into a separate business known by the shorthand name BAMTech. The unlikely pioneer was based in Manhattan's Chelsea Market, a former biscuit factory turned into a tony food court, shopping mall, and corporate offices for Google, the Food Network, and other tech and media companies. The game of baseball itself had never seemed more vulnerable, with shaky national TV ratings, steroid scandals, and diminishing appeal to young fans as it fell from "national pastime" status. Nevertheless, the sport managed to anticipate the future of video distribution. In 2002, BAM live-streamed its first game, a matchup between the Texas Rangers and New York Yankees, offering it free for anyone outside the teams' local metro areas (so as not to interfere with local telecasts). "The technology existed to do it, but of course, that doesn't mean it was good," said Bob Bowman, who headed up BAM. The initial streaming images "looked more like a flip book." Even so, ESPN's Skipper, then overseeing ESPN.com, got to know Bowman and his operation well. By the time he rose to president of ESPN, he was a BAM evangelist and readily endorsed the idea of bringing it into the fold.

Despite launching at a time when most Americans still had dial-up internet connections, BAM's streaming offering quickly gained traction. MLB launched a subscription package in 2002, delivering out-of-market games during the pennant race in August and September. (Over the years, Amazon, Facebook, and YouTube have made streaming a familiar part of the game's media footprint.) With sports an engine of streaming growth, as it had always been in linear TV, BAM was able to white-label its technology (including patented geo-location methods, which helped determine who was allowed to watch what) to other companies. Streams of the NCAA March Madness basketball tournament, pro wrestling matches, and NHL hockey games were all powered by BAM. Entertainment proved a logical next step, with clients including Hulu and HBO, whose direct-to-consumer service HBO Now had been created on a tight timeline in 2015 for $50 million.

Mayer knew that building streaming platforms from scratch would take several years and bring Disney's costs well into the hundreds of millions. A better course, he determined, was acquiring a plug-and-play expertise in streaming. He envisioned a multistep deal with BAMTech: an initial investment of about $1 billion for a 33 percent stake, with an option to gain full control by 2020. The news became official in August 2016, with Disney revealing that along with the investment, BAM would build a new direct-to-consumer service for ESPN. Less than a year later, Iger would return from an Orlando board meeting and tell Mayer to accelerate the buyout of BAMTech and let other execs know "to prepare for a significant strategic shift into the streaming business."

As Staggs and Mayer had predicted in their memo more than a decade earlier, laying out the case for strong franchises and brands carrying the day in the digital era, Disney would need to continue its reinvention efforts. Viewers reckoning with the growing array of content emanating from hundreds of streaming services would gravitate to familiar channel markers. Marvel. *Star Wars.* Pixar. Two weeks later, over glasses of wine at Rupert Murdoch's Moraga Vineyards in Bel Air, Iger proposed the unthinkable: acquiring the media empire the octogenarian dealmaker had assembled from a handful of newspapers over four decades. Acquiring most of 21st Century Fox would arm Disney with even more major franchises and control of Hulu. Iger's autobiography says Murdoch surprised him with the unexpected solicitation, though a source familiar with the discussions said it was the younger media titan who pitched the combination, eager to cement his legacy.

After an unrequited overture from a party other than Disney, the Murdoch family and company stakeholders took stock of its mergers-and-acquisitions trajectory, especially its regulatory profile, according to one former executive. Twice, it had been unsuccessful in acquiring Sky, the satellite distributor that had been a key building block for Rupert Murdoch as he formed his empire. In both attempts, regulators had seized on the activities of Murdoch in the news business—in the earlier one, the tabloid phone hacking scandal, and in the later one, the negative cloud around Fox News. It became increasingly apparent that Fox would have limited freedom to maneuver.

Iger, on the other hand, framed the $71.3 billion deal as the ultimate sign of Disney's maneuverability. He called it the culmination of a series of bets placed on streaming. Unlike others in the media space, Disney had run theme parks, hotels, and cruise ships, and made its direct connection with consumers a point of pride. Customer acquisition, fulfillment, and retention—the essential components of streaming—would become an even higher priority. After emerging victorious from a bidding war with Comcast and overcoming a series of regulatory tangles, Iger reflected on the shift of mindset that had enabled the company to embark on the transaction that reshaped the media landcape. Instead of viewing Fox as a collection of TV network and film studio assets, the deal was seen in terms of filling the streaming pipes. Maybe Disney wouldn't ever get to Netflix's seven hundred shows a year, but it now had *The Simpsons*, *Avatar*, and National Geographic to add to its already-impressive vault.

"By the time the acquisition opportunity came up, and we knew we were going in this space, we evaluated what we were buying through this new lens," Iger told CNBC. "What could it mean having access to [Fox's] library, not to monetize it through traditional means, but to do it through this?" Iger added. "Bam! I mean, the lightbulb went off."

CHAPTER 6

▶ Live from Cupertino

On a cool, overcast morning in March 2019, Hollywood celebrities, studio executives, and lawyers gathered in Cupertino, California. While many of the A-listers had grown accustomed to lead roles and final-cut privileges, they would find themselves relegated to supporting players and directors-for-hire. Apple and its soon-to-be-announced streaming service were the unquestioned stars of the show.

Anticipation had been building since Apple emailed invitations featuring an animated GIF of an old-time film leader counting down the seconds, 3-2-1, to "show time," telegraphing the tech giant's long-anticipated Hollywood debut. The customarily secretive Apple had done little to disguise its intentions to launch a video streaming service. It's hard to tamp down speculation when you strike a deal with Oprah Winfrey. But big questions remained unanswered: How much would it cost? When would it launch? How would Apple leverage its 1.4 billion active devices to grab market share? And would it ever be able to compete with other services that offered a dramatically deeper selection of movies and television shows?

The assembled agents, studio executives, and talent—usually looped into behind-the-scenes plans of anything they were participating in—found themselves frustratingly in the dark. They hoped to finally fill in a lot of the blanks.

Apple had signaled its seriousness about breaking into Hollywood in November 2017, when it outbid Netflix for *The Morning Show*. The prestige drama represented a departure from Apple's earlier, forgettable stabs at making original content, like *Planet of the Apps*. That reality series featured tech entrepreneurs pitching their app ideas to a panel of celebrity mentors, including Gwyneth Paltrow, Jessica Alba, and Will.i.am. It was canceled after one season.

The transformation occurred when Apple poached two former Sony Pictures Television executives behind such hits as AMC's *Breaking Bad*, FX's *The Shield*, and Netflix's *The Crown* to lead its original programming. Zack Van Amburg and Jamie Erlicht weren't looking to match Netflix's entertainment smorgasbord. Rather, they sought out a handful of caviar projects worthy of how Apple viewed its premium consumer brand. Though the pair had spent the bulk of their careers as sellers, not the buyers they would be at Apple, they were well known to Hollywood's creative community and dealmakers. The consensus view was that they seemed capable of overcoming the industry's reflexive wariness of tech bros blowing into town from Silicon Valley, flashing cash and bragging about reinventing entertainment.

Over two years, the duo struck deals with a who's who of Hollywood, among them filmmaker Steven Spielberg, talk show host and media mogul Oprah Winfrey, and Academy Award–winning actress Octavia Spencer. The *Morning Show* package was exceptional, too—Oscar winner Reese Witherspoon playing the lead opposite Jennifer Aniston in her first regular series role in almost twenty years. Steve Carell and Billy Crudup also had sizable roles.

Several marquee names—Winfrey, Aniston, Witherspoon, Spielberg, and filmmaker J. J. Abrams—were rumored to be making the trek to Northern California to participate in Apple's March 2019 event. But this Silicon Valley debut would represent a significant departure from the familiar rituals of Hollywood. If they had a show or movie to promote, or an award to collect, these show-business figures would be walking the red carpet, posing for photos, and doing interviews. Autograph hounds would track their moves. Sound bites, photos, and video clips would blanket the world in the hours after the event. On this gray Monday morning in Cupertino, by contrast, they were completely out of view.

Instead of fronting the event, Hollywood power players—including powerhouse entertainment lawyer Ken Ziffren and Universal's vice chairman of the filmed entertainment group, Peter Levinsohn—congregated in the ground-level lobby of the Steve Jobs Theater. They indulged in parfaits, espresso drinks, and lively speculation alongside members of Silicon Valley royalty, including angel investor Ron Conway and Laurene Powell Jobs, widow of the late Apple cofounder. They appeared, to the outside observer, like so many exotic fish impatiently swirling around inside the theater's circular glass structure, which affords an unobstructed, 360-degree view of Apple's sprawling, verdant 175-acre campus. Its design deliberately evokes the modern, airy aesthetic of an Apple store, with its lens-shaped roof resting atop an enormous glass cylinder that's 22 feet tall and 135 feet in diameter.

The thousand-seat theater itself is hidden underground, so as to better deliver an on-brand "element of surprise."

It had been eight years since Walter Isaacson's biography of Steve Jobs had tantalizingly hinted that Apple would do for television what it had done for computers, music players, and phones—make them simple and elegant. Jobs said his television would render complex remote controls obsolete.

The yearned-for Apple TV set never materialized, although a prototype existed in Apple's labs. The ailing Jobs would meet with executives in his Palo Alto home and discuss his vision for a television that could be controlled through voice and touch, said one former Apple executive. Internal design teams worked through various prototypes that would deliver on Jobs's ambition to create a simplified TV interface. Brainstorming sessions contemplated various features, such as a truly smart television that could recognize a consumer when they entered the room and begin personalizing the viewing experience.

"The problem was, A, the cost was going to be really, really high—

and people only upgrade their televisions every seven years," said the former Apple insider. "Then, everybody has different-sized televisions in their homes. Apple at that time was like, 'We're only going to do two, tops, of anything.'"

After Jobs's death from complications of pancreatic cancer in October 2011, CEO Tim Cook's executive staff—software vice president Craig Federighi, operating systems guru Scott Forstall, software and services head Eddy Cue, and design chief Jony Ive, among others—debated the fate of an Apple-branded television. Cue questioned how the company could sell a $7,000 device and make any profit on high-end screens that delivered low margins. Cook wondered about how Apple might build a business around a piece of glass in the living room.

It didn't fit with CEO Tim Cook's vision for building out Apple's ecosystem. The executive who first made his mark smoothing out Apple's supply chain isn't known for introducing groundbreaking new wares, but rather, for building an array of products and services around his predecessor's creations. He's a smart, steady operator—and that's precisely what Apple needed after its iconic founder's death. Cook's calm, hands-clasped stage presence, leavened with a warm Alabama lilt, lacks the crackle of electricity that Jobs generated. Building the audience into a state of frenzied anticipation, the Apple cofounder would culminate with the day's big product news, casually underselling it as just "one more thing."

The days of Steve Jobs's euphoric introductions of Apple's "insanely great" creations were gone. Instead of chasing "the new hotness," Cook favored iterating on the Apple TV set-top box the company had unveiled in 2006, betting that the comparatively inexpensive product could find its way into consumers' living rooms.

Launching a physical product is one thing. Bringing to life a rumored subscription video streaming service is another matter. It would fit neatly with Apple's burgeoning, multibillion-dollar services business, which by March 2019 had brought in more revenue than sales of Mac computers and iPads combined. And it would prop up revenue at a time when iPhone sales were slowing and provide another reason for consumers to hang on to their Apple devices.

Some studio executives predicted the opaque Apple was playing the long game: investing a couple of billion dollars in a handful of eye-catching projects to draw attention to the Apple TV app, which had languished, mostly unnoticed, on millions of iPhones and iPads. Once consumers grew accustomed to using the TV app, the calculus goes, it would become the logical leaping-off point for accessing other streaming services or renting movies. Apple would happily take a cut of the new subscriptions accessed through its app (often a healthy 30 percent of revenue). Eventually, the constellation of TV apps would disappear, leaving a singular Apple TV app.

"I think this is a play to reaggregate content," says one television executive with experience operating on-demand services. "The cable operator was an aggregator of content . . . That's what [Apple's] trying to do in digital, with their devices. It would be the place to go."

Indeed, Cue tried unsuccessfully to partner with Comcast, in hopes of becoming the cable giant's set-top-box provider. Comcast decided to go it alone, investing in its own X1 platform to deliver advanced search, personalized recommendations, and internet video apps. Cue's subsequent efforts to go around Comcast and strike deals directly with programmers similarly fell flat. "Some of them didn't like him," said the Apple source. "They're like, 'He's arrogant.'"

Repeatedly rebuffed, Cue decided to build a television subscription service from scratch.

Apple spent years discreetly working on the video service in-house, to avoid a repeat of the culture clash that followed its $3 billion purchase of Beats Electronics in 2014. That uncharacteristic deal, Apple's largest acquisition by far, was intended to accelerate its belated entry into music streaming, where upstart Spotify was attracting millions of subscribers. Apple also would benefit from a much-needed injection of cultural cachet in the form of Beats's cofounders, rapper-producer Dr. Dre and Interscope Records founder Jimmy Iovine.

Dre and Iovine's acclaimed personalized music streaming service, Beats Music, helped establish the superstructure for Apple's entry into the streaming business. But it was a complicated birth. The iTunes team in Cupertino butted heads with the music guys in Culver City, producing a compromise product that neither critics nor users loved. Eventually, Iovine, the profane, Brooklyn-born son of a longshoreman, wore out his welcome at Apple, which had become a more circumspect—and rich—company since the hot-blooded Jobs era. "When I went to Apple, it was a new creative problem for me. How do we make this the future of the music business? How do we make it not ordinary? But I ran out of personal runway," Iovine told the *New York Times*. "Somebody else will have to do that."

This time around, Cue opted for workhorses, not show horses, embodied by Van Amburg and his longtime collaborator, Erlicht. When professional associates asked why they'd abandoned Sony, the duo cited the example of the Sony Trinitron. Once a living room status symbol, the Trinitron was known for delivering a superior-color picture (in fact, it was the first consumer electronics device to win an Emmy). Sony went on to sell 280 million Trinitrons but eventually failed to keep innovating. When its patent expired in 1996, competitors like Mitsubishi were able to manufacture cheaper models, harnessing the same technology, and the Trinitron faded from the home. It's the Darwinian law of the consumer technology jungle: products that fail to evolve die.

"While they were at Sony, they watched that happen. This product, the single biggest generator of revenue, became irrelevant," says one agent to whom Van Amburg and Erlicht recounted the story. "Apple's mindset, not just about Apple TV, but about the Apple brand . . . [is] you can't just rest on your laurels. This is their next evolution. How do we get people to want to buy our device more?"

Before the curtains parted on Apple's new streaming service, at the unveiling in Cupertino, there was an hour-long opening act of incremental product news that the Hollywood guests were largely indifferent to: a new Apple credit card, an Apple News subscription service, a mobile game service dubbed Apple Arcade, and enhanced features for the Apple TV app, which would appear on screens everywhere.

When the moment arrived, Cook borrowed some of Steve Jobs's hyperbole, describing the new streaming service as nothing short of a world-changing event. "We feel we can contribute something important to our culture and to society through great storytelling," said Cook. "So we have partnered with the most thoughtful, accomplished, and award-winning group of creative visionaries who have *ever* come together in one place to create a new service unlike *anything* that's been done before."

Biblical clouds parted on the projection screen behind Cook to reveal the name: Apple TV+. Erlicht and Van Amburg continued the braggadocio as they talked about attracting a roster of "incredible artists" who were "thoughtful enough and brave enough" to share their best work with Apple. The service, they said, would be dedicated to (with apologies to Max von Sydow) "the best stories ever told."

A promotional reel, atmospherically filmed in black and white and dedicated to the art of storytelling, featured several of Hollywood's heavy hitters—Spielberg, Abrams, Sofia Coppola, M. Night Shyamalan, Ron Howard, Spencer, Witherspoon, and Aniston—talking about their creative process to a soaring symphonic accompaniment. The stage lights came up to reveal Spielberg, in his inaugural appearance in Apple Park, grinning to boisterous cheers and applause. That dramatic reveal would be repeated, over and over, for the stars of Apple TV+'s debut lineup taking the stage: *The Morning Show*'s Witherspoon, Aniston, and Carell; *See*'s Jason Momoa; *Little America*'s Kumail Nanjiani; *Sesame Street*'s Big Bird; and Abrams with his *Little Voice* collaborator Sara Bareilles.

Cook returned for the capstone moment: Oprah Winfrey, in a flowing white blouse, touted the inescapable allure of joining forces with Apple. "Because, they're in a billion pockets, y'all! A billion pockets."

The timing of the event, held two weeks ahead of Disney's planned investor day, seemed motivated by the desire to capture first-mover advantage. If the world of streaming music was noisy, streaming video was getting to be a cacophony. There were already 235 subscription services operating in the U.S. Apple seemed ready to turn the volume up before it even had the melody down.

But the nearly two-hour extravaganza concluded with major questions still unanswered: How much would Apple TV+ cost? When would it launch? Remarkably, only a few fleeting seconds of footage played from the shows being promoted, the opposite of the tried-and-true entertainment tactic of orchestrating buzz with extensive clip reveals.

Nonetheless, Apple considered the event a success. Organizers felt they'd successfully bridged the stubbornly distinct cultures of Northern and Southern California. The tech hosts feted guests at an evening reception, held for travelers who'd arrived the night before the event, and indulged Hollywood's impulse for self-promotion with a social-media-friendly reception at the café in Apple Park, which celebrity guests like Winfrey and Witherspoon shared with their millions of followers on Instagram. It arranged a *Vanity Fair*-style portrait of the thirty celebrities who'd made the pilgrimage three hundred miles north for the event—a gesture intended to assuage the egos of those who'd never made it onstage.

But most important, from Apple's perspective: none of the key details leaked ahead of the event.

The feeling of triumph was hardly mutual, as was plainly registered on the less-than-ebullient faces of Chris Evans and Michelle Dockery, stars of the forthcoming Apple TV series *Defending Jacob*, and *Dickinson*'s Jane Krakowski, who were captured on video during the Apple event, gamely applauding the day's announcements from their seats in the audience—away from the spotlight.

One agent cornered Van Amburg and Erlicht immediately after the presentation to angrily express displeasure. In the heated conversation that followed, the agent made it clear his clients were offended that they didn't make it onstage and that their projects failed to merit even a mention. "I think that they regret that," the agent said of Apple.

Another agent was more blunt: "That was fucking terrible. I wanted to kind of go, 'Are you fucking kidding me?'" The television agent was taken aback that Apple devoted so much time to details of its monthly magazine subscription service without even bothering to show trailers for its original shows. "I was like, that's just, you're giving the wrong, wrong message to this town."

While Hollywood was both irritated and baffled, the press was scathing.

"If the shows on Apple's new TV service turn out to be as smugly evangelistic, self-indulgent and editorially undisciplined as the launch event for the product . . . then it will be very bad news for Apple subscribers and very good news for Netflix, the current market leader," the *Guardian*'s Mark Lawson wrote. "Apple has often seemed at risk of mutating from technology company to quasi-religious cult, and its full-scale entry to the TV content market went very close to full Media Moonie." In his recap, which was headlined "Apple's Big Event Felt Small," CNN's Frank Pallotta marveled that the star power amounted to "a collective meh." One of the few dissenters from the general rebuff of the presentation was Josef Adalian of *Vulture*. "Apple wasn't trying to win Twitter on Monday, or even get anyone to subscribe to Apple TV+ quite yet," he wrote. "Apple doesn't need to woo Madison Avenue, and given how many top creatives it has onboard already, it didn't need to convince anyone in Hollywood its TV effort is for real."

A ghost from Apple's product closet was set loose by the proceedings in Cupertino, however, at least for some Hollywood players, for whom it conjured an earlier bungled entertainment offering. Specifically, in 2014, when Tim Cook welcomed Bono and the Edge onstage to announce that a free copy of the U2 album *Songs of Innocence* would be downloaded to everyone with an iTunes account—whether they wanted it or not. A wall of customer objections, ranging from bemused to outraged, greeted the move, which had cost Apple more than $100 million. U2 front man Bono later apologized in an interview with ABC News. "Drop of megalomania, touch of generosity, dash of self-promotion, and deep fear that these songs that we poured our life into over the last few years might not be heard," he said by way of explanation. "There's a lot of noise out there."

The introduction of Apple TV+ vividly illustrated the perils of trying to merge tech and entertainment. The tech industry generally is obsessed with avoiding the "Osborne effect," in which customers postpone buying a current product as they wait for a new, better model to arrive. It's a term that was coined after the bankruptcy of the Osborne Computer Corporation, a pioneering maker of a briefcase-sized personal computer, which saw its sales collapse as word leaked of a next-generation device with a bigger screen and enhanced capabilities. That 1983 bankruptcy serves as an enduring cautionary tale for Silicon Valley tech companies to remain mum about a new device until it's ready to hit store shelves. At Apple, the Osborne effect is gospel.

Hollywood, by contrast, relies on a series of teases building in a crescendo toward launch. "First looks," trailer drops, and social media froth all help stoke anticipation for a forthcoming television show or movie. In the entertainment world, silence equals professional death.

CHAPTER 7

▶ Cooking Up
"Quick Bites"

Jeffrey Katzenberg's grand vision first surfaced, aptly, at the ultimate blue-sky venue in media and technology: the Allen & Co. Sun Valley Conference. The annual summer gathering, convened by an investment bank involved in a number of tech and media deals, brings together a range of potentates for a private exchange of ideas. A few major transactions have taken root at the conference over the years, including Disney's purchase of Capital Cities/ABC and Amazon founder Jeff Bezos's scooping up the *Washington Post*. Mostly, though, the posh setting far from the prying eyes of the press is for schmoozing and the collective embrace of athleisure wear.

At the July 2017 retreat, the voluble Katzenberg had been talking nonstop since touching down in Idaho about his vision for revolutionizing entertainment on mobile phones. He didn't yet have a final business plan but enthusiastically sketched out for fellow moguls the broad contours of a concept he was calling "NewTV."

The idea was to bring Hollywood talent to the small screen, delivering movies and television shows in seven-to-ten-minute installments. These morsels of entertainment were designed to fill those fallow moments spent seated in the waiting room at the doctor's office, standing in the supermarket checkout line, or waiting for the barista to hand over a

latte at Starbucks. YouTube and social media networks had been delivering addictive doses of videos for years, of course, but NewTV would
raise the quality bar and deliver splashy programming worth the price of
a subscription. Katzenberg, in other words, wanted to take short-form
video upscale. And he pledged to raise an audacious $2 billion to realize
his vision. "Is this a gigantic undertaking? The answer is yes," Katzenberg told *Variety* when he went public with the idea he had been incubating since his forced departure from DreamWorks Animation upon
its sale to Comcast's NBCUniversal. "Is it bigger than DreamWorks? I
hope so."

Less than three years after his NewTV trial balloon at Sun Valley,
Katzenberg was back in Los Angeles, presiding over a meeting in a
crisp, white conference room whose dominant feature was a projection
screen. Just five weeks later, on April 6, 2020, Katzenberg's entry into
the streaming derby would officially launch. It was christened Quibi,
a portmanteau of "quick" and "bites," suggesting appetizingly short,
snackable content. While the name raised plenty of eyebrows, it was
at least an improvement over Katzenberg's original choice: Omakase,
a Japanese word for a "chef's choice" meal, often in a sushi restaurant.

The purpose of the seventy-five-minute meeting was for a creative
team of twenty to run down the status of unscripted programs ahead of
the launch. The session was vintage Katzenberg. The wiry and energetic
seventy-year-old is famous for his deep industry connections, cultivated
across an entertainment career now in its sixth decade. Even more than
other hard-charging personalities in Hollywood, Katzenberg was known
for booking multiple breakfasts on the same day and maintaining an
obsessive work ethic. As a young teen, Katzenberg began his lifelong
infatuation with politics, working as a youth coordinator for New York
mayoral candidate John Lindsay. He dropped out of New York University after his first semester and worked in the mayor's office until age
twenty-one, when he heeded the siren song of Hollywood. He hit Los
Angeles like he had been shot out of a cannon. A protégé of Barry Diller,
Katzenberg became one of the youngest-ever studio chiefs when he was

named head of Paramount Pictures at age thirty-one. A run at Disney followed, during which he spearheaded the resurrection of its moribund animation studio with *The Little Mermaid*, *Aladdin*, *The Lion King*, and many more hits as chairman of Walt Disney Studios. Along with David Geffen and Steven Spielberg, he founded DreamWorks SKG, which set out to be the most artist-friendly new studio since United Artists formed in 1919, and then ran its animation arm. There are MBA types in the corner office crunching numbers, and there are executives in the Irving Thalberg mode, reading scripts and suggesting changes. Katzenberg was capable at both but leaned toward Thalberg. At DreamWorks, he often sat in on recording sessions to punch up jokes or recommend line readings. One memorable remark to direct reports, when he took charge of Disney Studios, distilled his extremely high expectations: "If you don't come to work on Saturday, don't bother coming on Sunday."

Katzenberg opened the (weekday) Quibi staff meeting with an anecdote about the startup's courtship of a pair of Instagram influencers, sisters Claudia Oshry (Girl with No Job) and Jackie Oshry (JackieOProblems). He had surprised them with an order of "life-changing," off-the-menu sliders delivered to their table at the beachfront restaurant, Nobu Malibu, which the duo promptly dubbed "the Katzenburger" in posts to their millions of social media followers. He recounted a Sunday dinner party at which he found himself seated at a table with *America's Next Top Model* creator Tyra Banks. He coyly acknowledged her with a wave, unsure of the status of a proposed docuseries, *Beauty*, that she would host and executive produce for Quibi.

The mogul's brio never waned, as Katzenberg listened to casting updates, tossed off notes ("the end of Chapter Two was funky, it kind of fell off"), and brainstormed promotional stunts with the team. There was talk of hosting fashion designer Alexander Wang's celebrity talk show, *Potty Talk*, from the bathroom of the Met Gala and inviting *Dummy* star Anna Kendrick to join Katzenberg courtside at a Los Angeles Lakers game, accompanied by her comedic sidekick in the series, her boyfriend's sex doll, Barbara.

The coronavirus, which was the source of growing anxiety in New York City, as the number of confirmed cases reached thirty-three, was a gnawing background concern. Talent's worries about COVID-19 would be accommodated, with *Most Dangerous Game* star Liam Hemsworth expressing qualms about leaving Australia to attend the South by Southwest media festival in Texas. In a matter of days, the pandemic would hobble Hollywood, torpedoing live events such as South by Southwest and other festivals. Theaters shuttered and the releases of major films such as *Mulan*, *F9*, and the latest James Bond outing *No Time to Die* were postponed. Studios suspended production on hundreds of television series.

"I've never seen an environment change this fast. Every day is a new day, with new data and new concerns," said Quibi CEO Meg Whitman, whom Katzenberg had personally recruited to run the startup. They'd known each other since Whitman was a hotshot Harvard MBA working in Disney's strategic planning group, interacting with him as Disney Studios chairman. He later invited her to join the board of DreamWorks Animation.

Katzenberg initially sought to spin the calamity as potentially fortuitous for Quibi, which had been stockpiling fresh content in anticipation of a disruption of a different sort—a production halt triggered by a looming writers' strike. As the nation hunkered down at home, in the anxious hope of containing the virus's spread, people were craving a few moments of distraction to take their minds off the gathering doom, he said. That's precisely what Quibi promised: digestible "bites"—er, bursts of entertainment delivered to the smartphone. Movies unfolded in book-like chapters; fast-paced reality shows built to natural act breaks that served as logical bridges between episodes. News, another sought-after commodity in spring 2020, was also in the mix.

"Maybe the silver lining of what we are doing, and the pivot that we made, is this: Here is a moment in time when collectively—all of us— are stressed out, anxious, depressed, threatened. Life as we know it has just been turned upside down and inside out," Katzenberg said. "And depending on where you fall on this—it's from utterly dire to just plain unpleasant and uncomfortable and unrewarding—right at that moment in time, here comes something that's new, it's unique, it's different."

In a way, Whitman was Katzenberg's first convert. On the day she announced she would step down as chief executive of Hewlett-Packard Enterprise on November 21, 2017, her phone rang. It was her old friend Jeffrey. "[He] picked up the phone and said, 'So what are you doing?' And I said, 'You know, I don't know. I'm the chairman of Teach for America. I probably will do stuff with my husband and travel,'" Whitman said. "He goes, 'No. What are you doing *tonight*?' And I said, 'Knowing you, Jeffrey, I'm having dinner with you.'"

Katzenberg flew to Palo Alto and, over a three-hour meal at Nobu, gave his pitch for delivering short-form video to the phone. He would talk about the confluence of technology trends, with wireless cellular networks growing fast enough to deliver high-quality video to the ubiquitous portable device sitting in everyone's pockets—the smartphone. Consumers had developed the appealing habit of watching video on the go, with time spent increasing from about six minutes a day in 2012 to forty minutes five years later, representing a "singular entrepreneurial moment" that he sought to capitalize on with the introduction of a subscription service that would deliver premium entertainment.

In interviews, Katzenberg would draw on the example of HBO, a subscription service that launched at a time when free broadcast television ruled the living room. HBO began producing expensive original programming, such as the critically acclaimed mob drama *The Sopranos*, in the 1990s, when popular sitcoms like *Friends* and prime-time dramas like *ER* commanded huge audiences. "HBO comes along and says, 'We're not TV. We're HBO.' They're not putting television down. By the way, how could you? That was at the height of its moment. It was fantastic TV," the founder said. "They just said, 'We're going to give you something different. Because we are a subscription service . . . we can do things that broadcast TV cannot do.'"

On-the-go video represented a similar opportunity to reimagine the medium. The analytical Whitman has a mental model of what constitutes a great consumer business, refined over a career of working for some of America's most storied brands: Procter & Gamble, the Walt Disney Company, Hasbro, and eBay. This checked all the boxes.

"I ultimately said, 'You know what? I think I have another startup in me,'" says Whitman, who'd worked as CEO alongside another visionary founder, eBay's Pierre Omidyar. She joined as Quibi's first employee on March 1, 2018, and initially moved to a shared workspace called Serendipity Labs, with a youthful WeWork vibe that may have evoked eBay's earliest days. Those Silicon Valley offices' casual atmosphere—with their beach chairs and young employees clad in jeans and T-shirts—represented "a far cry from the stuffy marble and mahogany conference rooms full of pin-striped suits that Harvard prepared us to navigate and command," Whitman observed in her account of her decade leading eBay, *The Power of Many*.

Within five months of Whitman's arrival, Katzenberg announced that the startup had raised an astounding sum, $1 billion. The haul came from Madrone Capital Partners, the investment arm of Walmart's Walton family; Alibaba, the Chinese e-commerce giant; and the investment banks Goldman Sachs and JPMorgan Chase. Noticeably absent was the Samsung heiress turned media mogul Miky Lee, who had advocated that the family invest in Katzenberg's earlier studio venture, DreamWorks.

All the major Hollywood studios invested, their participation incentivized by what one banker called "schmuck insurance": keeping a chunk of whatever you're selling in case you've misjudged the opportunity. If NewTV failed, the studios would be free to stitch the content together into more traditional films or television shows and sell it elsewhere (after Quibi's two-year exclusivity period lapsed)—because they owned the IP.

Quibi's prodigious fundraising, which would eventually reach $1.75 billion, immediately caught Hollywood's attention. Anyone with programming to offer looked upon the startup as a giant, untapped development fund.

"I sold as much to Jeffrey as I possibly could, as quickly as I possibly could," says Jason Blum, the chief executive of Blumhouse Productions, who's carved out a lucrative niche as a producer of some of Hollywood's most successful horror movies, including Jordan Peele's Oscar-nominated *Get Out*. He signed on to make *Wolves and Villagers*, starring Naomi Watts, and two other series.

Blum wasn't alone. Quibi attracted a roster of A-listers, including filmmakers Guillermo del Toro and Sam Raimi; actors Jennifer Lopez, Idris Elba, Kevin Hart, and Queen Latifah; athletes Cam Newton and LeBron James; and musicians Joe Jonas, Demi Lovato, Lil Yachty, and Chance the Rapper. One big draw for feature film talent, especially, was that Quibi deliberately structured their deals so that rights would revert to the creator after seven years. That afforded far more flexibility than elsewhere in streaming. Netflix, for example, paid handsomely, but that was because it generally owned rights in perpetuity.

Quibi's enormous cash haul came with hidden peril, according to one senior member of the team. Almost overnight, the mobile upstart pivoted from a scrappy startup willing to take risks on emerging talent that might resonate with its youthful audience and gradually build buzz—like Kansas City's Morgan Cooper and his gritty reboot of *The Fresh Prince of Bel-Air*—to one inclined toward inoffensive, mainstream fare from NBC News and the Weather Channel, well-established TV brands capable of reaching large audiences that would make advertisers happy and reassure investors.

"Sometimes too much money is a bad thing," said the former executive. "Because [Katzenberg] raised two billion dollars, they're now beholden to two billion dollars in a return, whereas if you were to start up with, let's say, one hundred million dollars, and go under the radar—and not have to be something to everyone."

Despite Quibi's theoretically talent-friendly setup, there were whispers that it had become a haven for other studios' cast-offs. Take the comedy *Dummy*, which had been set up years earlier at TBS as part of a planned late-night programming block akin to that of the network's corporate sibling, the adult-oriented Adult Swim. Writer Cody Heller had completed seven of eight scripts when TBS abandoned its plans, stranding the project, which was inspired by Heller's reaction to discovering partner Dan Harmon's sex doll.

Dummy was revived when former Turner development executive Colin Davis, who'd championed the project at TBS, joined Quibi.

"I got a call [from Davis]. 'Hey, so, I left TBS. I'm at this new place that you don't know, it's with Jeffrey Katzenberg. I took the liberty of giving him the scripts you wrote for *Dummy*. And he wants to meet right away,'" Heller recalls. "I met with Jeffrey. He was so super cool and supportive and quoted lines from the script."

Katzenberg expressed interest in green-lighting the show, provided it could attract the right "star power." Anna Kendrick signed on, and the show was shot in a compressed eighteen days to accommodate her schedule. *Dummy* garnered a warm reception from critics, one of whom called it "the hilariously filthy and raw show we need right now," as well as an Emmy nomination for Kendrick.

But as many doors as Quibi opened up for the creative community, its name and brash approach engendered a steady social media backlash. Many startups face a wall of skepticism, sometimes for good reason and sometimes not. With this new contender, the pedigree of the founder and CEO made ripe targets for ridicule. Despite the repeated assertions that Quibi had identified an uncluttered "white space" on the entertainment map, the streaming landscape had grown crowded over the service's three-year gestation. One notable rival, the compulsively entertaining video-sharing app TikTok, was stealing all the thunder, having surpassed 2 billion downloads around the time Quibi finally launched.

"The whole hating-on-Quibi thing became such a trend on Twitter, with everyone wanting to shit on Quibi, I found myself getting defensive and hurt," Heller said. "I got to make my show there. Jeffrey believed in me and allowed me to truly make the show I wanted to make."

Hollywood observers and people close to Quibi say Katzenberg, whom Whitman describes as a "right-brain storyteller," and the CEO, a self-described "left-brain analytical thinker," clashed as they sought to shape the platform. Some high-profile executives left, repelled, said one Hollywood lawyer, by Katzenberg's workaholic tendencies. Katzenberg came to see that his insistence on weekend work and other stipulations made his reputation but also painted him as a "Neanderthal" by current standards. "Working smarter, not harder, sometimes is better," he conceded in a 2018 talk with Stanford MBA candidates. That magnanimity was nowhere in evidence as Quibi entered launch mode, numerous insiders have said.

"I joked in the past that if we were twenty years younger, we might have killed each other by now," Whitman acknowledged. "But we also have the maturity to know that we only want Quibi to win. We're not marking territory . . . I think there's grace, forgiveness and trust. We really do trust each other. We trust each other's instincts. We trust each other's domain expertise. Great partnerships are built on trust."

That may well have been wishful thinking. A *Wall Street Journal* story revealed the stress fractures beneath the appearance of a professional working relationship. Whitman described Katzenberg as dictatorial, belittling her and treating her like an underling as opposed to a true CEO. She had even threatened to quit, the report said. Culture clashes were evident from the earliest days. One executive recalls, incredulously, how the Hollywood types became fixated on having an office and an assistant, an obsession with appearances that was anathema to Whitman's unpretentious, Silicon Valley cubicle sensibilities.

"It's a silly example, but it in some ways highlights part of the problems of Quibi," said the executive, who found the preening a stark contrast to the professionalism and relentless customer focus at Netflix. "It's more important—the size of your office, who you meet with, who sits where at the [conference] table, and who speaks up, those kinds of things."

Signs of the internal strife occasionally spilled out into the open, as a number of senior executives exited. Janice Min, the former editor of the *Hollywood Reporter*, left after reportedly clashing with Katzenberg over the direction of Quibi's news and information programming, dubbed Daily Essentials. Tim Connelly, the head of partnerships and advertising, departed as Whitman asserted control over advertising deals. The former Netflix director who headed Quibi's brand and content marketing, Megan Imbres, departed two weeks after launch, due to what Katzenberg termed a "difference of opinion" about strategy.

Katzenberg and Whitman had to leave the drama backstage and present a united front in Las Vegas as they unveiled Quibi to the public at the Consumer Electronics Show in January 2020. The keynote presentation opened with a promotional video that, months later, would look like a time capsule preserved from another, pre-COVID era. It featured people watching videos on their phones as they went about their daily lives—lounging carelessly in a pool float, standing on a subway platform waiting for a train, or sipping coffee in a café.

The future of entertainment, it promised, was in your hands.

"Mobile phones are the most widely distributed, democratized entertainment platform the world has ever seen," said Katzenberg, standing alone at a podium onstage. "And innovation in mobile technology and network capability mean that we now have billions of users watching billions of hours of content every single day. And those numbers, which are huge—they're only growing."

Katzenberg presented Quibi as the next evolutionary chapter in the long-running saga of technological innovation sparking Hollywood's creativity, with a service that would deliver movie-caliber stories created expressly for viewing on the go. Whitman talked about building a platform that would enable storytellers to take full advantage of the phone's capabilities—its touchscreen, its camera, its built-in awareness of location and orientation—to tell different stories.

"From Day One, we wanted to make clear that we are creating a mobile-only platform," said Whitman. "Why? Because we're not shrinking TV onto phones. We're creating something new." Whitman cited, as one example, a horror series from Spielberg that viewers could only watch after the sun set. "The episodes can unlock just as it gets dark," she said. "And the virtual film can melt away right before your eyes when the sun comes up in the morning." That project, *After Dark*, never made it into production.

The centerpiece of Quibi's presentation was its technology, dubbed Turnstyle, which let viewers switch fluidly between full-screen portrait and landscape video when they rotated their phones. Though video on YouTube flips from horizontal to vertical, depending on how someone holds their phone, Quibi was different. Every film was shot and edited in portrait and landscape, then stitched together and delivered in a single package to the phone. The video instantly switched when the user rotated the phone—allowing viewers to shift narrative perspective with a flip of the wrist.

Director Zach Wechter exploited the ability to tell one story from two viewpoints in the Quibi film *Wireless*, a drama where the medium is the message. *Ready Player One*'s Tye Sheridan stars as a self-obsessed college student who is stranded in the Colorado mountains after crashing his car. His only hope of escape is his quickly dying phone.

"When you hold the phone horizontally, you'll see a traditional cinematic perspective of the story," said Wechter, who used a special rig to capture a phone's forward-facing and rear-facing cameras as well as the phone screen. "But when the viewer rotates the phone vertically, it's as if the character's phone takes over your own."

Wireless illustrated both the promise of Quibi and its programming disconnect. The show took deft advantage of the app's technical features to deliver a unique experience. But it wasn't offered at launch—it debuted months later, in September. Other shows leaned into the phone's interactivity, such as a planned update of the TV dating genre, *The Hot Drop*, in which the audience would submit videos for a chance to date the eligible single and the Quibi community would vote on which of the top three candidates would get shot. It never got a first date.

"There was an entire tech infrastructure to allow for interactive storytelling that never saw the light of day," said one former insider.

Instead, Quibi turned to Katzenberg's Hollywood connections. The

star-studded launch lineup included *The Most Dangerous Game*, starring
Liam Hemsworth and Christoph Waltz; a *Judge Judy*–esque courtroom
reality series, *Chrissy's Court*, starring Chrissy Teigen; a reboot of MTV's
prank show *Punk'd* with Chance the Rapper, and a cooking competition, *Dishmantled*, hosted by Tituss Burgess. Coming titles included
Kiefer Sutherland in a remake of *The Fugitive*, Don Cheadle and Emily
Mortimer in futuristic thriller *Don't Look Deeper*, and Kevin Hart in
comedic action meta-show *Die Hart*.

"It's hard to believe that it was less than eighteen months ago that we
first announced Quibi to the world," said Katzenberg as he crossed the
CES stage in front of a backdrop filled with colorful celebrity portraits.
"I actually could not be more proud that in that very short amount of
time this incredible wall of entertainment—and many, many more—
have agreed to be a part of it."

Here was the challenge, though: The millennial viewers Katzenberg hoped to entice with Quibi's marquee names couldn't have cared
less. They hardly needed Quibi to connect with celebrities through the
phone. Stars could readily be found in abundance elsewhere, on TikTok
or Instagram.

Katzenberg returned to the stage to acknowledge the difficulty
of launching a subscription service without a rich catalog of familiar
movies and TV shows. Quibi's bespoke programming strategy wasn't
something it could find off-the-rack. So, it would create every piece of
content from scratch, planning to launch a prodigious 175 new original
shows over the course of the year—the kind of production slate associated with Netflix, though with a fraction of the streaming giant's $13.5
billion budget.

"We realize not every in-between moment of your day calls for the
same kind of entertainment," Katzenberg said. "So our approach to the
content is meant to assume that we have something for every moment."

There would be three types of content on Quibi, executives explained: movies told in chapters of seven to ten minutes in length, episodic and unscripted series and documentaries, and Daily Essentials.

The last component would combine national news, sports, and weather updates with lifestyle content like *The Daily Chill*, a meditation show. Just as in other arenas, partnerships for Daily Essentials were set with outlets that were hardly run-of-the-mill. ESPN planned a custom, six-minute highlight show, and news mainstay *60 Minutes* would do the first shortened version of its fifty-two-year-old show, *60 in 6*, with all-original reports distinct from the weekly CBS broadcast.

As Quibi neared launch, reservations appeared to fade—though there were still doubters. One investment banker who attended CES talked about the sentiment expressed at one private dinner in Vegas: "DBA Jeffrey," short for "don't bet against Jeffrey." It was a nod of respect but far short of a ringing endorsement.

CHAPTER 8

▶ The Kid
with the Cartoons

A lot of grade-school kids dream of being astronauts, athletes, or fire-fighters. Matt Strauss just wanted to be able to watch cartoons on demand. While he didn't know it at the time, growing up in the 1970s in the New York City suburb of Oyster Bay, making that commonsense idea a reality would become his career. Taking the measure of Strauss's arc, from childhood obsession to head of NBCUniversal streaming service Peacock, helps shed some light on how the television business has reckoned with the digital age.

In the era of broadcast TV dominance decades ago, Strauss would keep track of when all his favorite cartoons were scheduled to air on Saturday mornings. On the occasions when he wasn't home or didn't get up early enough to watch live, though, there was no way to summon them another time, another way. Such a fate "just seemed incredibly unfair," he recalled a long while later, a note of childhood resentment still registering in his voice. "It bothered me to the point where my parents, they didn't know what to do because I kept complaining about it while other kids were collecting baseball cards."

Enter the videocassette recorder. As it became widely available to U.S. consumers over the latter part of the seventies, the Strausses took pity on their son and sprang for one. It was a transformative event for the eight-year-old. "I just went to town," Strauss laughed. "I recorded everything, I cataloged everything, I literally built *hundreds* of tapes. I built a database and I would catalog everything. I didn't even realize it at the time, of course, but I was in some ways trying to create more of this on-demand experience. All my friends would come over to my house and they knew I was the kid with the cartoons."

Oyster Bay was the same Long Island town where Chuck Dolan, the founder of Cablevision and media pioneer who created HBO, also lived. Perhaps not surprisingly, it ended up being one of the first communities in the U.S. to get cable TV, which followed soon after the VCR. Strauss instantly expanded his database tenfold, recording thirty networks compared to just three. He also started collecting TV gear, a hobby that continued into adulthood. "I have the very first remote control that was wireless, which was the Zenith—the Zenith Flash-matic," he said, conceding with a laugh that it was "very nerdy" information to share.

After graduating with a business degree from NYU, Strauss talked his way into a job at ABC's New York City headquarters. Idolizing Bob Iger, who was then running the network, Strauss climbed the ladder in the strategic planning division, leveraging his business knowledge but harboring much loftier ambitions. Ever since his catalog-and-database days, he "always had this interest in trying to make TV better." It was more serious than just incremental improvement or percentage gains, the way his classmates thought of it in business school. There was an unusual sense of justice, of confronting the vexing question, why did cartoons have to only appear live on Saturday mornings? "I was trying to right a wrong," Strauss explained. "To me, the wrong was the way TV worked. I could not accept the fact that it was this bad, that that was the only way we were going to be able to watch television, so I wanted to do something about it in my own small way."

Having learned the industry ropes at ABC, Strauss was offered a chance to come home and make a deeper mark on the medium. Cablevision wanted him to help develop an ambitious on-demand concept.

Strauss wrote a business plan outlining a service called Mag Rack, which wound up launching in 2001. The suite of offerings took its name from the idea of browsing through magazines on a newsstand or in a bookstore. As the internet spurred cable companies to allow catch-up viewing via video on demand, Mag Rack produced "video magazines" focused on niches like science, health, cars, and wine. Because it was free for customers, Cablevision told customers it enhanced the value of their cable subscription—and it even got other cable operators to license it. Despite such glimmers of innovation, Chuck Dolan shaped Cablevision into what the business world would call a "fast follower," often mainstreaming technology developed by small, marginal players. The company was in hot pursuit of digital video recorder technology, though its embedding of DVR technology in its cable boxes landed it in court for years in a fight with TiVo and other companies. It also swung a risky deal with Sony to build set-top boxes whose sophisticated design had never been seen in the industry. "It was almost like a Ferrari box," Strauss said, pausing to appreciate the craftsmanship. "But it turns out it was just too expensive to scale. But it gave us a little bit of a glimpse into what was possible." Strauss, still in his twenties and working directly with Dolan as an executive vice president on all of these innovations, seemed to have found his tribe. "I always believed the future would be on demand," he said.

Over time, the Long Island cable company started to feel a bit provincial. It had a sizable market share in New York, but it was still just the sixth-largest cable provider in the U.S. It wouldn't be able to right all of the wrongs of television. Strauss decided to make a move that would pave the way for him to eventually run Peacock. He cold-called Steve Burke, head of Comcast Cable in Philadelphia and son of legendary media figure Dan Burke, who ran Capital Cities and had merged it with ABC during Strauss's tenure there. The younger Burke had also been at Capital Cities/ABC before decamping for Comcast, which had become the number one cable provider in the U.S. by the time Strauss's call came in.

When Burke picked up the phone, to the surprise of Strauss, the rising executive said he had been following Burke's public comments as well as those of Comcast CEO Brian Roberts. They had professed the future of the TV business was empowering viewers to watch what they wanted, when they wanted. "I just said to him, 'I know what you're trying to do with on demand.' I said, 'I can build this for you. I know exactly what you need to do.'" Burke told Strauss to hop on a train to Philadelphia to tell him more.

Strauss articulated a vision for on-demand programming that would not simply be an improvement over pay-per-view, which had existed since cable's earliest days. "We should be producing original programming, we should be packaging it up and using it as a differentiator and as an added value to the cable bundle," he remembers telling Burke. Not only would Comcast "change the way people watch television" but it would have an edge over satellite rivals like DirecTV and Dish Network, whose "one-way" technology limited their ability to offer much on demand.

Two weeks after the meeting, Strauss was hired, "essentially without a job description." Thus began a run of seventeen years (and counting, as of this writing) for Strauss at Comcast. He spearheaded a range of projects that positioned Comcast as an innovator, even if it was, yes, still a cable company with a somewhat checkered record of customer service. As one of the executives working on the Xfinity cable system, Strauss oversaw the integration of Netflix, Amazon Prime Video, YouTube, and other streaming apps into the X1 interface. That meant that instead of forcing viewers to go through a laborious series of steps to toggle between TV and streaming, Comcast reduced friction and made streaming services just another button on the remote. Their against-the-grain theory: by keeping customers inside the Xfinity X1's set-top experience, even if they didn't watch traditional TV, the net effect would be positive for Comcast. The theory was that happier customers able to easily sample video services would be less likely to cancel their Comcast subscriptions.

A similar venture led by Strauss was the Xfinity Flex video service, which was free for broadband customers. Similar to free streaming packages like Pluto TV, the Roku Channel, and Amazon Fire TV, Flex brought together dozens of channels and streaming services, catering to the very cord-shavers whose resistance to the big bundle posed a threat to cable operators. Selling broadband, of course, had become a brisk business, so it made sense for Comcast to lure customers there even if they didn't want conventional pay TV. Flex gained traction quickly, passing three million set-top boxes installed two years after it launched.

Comcast took full ownership of NBCUniversal in 2013 after buying out General Electric's remaining stake. As streaming rose and the pay-TV bundle faded, the notion of direct-to-consumer streaming had never gained traction at the company. Unlike rival media companies like Disney and Time Warner, NBCUniversal was not inclined to disrupt itself. It was content with operating TV Everywhere apps, which allowed streaming only to pay-TV subscribers, as well as licensing its own programming around the world for significant fees. Even by early 2019, after Comcast announced it would follow Disney and WarnerMedia into streaming, Roberts struck a moderate note during an appearance at a Wall Street conference. Without naming names, he took pains to point out differences between the Comcast and Disney approaches to licensing out content versus reclaiming it for its own purposes. "We're very much focused on not just, as others have said, going completely cold turkey and taking it off all these other platforms," Roberts said. "I don't think that's our mindset at the moment. We like those relationships." Strauss put a finer point on it. "Comcast generally tends to be very methodical in how we execute our decisions," he said.

The company's methodical approach stemmed from the many legacies it had to preserve—especially at NBCUniversal, whose base at 30 Rockefeller Plaza is a monument to media history. In 1935, for example, one thousand square feet of office space on the third floor was transformed into something the world had never before known: a commercial television studio. Studio 3H had low ceilings and cameras that barely budged. But NBC was eager to show off its state-of-the-art facility when it opened, so it staged a demonstration for the press, setting up a monitor on the building's sixty-second floor. Commentator Betty Goodwin, comedian Ed Wynn, and members of the Rockettes appeared, as did executives like RCA mogul David Sarnoff, who teased a more ambitious exhibition planned for the 1939 World's Fair. The demo show had an uneven rhythm, with newsreels and movie clips mixing with live performances. Primitive, sweltering stage lights loomed perilously close to the talent, at one point making mascara run down the cheeks of a cabaret singer named Hildegarde. Reviewing the event for the *New Yorker*, E. B. White described feeling disoriented by the aesthetics, which made faces look like they were "mounted on watered silk." The twenty-minute show "didn't make television seem any too practical for the living room of one's own home," he concluded, "although of course homes are changing."

As one of the prime movers of media and entertainment for nearly a century, NBC—known as NBCUniversal since the network merged with Universal Entertainment in 2004—has ushered in numerous changes to the living room. Unlike the era when it was leading the innovation cycle and convening proto-Apple product launches, this time it would have to play catch-up. Netflix, founded during the euphoria of the dot-com era, dominated the streaming business it had largely defined. It employed thousands of engineers to fine-tune its only product, an app available to 200-plus million subscribers in 190 countries. Traditional media companies had few clear advantages over spend-happy tech invaders, the main one being a significant portfolio of programming that they owned. Popular sitcom *The Office*, for example, was one of the most streamed shows on Netflix. Now NBCUniversal could reclaim it and use it as an anchor of its own competing service, though doing so would cost more than $500 million.

Steve Burke spearheaded the streaming initiative as NBCUniversal's CEO. The sixty-two-year-old media executive wore a suit well, possessed of both conventional good looks and a shrewd analytical mind. He conceded to being driven, even a taskmaster, as a leader, but had developed a lot of loyalists both in his company and in industry circles. Unlike other media CEOs, he was no Hamptons-and-Malibu-haunting grandee. When in need of recharging, he would head to Montana to fish. Burke had an early career stint at Disney working with his father, Dan Burke, co-head of Capital Cities, which bought ABC in 1986 and in turn was swallowed up by Disney a decade later. Bob Iger, then ABC's president, had been grooming the younger Burke to succeed him at the network—but Burke had no interest in decamping to Burbank and took a job running Comcast Cable instead. "It felt like a knife in my back," Iger wrote in his biography, *The Ride of a Lifetime*, remarking, in a rare dig for the self-professed nice-guy CEO, that Steve lacked his father's "natural warmth."

Burke remembers 2017—the year when Iger shocked the media world with the announcement that Disney would pull its content off Netflix and launch a competing service—as the time when active planning began in earnest for NBCUniversal's own service. "We started having meetings. Once every two weeks we would meet for a couple of hours," he recalled. "I would meet with our CFO and our strategy people, and then there were certain meetings I would have with my executive committee, which are all my direct reports, and we would look at everything and try to figure out what to do." One option was to amass the scale by combining NBCU's assets with Discovery's popular reality programming and Time Warner's deep repository of television sitcoms and dramas. Burke and Comcast CEO Brian Roberts called Discovery CEO David Zaslav to float the idea, saying each partner would benefit equally, according to one well-placed source. The potential deal evaporated when Comcast expressed interest in acquiring the two smaller media companies.

Burke and team went to school on Disney, seeking to reverse-engineer the business model for a financially viable streaming service. "We said, 'Well, Disney, they're smart and they must have some insight that makes sense. What are we missing?' And so we called a bunch of people who'd left Disney and consulting firms who had done work for

Disney and we just couldn't figure out a plan that we thought made sense," Burke recalled. "Then one day . . . a guy walked in and said, 'What if we made it free and ad-supported?'"

It was an utterly logical question for a company heavily invested in the status quo. Given NBCUniversal's massive advertising business, which reaped between $12 billion and $13 billion a year from linear, digital, and streaming worldwide, the idea of preserving the decades-old presence of sponsor pitches in streaming was attractive. After all, viewers had been watching free, ad-supported television since Bulova aired the first TV commercial on July 1, 1941, hawking its watches during a Brooklyn Dodgers–Philadelphia Phillies baseball game. Despite the conventional wisdom that the TV spot was dying out—a casualty of an earlier home entertainment innovation, ad-skipping digital video recorders—CBS All Access and Hulu's basic tier had shown that large-scale streaming services with ads were viable. Viewership was growing on free, ad-supported outlets like Pluto TV and Tubi, which were enticing to customers unboxing a new smart TV or any of the millions of Americans looking to cut the pay-TV cord. Mounting a pure subscription offering to challenge entrenched players like Netflix, in Burke's view, seemed daunting. "The math is very challenging. With a subscription business, the one thing you know is you start with zero and then at the end of the year you might have three million subs or whatever. And then the second year, you go from three million to six million. It's a slow ramp for a subscription business. . . . You have to show up with the product and cost of it on day one, despite the fact that you haven't yet built the subscriber base. So, it's an economically painful model."

As the advertising-oriented strategy took shape, Burke did not initially turn to Strauss to make it happen. Instead, he tapped a trusted lieutenant to steer the day-to-day operation: Bonnie Hammer. After starting out in documentaries and public television (one of her early producing credits was on *This Old House*), Hammer went on to hold key positions at Universal Television and then NBCUniversal. She really hit her stride fortifying and rebranding well-established cable TV operations, among them E!, USA, and Syfy. A petite, fast-talking dynamo born and raised in Queens, Hammer had joined the top tier of TV executives by grooming networks into cash-generating machines. At their peak, at the start of the 2010s, the networks she had revamped were bringing in almost $2 billion in annual profit.

Despite Hammer's keen radar for hit shows and knack for spotting and wooing talent, she had never immersed herself in the nuts and bolts of technology. Mounting a streaming service would require her to grapple with concerns about latency, user interfaces, distribution rights across hundreds of properties—all on an accelerated timeline of fifteen months from shoulder tap to launch. The seventy-year-old executive found herself thrust into the erratic metabolic rhythms of a startup. Amid all the novel challenges, Hammer leaned into what she does best: creating a brand out of nothing, while taking advantage of NBCU's assets and heritage.

"'Take a look at the portfolio and try to determine the strengths of NBC content, both in library and potential originals,'" she remembers Burke asking her. "We were challenged to look for content that would be interesting and noisy to help launch." The goal, Hammer said, was to tap into the power of NBCU, while at the same time creating something unique—"something original that had credibility and gave a nod to NBCU and its history."

NBC had a more complex view of streaming than its network peers. It joined with Fox to launch Hulu, a pioneer in delivering TV shows via the internet. But that was in 2007, well before the nation's largest cable company, Comcast, took over the venerable broadcaster, its local television stations, its cable channels, and the Universal movie studio in 2011. The conglomerate's cable operations—which include high-speed internet access as well as video—dwarf its entertainment unit, with twice the revenue and four times the earnings. So its business interests are paramount.

In 2018, having lost out on the 21st Century Fox assets in a takeover battle with Disney, Comcast placed a fairly extravagant bet on an asset that would be central to its streaming strategy. It paid $40 billion to acquire Sky, the UK-based satellite broadcaster, after a separate duel with Disney. While satellite was in decline in Europe, just as in the U.S., the efforts by Sky to transcend that gave Comcast confidence in the deal. It also controlled a large amount of sports rights and had exclusive distribution deals with HBO in the UK and Germany. The architects of the British company's Now TV streaming service—widely seen as the best in class of the European field—would apply their skills across the pond.

One reason Comcast was not yet pushing to demolish its existing model is that it controlled TV and digital rights to large-scale events like the Olympic Games. Traditional gauges of Olympics viewing show their numbers are slipping, but social media has helped them continue to be one of the last global watercooler properties in media. NBCUniversal has held exclusive U.S. broadcast rights since 1988, shelling out more than $12 billion since 2011 to lock them up through 2032. NBCUniversal already had been spreading coverage around cable networks and digital platforms, but it insisted on preserving the decades-old concept of a nightly prime-time broadcast. Time-zone delays of coverage—all the more glaring in the era of instant social media gratification—made the coverage seem even more anachronistic. Across its digital and linear platforms, NBCU pumped out thousands of hours of coverage. Live ratings continued their downward trajectory, but the company reported solid profits thanks to catch-up viewing and advertisers willing to pay a premium for high-profile inventory.

NBCUniversal had also had a decidedly mixed experience with subscription streaming services. It had a solid niche performer in NBC Sports Gold, but it laid an egg with a comedy-focused streaming service called Seeso. Launched in early 2016 as what the company said would be the first in a portfolio of targeted offerings, it aimed to trade on the heritage of NBC properties like *SNL* and Thursday night sitcoms, charging a modest $4 a month. The price was reasonable, but there was no compelling reason for new customers to take the bait. By the fall of 2017, the service had shut down after accumulating just 250,000 subscribers. The failure did not come cheap. A person familiar with the books said about $300 million was invested overall—80 percent of it in customer acquisition and the rest in original and acquired programming. Bob Greenblatt, who was chairman of NBC at the time, told reporters at the 2016 Television Critics Association summer press tour that "toe in the water" initiatives like Seeso were just a precursor to something much broader. "We know this OTT-digital strategy is going to happen," Greenblatt said, referring to "over-the-top" media services that bypass traditional cable. "It's happening in a lot of places already. It's kind of where the audience is going and where they demand us to go. We spend a lot of time talking about what we're going to do in the space."

Despite the starts and stops in streaming, the 2016 Rio Olympics wound up being the most profitable in the company's history, netting $250 million. Broadcast television remained the primary engine, accounting for roughly 75 percent of profits due to the premium ad rates. A month after the closing ceremony in Rio, NBC premiered a sentimental new drama about a family's interactions across generations, told in time-skipping fashion. *This Is Us* would draw blockbuster ratings and critical praise, averaging nearly fifteen million viewers in an era when prime-time broadcast shows garnered a fraction of that. With two of television's other top draws, the NFL's *Sunday Night Football* and *The Voice*, defying gravity and pulling in large linear ratings, NBC had reason to place continued faith in the traditional model. Streaming had brought mostly headaches.

"We're playing to our strengths," Burke said of the company's philosophy regarding Peacock. "We happen to be part of a company that has fifty-five million video customers and is the biggest provider of television advertising in the United States." By the time the Rio Olympics came around, Burke had developed scar tissue from handling a series of scandals. He personally managed the response to an outcry over NBC News anchor Brian Williams's exaggerating and misrepresenting his coverage of the Iraq War, striving at every turn to stay out of the headlines. "He's not shy, he's not reticent, he's just not voluble like me," longtime friend Warren Buffett told the *New York Times* soon after Burke took the job.

It's not that Burke was ignoring the streaming revolution; he fully anticipated other major media companies would launch Netflix-like subscription services. But the notion of losing billions a year—at a company known for reliable cash flow and conservative management—was unworkable. As a Harvard MBA who had learned from his father's business trajectory, Burke had long enjoyed a reputation as a seasoned dealmaker. As 2017 drew to a close, economic conditions favored mergers and acquisitions, and traditional media companies were fretting about the effects of cord-cutting and the decline of TV viewership. The iceberg was officially melting, and the response was a familiar one to students of business history: consolidation. AT&T announced a deal to buy Time Warner, a merger soon followed with Lionsgate swallowing Starz, and Discovery revealed plans to acquire Scripps Networks Interactive in a $14.6 billion cable combination. The biggest blockbuster, though, was revealed in November 2017: Disney was in talks to buy most of 21st Century Fox. That deal would reshape the movie and TV landscape and also give a single company majority control of Hulu for the first time since its 2007 launch—a setback for NBCU. Streaming was the prime motivator of the acquisition flurry, with companies aiming to assemble a roster of programming potent enough to lure fickle consumers.

Comcast, which had made a hostile bid for Disney in 2004, dueled again with the company in 2018 over the 21st Century Fox assets but came up short. Comcast then decided to aggressively pursue a different piece of Rupert Murdoch's media empire: European satellite TV giant Sky, winning a separate bidding war with Disney with a $40 billion offer. Sky owned important sports rights and had a well-established brand in Sky News. But its main value in streaming, compared with Fox's stable of properties like *The Simpsons*, *Avatar*, and the X-Men franchise, was product expertise. Sky's Now, a streaming service in the UK, was an acknowledged leader. The team that built it would be tasked with replicating the service for NBCUniversal's long-awaited entry into streaming.

Once the ink had dried on the Sky deal, Burke unveiled a long-awaited streaming service in the U.S., which was eyeing a launch in early 2020. Burke chose to "zig when everyone else was zagging" and offer a free, ad-supported service. Owning Comcast and Sky gave the initiative an inside track, Burke argued, with millions of customers instantly able to access the new streaming offering for free.

He made it clear that NBCUniversal was not going to chase new subscribers the way WarnerMedia and Disney were setting out to do. "About eighty percent of the viewers are in the pay-TV ecosystem," he said. "That's already where we live."

CHAPTER 9

▶ Long Game

When he isn't mapping out new products or services for Apple, Eddy Cue is an avid golfer. "I've become an addict," Cue confessed with a bashful grin during an episode of *Callaway Live*, a YouTube series hosted by the golf equipment maker. "I love doing it any time I have time off." He added that he'd made some of his "closest friends" while playing golf.

Two friends he evidently looked forward to making on the links in 2018 were Tiger Woods and Phil Mickelson. The Hall of Fame pros were set to take part in a novel live streaming event: the Match, an eighteen-hole faceoff over Thanksgiving in Las Vegas. Players would wear live microphones and would be encouraged to trash-talk (not a stretch for Woods and Mickelson, who weren't friendly). The winner would earn $9 million. Cue was among multiple parties who looked to acquire rights to the showdown, according to people familiar with the negotiations. Apple hadn't even launched its streaming service, Apple TV+, at that point, so it's not clear how they would have packaged it. But for Cue, the Match seemed too good to resist. "Eddy was definitely really interested and almost made an offer," one of the agents representing it recalled. "He wanted to hang with Tiger for the weekend," the agent added with a chuckle.

The rights, which were hotly contested but cost just a fraction of the full-season, multibillion rights packages that are common in sports media, didn't dangle for long. ESPN came close to a deal, but it fell apart at the last minute. AT&T prevailed, acquiring rights for Turner Sports and DirecTV, which would also offer the event as a $20 pay-per-view attraction. The motives of AT&T executives were similar to Cue's, the agent said. Turner Sports chief David Levy and AT&T's then-CEO Randall Stephenson both came to the event and had pictures taken with the players and seemed eager to spend time with them—though the official strategy of the high-stakes duel was to lure younger viewers. "This is funny," the agent remembered thinking. "Are you guys just buying your way into hanging with celebrities? I thought you guys were masters of the universe!"

In the end, the Match became an ignominious footnote in streaming history when it ran into major technical glitches. Levy blamed "insufficient memory" and a high volume of requests coming in at the same time shoppers were making Black Friday purchases. AT&T wound up dropping the pay-per-view gate in real time, allowing viewers to tune in for free and issuing refunds to the reported 750,000 viewers who had shelled out $20. Other distributors followed suit. By the time Mickelson edged Woods in extra holes, even many die-hard fans had tuned out.

The unsatisfying outcome for the Match owed plenty to golf-obsessed executives and celebrity players eager to cash in, while no one managed the blocking and tackling of executing the broadcast's technical aspects. It also reflected the urgency driving dealmakers to put sports—the still-beating heart of the pay-TV bundle—into the stream. Every company trying to go after Netflix in the streaming race had a major stake in live sports, but the trick would be to see how they could compel sports fans—who, history had shown, would pay dearly to watch their team—to think digital.

Amazon, Twitter, Facebook, and YouTube all began taking a page from BAMTech's playbook and streaming live games starting in the 2010s. Today, Amazon owns exclusive rights to *NFL Thursday Night Football* and is a part owner of the YES Network, streaming twenty-one New York Yankees games a year. Globally, it carries Premier League soccer and major tennis tournaments. Apple has held talks with major college conferences and regional sports networks but, as of this writing, has not pulled the trigger. NBCUniversal's Peacock and Disney's ESPN+ have live sports at their core, and WarnerMedia's HBO Max added NHL hockey rights in 2021. Paramount+, which ViacomCBS has positioned as a next-tier streaming contender, has made soccer, college sports, and the NFL a central part of its pitch.

To understand the complicated brinkmanship of the sports-licensing game in the era of streaming, there are few more sage guides than John Skipper. The lanky sixty-five-year-old media veteran followed a twenty-seven-year run at Disney and ESPN with a stint as executive chairman at a sports streaming outlet called DAZN (which is pronounced, yes, "da zone"). Backed by billionaire Len Blavatnik, the sports service operates in the U.S., but most of its nearly eight million subscribers are overseas. In its few years of existence, DAZN has scooped up rights to major soccer leagues, elite boxers like Anthony Joshua and Canelo Alvarez, and, in certain parts of the world, the NFL.

Skipper, who left DAZN to found a boutique production entity called Meadowlark Media in 2021, had an eventful final stretch steering ESPN. His six-year run as president ended with his resignation due to a cocaine addiction, a revelation that stunned the media industry. The beginning had been inauspicious as well, Skipper blithely pointed out over a leisurely lunch recently in Manhattan's West Village. The pay-TV bundle hit its peak in 2012 before recording its first annual decline in decades the following year, a downturn that has only accelerated since. "I assumed my job on January 1, 2012, and I told people in jest years later that the day I got there was the first day it leveled off," Skipper says with a laugh, his long-voweled accent revealing his upbringing in central North Carolina. As cord-cutting quietly accelerated, Skipper's task was to somehow wring greater profits out of fewer and fewer subscribers as a machine engineered for the twentieth century crashed into the realities of the twenty-first.

ESPN remains highly profitable even today, but the steady loss of traditional subscribers poses an existential threat and has heavily

influenced Disney's stance on streaming. Bob Iger, shortly before passing the baton as CEO, acknowledged that ESPN is fated to become
"far more of a direct-to-consumer product," though that transition is
expected to take many years. Stand-alone service ESPN+ launched in
2018 and verged on fifteen million subscribers three years later, but it has
remained a complementary service. The games and programming that
matter can only be seen on regular ESPN, via a pay-TV subscription.

As Disney and other media companies confronted the impact of the
internet in the 2000s and into the next decade, there was a lot standing
in their way to make a full pivot toward streaming. The internal debates
were vigorous, but the forces of ESPN had more reason than anyone to
be loyal to the traditional business model rather than going "over the
top," as streaming was initially called in the TV business. The company
was so powerful it could hike carriage fees at will and sell ads at premium rates on top of that. ESPN had invented the dual revenue stream
in 1983, persuading cable operators to pay to carry the network while
they also sold ads, a feat that other cable pioneers, like MTV, Nickelodeon, and CNN, had not managed to that point. That innovation
started extremely modestly. In the oral history *Those Guys Have All the
Fun*, by James Andrew Miller and Tom Shales, former ESPN executive
George Bodenheimer recalls persuading mom-and-pop cable operators
to pay a fee of four cents per subscriber per month. Eventually, those
fees ran into the billions and inadvertently created an obstacle to any
reorientation toward streaming. Media executives earned bonuses based
on their performance but also the performance of their division, as well
as the overall company. Forfeiting carriage fees would mean asking dozens of senior employees to forfeit six- and seven-figure annual sums.

The company "had very good and smart discussions" about the
need to shift to digital, Skipper recalled. "ESPN was probably a brake
on moving quickly. And I was part of that. Because it was like, 'Guys,
you can't go to the distributor and say, "I want another seven to eight
percent," if you're also over-the-top.'" As president, Skipper said, he
most often sided with his distribution chiefs. "As the head of distribu-

tion, you're naturally a voice going, 'Wait a minute, what are you *talking* about?! We get eight billion dollars a year [from pay-TV carriage fees] and you're gonna subvert that?'" he said. "We would have these discussions and we would say, 'Yeah, that is the future, but when is going to be the time to pivot?' You pivot too quick, you're just shooting yourself in the foot. So, Bob always made these decisions with regard to how we were going to keep the stock price up and return value to shareholders." In recalling those complicated days, Skipper notes that he helped spearhead the launch of broadband-only network ESPN3, which was an early sports streaming outlet. The spinoff network, stocked with an eclectic mix of live sports from college volleyball to cricket, was created to meet rising demand from pay-TV providers expanding into broadband. ESPN managed to wrangle a fifty-cents-per-subscriber fee from broadband providers, Skipper said, and they then offered it free to high-speed internet customers as a value-add. While it was a pioneering foray into sports streaming, the distribution model is significant. Like ESPN+, it was always a satellite orbiting Planet ESPN.

The question of when the big planet will become available outside of the pay-TV bundle has only grown more persistent nearly four decades after the first carriage fees were collected. Skipper's successor, Jimmy Pitaro, is likely considering it, says one source familiar with his thinking, adding that management teams "have been having that conversation for a while now." At the same time, change does not appear imminent. "I get why you would ask that and why you would think that," said the source. "'They are now prioritizing even more direct-to-consumer, so they must be wanting to take the flagship direct sooner.' The answer to that is no. We've been having these thoughtful conversations around 'if and when' we take our flagship direct."

Television's transition to streaming is generally considered to be inevitable. Before they became prime movers in the movie business, directing the last two *Avengers* films and other major titles for Marvel and Disney, Joe and Anthony Russo worked in the television business. They were producers and directors for years on network series like *Community* and *Arrested Development*, and they witnessed the disruption of linear networks and its effect on the creative community. "Anthony and I have been saying that to each other for well over a decade," Joe Russo says of the broader shift from the traditional bundle to streaming. TV networks were "built around brands and commercials, the content was driven by advertisers and advertiser dollars, which dictates the kind of content that you can put on the air," Anthony Russo says. "There's no question that that model is a broken model, because it corrupts the narrative, where you're dealing with other forms of distribution that don't corrupt. So they're being leveraged by the advertisers. To us, it was a broken model driving on a flat tire, and it's been driving on four flat tires for at least six or seven years. At some point, they just have to pull the car over to the side of the road and declare it a lemon, junk it, take the plates off and run." He punctuated the distended metaphor with a laugh.

Advertising, though, has been woven into the fabric of American television in a way that's different from how the medium works in other parts of the world. From the days of *Howdy Doody* and *Texaco Star Theater*, advertisers had called the shots, plastering their brand names on shows, running commercials, and having talent do on-air "reads" of sponsor messages. It is significant, then, that streaming's boom phase for U.S. audiences has to this point been defined by ad-free subscription services, chiefly Netflix. While the earliest digital video efforts in the 2000s (notably Hulu and YouTube) had advertising at their center, the essence of the internet-delivered video experience soon asserted itself, and it was about the viewer taking control.

"The 'immediacy' and 'liveliness' that had been believed integral to the experience of television was believed to be a by-product of its previous distribution technologies," observes media studies professor Amanda D. Lotz in her book *We Now Disrupt This Broadcast*. "Internet and other digital technologies allowed viewers to access television at their command—as had occurred with print and audio media. Viewers rejoiced, but television's business models now needed to catch up." Netflix, by contrast, ritualistically said it was seeking to "delight" its "members." Satisfied, dues-paying members of the club would not allow themselves to be bombarded with ads. Streaming's inversion of the CBS-before-HBO paradigm of linear TV was likely connected with the way the cable industry's TV Everywhere effort alienated viewers with a clumsy ad experience.

If the great shift is to happen, though, with marquee programming and mass audiences all moving from the traditional bundle to the internet, advertising dollars will be a requirement. Amazon's recent push into sports, as well as its investment in other streaming platforms—Twitch, Fire TV, and IMDb TV—is motivated by advertising. The company is now projected to exceed $20 billion a year in ad revenue, a figure that some Wall Street analysts see tripling by 2026. Once a distant also-ran compared with Facebook and Google, Amazon is now a colossus in video advertising as in other sectors.

Advertisers are indicating a willingness to explore streaming as a way of finding younger consumers with the superior targeting capabilities of the digital realm. The notion of streaming popularized by Netflix was ad-free and subscription based, but signs of "subscription fatigue" had surfaced by 2020. Especially given the financial burdens of COVID-19, survey data indicated consumers would pay for no more than three services at a time. Ad-supported streaming's time might finally have arrived, partisans believed. American viewers for decades had en masse made the trade-off of sitting through ads to be able to watch programming for little to no up-front cost. Why couldn't that same idea work in the streaming age?

Over time, the reconciliation of ad-free subscription video-on-demand services (SVOD) with a more sophisticated group of ad-supported ones (AVOD) will define the video experience. "True premium, first-run content today—because of the way the business works—needs SVOD or SVOD/AVOD as a business model," says Scott Rosenberg, general manager of Roku's platform business and a close observer of thousands of streaming apps of all stripes. "Pure AVOD—Google, Facebook, have played with it. They have some of the elements but maybe not the right screen to scale. I do think in pure, first-run AVOD, original, high-production-value content is feasible, at least in certain categories—food, lifestyle, reality. Deep, costly, dramatic episodic product, maybe not now, maybe someday with global scale. Maybe." The feasibility of high-end AVOD is being tested by Peacock and HBO Max, following a trail blazed by Hulu and, more recently, Paramount+ (*né* CBS All Access). The WarnerMedia service is attempting something only cable networks like AMC and Bravo have tried in the modern media era: adding commercials after starting out commercial-free. As promised in 2019, it added a $10-a-month ad-supported tier to its $15 ad-free version.

While Netflix co-CEOs Reed Hastings and Ted Sarandos have vigorously denied it, the accepted wisdom for many observers is that the company will one day need to incorporate advertising. Skeptics believe it is vulnerable to rivals charging a fraction of its monthly subscription fee, or even nothing at all. An array of free services, like Pluto TV, Tubi, Crackle, Amazon-owned IMDb TV, Xumo, and others, have blossomed, drawing tens of millions of monthly "users," in the common, tech-derived lexicon. Their growth has stemmed from the ubiquity of smart TVs equipped with internet access and also viewers cutting the pay-TV cord. Their economic model could not be more different from Netflix's, featuring limited original production and modest programming costs. Early AVOD services were crude and unsatisfying viewer experiences, with less stickiness than the Binge Times kingpins like Netflix. But the experience has steadily improved, and the offerings have multiplied. IMDb TV, for example, brings viewers prestige shows like *Mad Men* and Norman Lear's iconic seventies series at no cost to the viewer. Companies running free services are content to be the dollar stores next to the high-end retailers like Netflix. During the economic dislocation of the pandemic, they drew plenty of curious shoppers.

Sports-focused streaming will likely never be free, or free of advertising. How else to pass the time when there is a time-out on the field or yet another pitching change? "We do think advertising works in sports," Skipper said. "And we do think it's a dramatic second revenue stream. . . . And we need to have multiple revenue streams." DAZN has developed a dynamic insertion application with Google, a nod to streaming advertisers' obsession with using data to find specific customers. Internet-based distribution, unlike linear TV, is built on personalization and data-centric ad approaches. Dynamic ad insertion is the other side of the spectrum from shotgunning the same beer ad to tens of millions of living rooms. One reason for Skipper's interest in bolstering advertising's role in his streaming operation is the reality that acquiring rights alone is less apt to lead to profits, at least in the U.S., where the cost of rights is expected to keep rising. Billions of dollars are going to be spent on licensing fees by the same American media companies pouring vast resources into their own streaming efforts. Domestic rights packages in Europe and elsewhere for soccer and other sports have gone down markedly over the past year due to a mix of factors, including tighter regulation, fewer bidders, and a surprising, commonsense course correction of long-standing rights holders deciding to offer less to renew. The favorable deal climate is a big reason why DAZN is refocusing its attention outside of the U.S.

Pitaro sees more changes coming to the rights landscape. "For certain sports, it is time for a reset," he said. "Everything can't be up and to the right. Maybe a decade from now, things could get back into growth mode when these over-the-top services have proven their value, but . . . in a world where we are seeing cord cutting accelerate, it's a much more challenging environment to be operating in. And, at a certain point, the industry is going to have to accept that. That ratings are down and the number of subscribers are down. As a result, ad revenue is down. The fees that were the payments that media companies are getting contributors are down. It's not sustainable to have all of that down."

For all the hope for a reset, the NFL delivered a stunning demonstration of its power by commanding nearly $110 billion in a set of major rights renewals announced in March 2021. In eleven-year extensions, ViacomCBS, Disney/ESPN, Fox Corporation, NBCUniversal, and Amazon all locked up rights through the mid-2030s. The figure was not a complete surprise—NFL games accounted for seven of the top ten highest-rated TV programs in 2020—but it was a terrifying number. It kept "Big Iron," as traditional broadcast operations were called, in the mix for another decade. The dilemmas about when and how to fully wean themselves from the familiar source of revenue would continue.

Nick Khan, president of World Wrestling Entertainment and a former ICM and CAA agent, watches the sports rights space closely. Reflecting on the NFL renewals, he predicted the "death of more basic cable channels" in favor of streaming would be the near-term result. Already, NBCUniversal had announced that its NBC Sports network, whose DNA was decades old, would shut down in 2022 and much of its programming would shift to Peacock. When Disney won most rights to NHL hockey, the league decided to phase out its own channel, the NHL Network. What no one knows—even the great and powerful Amazon, Khan agreed—is how to guide sports viewers through this transition. Unlike in the traditional bundled world, "there is no channel surfing" in streaming, he pointed out. "When consumers look through their onscreen grid at night, they'll see certain things and think, 'Oh, I didn't know this next game was on.' With streaming, it has to be must-see TV."

CHAPTER 10

▶ The Birth of ClownCo

It was easy for Hollywood to dismiss YouTube in its early days, when the most popular videos on the site capitalized on the delight of discovery and the thrill of sharing some irresistibly quirky video with friends. Schlock science experiments with Diet Coke and Mentos, a "Star Wars Kid" awkwardly brandishing a lightsaber, and motivational speaker Judson Laipply's fluidly shifting dance styles to fit a medley of a dozen pop hits, dubbed the "Evolution of Dance"—all attracted millions of views.

None of that user-created ephemera seemed to pose a serious competitive threat to such television juggernauts as *American Idol; CSI: Crime Scene Investigation;* and *Grey's Anatomy* in 2005. But as often is the case with early-stage technology, the nature of the threat evolved quickly, as users found a new application for the video-sharing site— uploading favorite television clips. One of YouTube's earliest viral hits was ripped, literally, from TV: *Saturday Night Live*'s "Lazy Sunday" skit, featuring Chris Parnell and Andy Samberg as two slackers rapping about the virtues of New York's Magnolia Bakery cupcakes and going uptown to watch *The Chronicles of Narnia.* The two-and-a-half-minute short racked up five million views in a matter of days, though network parent NBC didn't see a penny and demanded it be taken down.

A number of suitors—including Viacom, Yahoo, News Corp, and, furtively, Time Warner—sought to acquire YouTube, in an effort to bring the unruly site onto the show-business reservation. Time Warner had some of its executives pushing for a deal, but CEO Jeff Bewkes nixed the plan. No matter. All the hopefuls would end up vastly outbid by the deep-pocketed Silicon Valley company that Hollywood loves to hate, Google. The $1.65 billion acquisition in October 2006 was a wake-up call. Sales execs from Google would be able to call on the same advertisers buying spots on broadcast and cable networks. Even worse, the growing platform would encourage video consumption outside of the realm of pay TV, the dual-revenue domain of traditional media. The first marriage of tech and entertainment, AOL Time Warner, may have crashed and burned, but Google's YouTube play, despite its loss-making economics in the near term, was genuinely unnerving.

"Everyone was worried that we needed to control our own destiny," says Mike Hopkins, who at the time was president of distribution for Fox Networks Group, "and not just license all of our content to third parties and then let the market develop without any exposure to it."

Executives at NBC came to a similar, jarring realization: suddenly cofounders Chad Hurley and Steve Chen had the resources to develop the already fast-growing site, which had amassed some fifty million worldwide users in less than a year, into a significant new entertainment platform. "We were sitting there at NBC going, 'Holy shit, these guys that started this company two minutes ago just got sold for a billion six—on our content," recalls former NBCUniversal digital executive Jean-Briac Perrette. "What are we doing?"

Perrette and NBCUniversal's then–new media chief, David Zaslav, set out to erect a fortress against the digital insurgent and started looking for allies. At the top of the call sheet was Viacom, whose collection of young-skewing cable TV shows—such as Comedy Central's *The Daily Show with Jon Stewart* and *South Park* and Nickelodeon's *SpongeBob SquarePants*—was found in unauthorized abundance on YouTube. It quickly became clear that Viacom was engaged in conversations with another media company with similar ambitions, News Corp.

NBC and News Corp began formal talks. Executives at Rupert Murdoch's media company were negotiating from a position of strength. Its Fox broadcast network was at the top of the prime-time heap, thanks to the pop culture phenomenon *American Idol*, which helped bring audiences to its other shows, including the spy thriller *24* and the medical drama *House*. It had outmaneuvered rival Viacom to capture the world's largest social media network at the time, MySpace. If a new video platform to be built on Hollywood content was going to emerge online, News Corp wanted to own it.

Fox was emboldened and ready to go. But the media-rivals-turned-partners were unable to win over other digital converts. CBS's Les Moonves politely declined after in-house advisors persuaded him it would dilute the Tiffany Network's brand. Disney-owned ABC saw it as a threat to the network's own digital initiatives and demurred, saying joint ventures don't work. Viacom ultimately got cold feet, choosing instead to fight YouTube in court—a battle it ultimately lost. NBC struggled over its inability to recruit a third media partner to the venture, known internally as "ScrewTube," but decided to push forward anyway, with the support of NBCU's chief executive at the time, Jeff Zucker.

"We all sat there and said, 'Shoot, what's the alternative?'" recalls Perrette. "'Let's give it a go.'"

Like any corporate initiative that shakes up the status quo to position a company for the future, the first iteration of Hulu faced massive internal opposition.

"What was interesting is that almost everybody in the company hated it," said one former News Corp executive. "The broadcast people, the cable people, the ad-sales people, the syndication people, the home video people, would all come into my office and say, 'You're going to destroy my business.'"

Broadcast executives at News Corp's Fox unit and at NBC worried about kicking the moorings out from under the $68.6 billion pay-TV ecosystem that subsidized the cost of programming (and network profits). Why would viewers pay for a monthly cable or satellite television subscription when they could stream popular prime-time shows like *House*; *Law & Order: Special Victims Unit*; and *24* for free? The syndication team worried, presciently, about their ability to license reruns to secondary cable networks in the U.S. or for international distribution, given their broad online availability.

Network advertising executives sweated meeting their sales targets as a separate digital sales team hawked ads for online distribution of the same shows. The home entertainment crew fretted about online availability gutting the lucrative market for digital downloads and DVD releases.

Then-president of News Corp Peter Chernin's "inspiration and strategy was, 'It's gonna happen anyway, right? We can't stop this train. We need to get it out there, we need to learn, we need to be where consumers are,'" recalls Hopkins, who later would be tapped to run Hulu and now leads Amazon's Prime Video and Amazon Studios. "He just really pushed it through the organization and just said, 'Okay. Everybody be quiet. We're gonna do this and get on board.'"

To lead this disruptive venture, News Corp and NBC recruited Jason Kilar, an Amazon executive who wrote the original business plan for the online retailer's entry into the video and DVD business. His name didn't appear on the initial list of candidates for the job, which consisted largely of media industry retreads. Chernin directed the recruiters to look beyond the usual suspects. Studio executives are wholesalers: they sell movies to theaters or, later, to cable networks, and hawk television shows to advertisers and pay-TV distributors. Hulu would need someone with an e-commerce background who would be thoughtful about the consumer experience.

Kilar came with the enthusiastic support of Amazon CEO Jeff Bezos, who'd met Kilar in a professor's office after a Harvard Business School class on "managing the marketplace" in which classmates predicted the online bookseller was destined for failure. Bezos acknowledged the prowess of Walmart and Barnes & Noble while gently asserting that e-commerce would require a different mindset. "At that point, it was very obvious to me that this was going to be one of the more important leaders of our time, because he was so focused and so thoughtful," said Kilar, who weeks later flew to Seattle for a formal interview with the two-year-old startup and accepted a job offer on the spot. He remained with Amazon for nine years, working alongside Bezos. It took plenty of cajoling to win over the Harvard MBA, who knew the disastrous history of joint ventures, a third of which fail within the first five years. Kilar, who as a child idolized Walt Disney and harbored ambitions to one day run a media company, agreed to take the job on one condition: that Chernin and Zucker would serve on the board of directors.

"He was smart. He knew he needed them directly involved to cut through the inevitable amount of bullshit and organ rejection that was bound to happen at each of the shareholder companies," says Perrette, who counts himself among Kilar's friends.

Kilar projects a Boy Scout persona. One *Fast Company* profile burnished the wholesome image of an executive who rouses at five A.M. to go running, returns home every night to tuck the four kids into bed, and eschews such mood-altering substances as coffee. He was born in Pittsburgh to an electrical engineer father who worked for Westinghouse and a journalist mother who wrote a humor column for the local paper, "Enough Is Too Much." Kilar remembered his mother "was trying to kill 'em in the aisles with jokes about our lives." One of her columns described school bus stops as "one of America's fastest-growing trauma centers," recounting the day when seven-year-old Jason missed the bus. "Seems like Jeff (an 11-year-old) devastated him at the bus stop by shouting the name of Jason's alleged girlfriend," Maureen Kilar wrote. "(Jason denies the existence of girls.) So, home he came . . . in tears." The bully, she revealed, was Jason's older brother.

Decades after those childhood brushes with unwanted media attention, the executive brought a singular vision to the Hulu venture, which had been derisively branded ClownCo by media and internet critics. Wary of having his futuristic vision squelched, Kilar's first act was to change the locks at the Santa Monica, California, offices. That barred entry to the one hundred traditional media types who'd been hastily assembled from NBC and News Corp to start work on the project.

He set out to build a team with a tech pedigree, starting with a friend and former Microsoft engineer, Eric Feng, who'd founded a video startup in Beijing, China. Together, they assembled two technical teams, one in California and the other in Beijing, to accelerate the development process. The U.S. team would send specs to China, which would turn around the code in time for the SoCal team the next morning. The trappings of startup culture were everywhere: foosball table, beer tap, an "Experience Team" that celebrated employees with cakes and Mylar balloons.

The site, dubbed Hulu (literally "gourd" in Mandarin, or, according to one Chinese proverb, the holder of precious things), launched in March 2008. Its swift success silenced skeptics.

Within two months, Hulu cracked Comscore's top ten sites for video streams, with eighty-eight million. Online viewers were attracted by an array of free content, from vintage NBC series like *McHale's Navy* to the latest episode of Fox's *The Simpsons*. Tina Fey's lacerating impersonation of Republican vice presidential candidate Sarah Palin during the 2008 presidential election campaign, in the former *Saturday Night Live* cast member's guest appearances on the show, served as a useful lure to attract viewers to the nascent service. As soon as the broadcast ended, Hulu encoded each *SNL* sketch for the web—beating pirate sites to the punch. Viewers came by the millions. By March 2009, Hulu pulled into the top three video streaming sites, and it enlisted another major network participant, the Walt Disney Company's ABC, which joined in April 2009.

A swaggeringly irreverent Super Bowl ad featuring *30 Rock* star Alec Baldwin sought to explain Hulu to the masses: watch TV "anywhere, anytime, for free." Directed by Peter Berg, the filmmaker behind hit films like *Friday Night Lights*, the special-effects-heavy spot was praised by numerous media outlets, but some viewers said they found the message confusing. And its tongue-in-cheek tagline, "Hulu: an evil plot to destroy the world," definitely hit too close to home for some TV executives. They saw Hulu's wildfire success as threatening to burn down the pay-TV ecosystem.

Hulu quickly became a victim of its own success.

Content began to disappear from the service. FX asked Hulu to pull all but the five most recent episodes of Danny DeVito's offbeat comedy *It's Always Sunny in Philadelphia*, a show that had languished on the network until Hulu's users discovered it and made it one of the site's most popular shows. That didn't sit especially well with cable TV providers, which balked at the notion of viewers' watching such shows free online.

Hulu's benefactor at News Corp, Peter Chernin, announced plans to leave the company after twenty years. His successor, News Corp's deputy chairman Chase Carey, began to pump the brakes, speaking publicly about the need to create a paid version of Hulu. "A free model is a very difficult way to capture the value of our content," he said at one industry summit in 2009, in comments that presaged the 2010 launch of a "premium"—that is, paid—version of the service. Other joint venture partners began pressing for an increased ad load—traditional broadcast and cable networks accompany their programming with sixteen to eighteen minutes an hour of ads. But would digital audiences sit still for that kind of experience, especially if they were watching on their laptops?

One board member hit on a potential solution: merging Hulu with Netflix. The combination would create a "freemium" model in which Hulu's ad-supported service would present opportunities to sell viewers a premium experience on Netflix. Early, exploratory talks with Netflix CEO Reed Hastings stalled because the idea never gained traction with the full board.

Tensions mounted at Hulu, which hardly comes as a surprise for a consortium of companies that compete with each other at the movie box office and in the Nielsen ratings. Studio executives grumbled about being forced to surrender their prime-time shows to Hulu while carrying losses that affected year-end bonuses. "As one studio executive said to me, 'I'm the dumbest fucker in town, because I'm losing money on my books plus I'm paying my competitors,'" recalled the former Hulu board member.

Ad-sales executives complained that marketers were bypassing them and approaching Hulu directly to buy time on the same popular prime-time shows. The executives operating network-run websites clamored for access to Hulu's sophisticated consumer data ("we were still horse-and-buggying it"). Network talent, including *SNL* creator Lorne Michaels and *Tonight Show* host Conan O'Brien, took meetings to explore how they could work directly with the hot new entertainment brand, prompting NBCU digital entertainment president Vivi Zigler to prohibit such talks.

Disagreements over Hulu's future spilled out into the open when Kilar published an essay called "The Future of TV," which wags dubbed his "*Jerry Maguire* manifesto," a reference to the 1996 film about a sports agent who pens a heartfelt memo that gets him fired. Kilar, indulging in some classic tech-exec sloganeering, alluded to "thoughtful stubbornness" and the "relentless pursuit of better ways." Without quite naming names, he effectively called out the joint venture owners for their short-sightedness, declaring that consumers had demonstrated they wanted fewer ads and greater control over their viewing experience.

"History has shown that incumbents tend to fight trends that challenge established ways and, in the process, lose focus on what matters most: customers," Kilar wrote at the time in a blog post that has since disappeared from the Hulu site. "Hulu is not burdened by that legacy." His team, he vowed, would continue its against-the-odds quest to "reinvent television."

The memo did not go over well. Fox's Carey was none too pleased. Disney CEO Bob Iger, who considered himself to be digitally savvy, felt personally impugned, and Hulu board members discussed firing Kilar. The provocative change agent, once proclaimed by *Fast Company* as a putative "savior" of TV, left of his own accord in 2013, pocketing a reported $40 million when one of Hulu's owners, Providence Equity Partners, sold its 10 percent stake in the joint venture.

Other executives would follow the charismatic leader out the door, leaving its fate up in the air. Disney and News Corp considered selling its migraine-inducing streaming service and received offers approaching $1 billion. But as prospective buyers, including Chernin, laid out plans for revitalizing Hulu, the owners began to reconsider.

"Internally at Fox and at Disney, everybody was starting to go, 'Hmm. Maybe instead, we should just really go for it,'" recalls Hopkins, who spoke with his Disney counterpart, chief strategist Kevin Mayer, about more seriously competing with Netflix.

News Corp's Carey and Disney's Iger agreed with the strategy and consulted with Comcast CEO Brian Roberts, who had relinquished management rights to its minority stake in Hulu to win regulatory approval of its takeover of NBCUniversal in 2011. "Ultimately, I think everybody kind of got in the same place with a lot of different things happening. Chase and Bob went to Brian and said, 'We're gonna keep it. We think we should all throw in a bunch of money, are you in?' And he said, 'Absolutely.'"

The owners announced in July 2013 that they would not only retain ownership in Hulu but recapitalize it with a $750 million investment. The message from the board was clear: "You're not going to be a hedge anymore, go out and do things," said one former insider. The pivotal decision would return Hulu to a growth trajectory, after years of virtual suspended animation.

Subscriptions rose to thirty million by January 2020, up 20 percent from the previous January, thanks to the lure of original programs like the Emmy Award–winning dystopian series *The Handmaid's Tale*, which Hopkins acquired from MGM Television. Blame lingering resentment or simple aversion: the parent companies' studios resisted selling shows to Hulu, says former CEO Randy Freer, forcing it to look elsewhere to buy content.

Hulu eventually found itself bidding against deep-pocketed rivals like Netflix and Amazon to win rights to distribute original series like the acclaimed historical drama *The Great*, starring Elle Fanning as the Russian empress Catherine II, from Thruline Entertainment. It successfully snagged another high-profile project, a limited-series adaptation of Celeste Ng's bestselling novel *Little Fires Everywhere*, starring Reese Witherspoon and Kerry Washington. But the competition among streaming services was driving up the price for coveted shows, a pace of check-writing that Hulu would not be able to maintain.

"In the world we live in today, you can't exist that way, because if you're at Hulu, at least, you're not going to win every auction," said Freer in a 2019 interview. He was speaking shortly after losing out to Netflix in a bidding war for a screen adaptation of Neil Gaiman's *The Sandman* comic book series in a pricey deal with Warner Bros., with a budget of as much as $15 million per episode.

Disney's $71.3 billion acquisition of 20th Century Fox's entertainment assets in March 2019 gave the Burbank entertainment conglomerate a controlling interest in Hulu. Disney quickly consolidated its control, striking deals to buy out the other equity partners, Comcast and AT&T's WarnerMedia.

Hulu has emerged as the critical component of Disney's launch strategy, with its sizable installed base providing a springboard from which to launch the newer streaming services, Disney+ and ESPN+. Hulu also gained access to in-house development, with ABC Signature developing an adaptation of the sci-fi classic *The Hitchhiker's Guide to the Galaxy* with showrunner Carlton Cuse (*Lost, Tom Clancy's Jack Ryan*). In March 2020, it became the official home of FX's prestigious titles, like *American Crime Story*, *Pose*, *Fargo*, and *The Americans*.

But after the successful launch of Disney+, and its galloping global popularity, industry observers wondered how long Hulu would remain a stand-alone service. Just as many of Hulu's business operations have been absorbed by its Burbank parent, Hulu seems destined to become a programming tile on Disney+.

CHAPTER 11

▶ The Flywheel

A phalanx of top executives at AT&T took their seats in front of an audience of Wall Street analysts. It was the week after Thanksgiving 2018 in Time Warner Center, the twenty-four-year-old skyscraper erected on the site of the old New York Coliseum on Columbus Circle. The gold-and-tawny treetops of late-autumn Central Park unfolded like a welcome mat outside the floor-to-ceiling windows. Just days earlier, the floats and giant balloons in the Macy's Thanksgiving Day Parade had passed by those same windows. The mood in this corporate presentation wasn't quite as festive as a parade, but it qualified as upbeat.

AT&T had prevailed a few months earlier in a nearly two-year battle with antitrust regulators at the U.S. Department of Justice, closing its $85 billion acquisition of Time Warner. The government had ignored the explicit advice from the judge who ruled against its lawsuit and decided to appeal the verdict in a federal appeals court. The appeal cast a shadow over the company's operations and held investors' enthusiasm in check, but the analyst day was intended to put a spotlight on the vision for the merger. The elevator pitch: It married top-shelf entertainment content from Time Warner's HBO, Warner Bros., and Turner Broadcasting with the distribution might of AT&T. The telecom giant's 170 million customer relationships spanned cable and satellite TV, wireless and broadband, around the world. AT&T CEO Randall Stephenson and Time Warner CEO Jeff Bewkes had first revealed the merger plan in October 2016. The government's lawsuit, Stephenson explained to analysts, "caused [them] to put on hold a number of plans." After moving sideways for nearly two years, he said, the company looked forward to the chance to "talk a little bit about AT&T and where we stand and what our plans are."

Stephenson sometimes referred to his senior management team as "the Johns." In his Great Plains twang, the moniker shed any family-unfriendly overtones. It was a straight-ahead shorthand for Warner-Media chief John Stankey, chief financial officer John Stephens, and wireless and pay-TV head John Donovan. These middle-aged white men leading the newly enlarged company were united by more than their given name. They shared a workmanlike ethos, a predilection for blue dress shirts, and a relentless drive to achieve higher profits quarter after quarter.

The tableau differed substantially from a legendary AT&T gathering held about a century earlier at the New Willard Hotel in Washington, D.C. As Tim Wu details in his indispensable book, *The Master Switch*, about eight hundred executives and politicians attended the celebration of the Bell telephone system, an innovation that had changed the world. AT&T president Theodore Vail, a bravura, Teddy Roosevelt–like figure who personified telecommunications might, presided over the first public demonstration of long-distance calling. While that alone drew gasps, the night's grand finale brought the house down. In order to show off a device that was essentially the forerunner of today's mobile phones, Vail combined radio, phonograph, and telephone technology with an even newer invention: a motion-picture projector. As a radio station miles away in Arlington, Virginia, played "The Star-Spangled Banner," hundreds of wireless receivers relayed the sound into the banquet hall as the projector beamed a waving-flag image onto a large screen. *National Geographic* later wrote that the spectacle "brought the guests to their feet with hearts beating fast, souls aflame with patriotism, and minds staggered."

The AT&T of 2018 wasn't aiming to stagger minds or set souls on fire. Instead, it ruthlessly zeroed in on concepts with enduring appeal to Wall Street: efficiency, synergy, and long-term growth. Unlike wildly fluctuating technology stocks, AT&T's had been a quintessential defensive play for decades. Its dividend payments were as predictable as the sun's rise and set. While institutions controlled most large public corporations, AT&T still had about 48 percent of its shares in the hands of individual investors. That dynamic made consistency in the form of regular dividends yielding a healthy 7 percent a necessity given how many people depended on their shares as a source of income. Streaming was, of course, the major new element in the overall narrative, but Dallas-based AT&T didn't go in for the razzle-dazzle favored by Netflix and other digital aspirants. Saddled with $181 billion in debt after the Time Warner deal, it wasn't going to throw money around indiscriminately. Its entry would be as precisely engineered as the cell towers that power its wireless networks, leveraging the company's hundred-year history of entertaining the world.

Stankey summed up his plan to make streaming the hub of a virtuous financial circle he called a flywheel, in which content supplies networks, which in turn drive more people to content. In mechanical engineering, a flywheel is a heavy, revolving wheel in a machine that increases its momentum. With more momentum comes more power and stability. While some management consultants and MBAs favored the term to describe business dynamics, it's hard to imagine its ever passing the lips of Time Warner founding fathers like Jack Warner, Ted Turner, and Henry Luce. Three times during Stankey's fifteen-minute remarks, he circled back to the concept, driving it home in an insistent style redolent of PowerPoint. "What do we need to do? We need to build a better product, a better experience," he said. "A better product through experience ultimately drives more engagement. More engagement drives more data. And then, ultimately, when you get that kind of a flywheel going, you have an opportunity for better and more monetization."

AT&T executives had largely talked in generalities about their streaming plans to this point, saying only that their timeline for launching their new service was the fourth quarter of 2019. Stankey was finally ready to get more specific and investors leaned forward in their seats. The offering, he said, would feature a "three-tier structure," with distinct price points and levels of programming. The cheapest tier would focus on movies, with the middle offering original programming and more film titles, while the highest end would add library selections including classic films, comedy, and children's programming. News and sports were not mentioned, despite the company's decades of experience in those arenas. With no pricing information and no name for the service, it still felt a bit vague.

In Time Warner, AT&T had taken over a company with other irons in the streaming fire. Since 2015, Time Warner had a stand-alone streaming service called HBO Now in the market, plus various other targeted services, like FilmStruck for cinephiles and Crunchyroll for anime fans. Just two months before the analyst gathering, the company had launched DC Universe, an $8-a-month home for superhero content featuring Batman, Superman, and other characters.

In the same week as the analyst meeting at Time Warner Center, FilmStruck had been shuttered, eliciting howls from classic film lovers. The service, which drew from the Turner Classic Movies library and also had rights to hundreds of art house films from the Criterion Collection, left a notable void. Worse, according to multiple WarnerMedia executives familiar with the financials of FilmStruck, it wasn't shut down because it had missed subscriber targets or because of a corporate rethink of how to leverage the film library. It was because unplugging it would generate a $30 million write-off, which would help the company's balance sheet. "You're going to make enemies of the most powerful creative people in the business and you're going to need them to make content for you," one former executive said he warned Stankey. Sure enough, a group of notables, among them Steven Spielberg, Martin Scorsese, Francis Ford Coppola, and Wes Anderson, wrote letters directly to Stankey. Another group, including Christopher Nolan, Paul Thomas Anderson, Guillermo del Toro, Alfonso Cuarón, and Leonardo DiCaprio, signed a letter to Warner Bros. seeking a reprieve. Twitter was ablaze with anger, including from a wide range of filmmakers and Hollywood figures. When Stankey asked one of the leaders of FilmStruck why the blowback was so intense, the executive told him, "'This is about the curation of film. It's not just the Criterion Collection—that's one-third of the viewing. The rest of it are classic movies from twenty-three studios. People are lamenting the curation of the service and what the service means to them. It's a time machine—movies are time machines. It's different than a hot show. You have to think of content differently.' And I'm like, 'Stankey's not getting any of this.'"

By his own admission, Stankey is no student of the popular arts. He told *New York Times* columnist Andrew Ross Sorkin that he suffers from "Catholic guilt" when it comes to watching television. His parents forbade it when he was growing up, so he would sneak downstairs on Saturday mornings to watch cartoons with the volume barely audible and anxiously snap off the TV set as soon as he heard his parents' bedroom door crack open. "Getting over the hump on this has been a little bit of a challenge," Stankey conceded to Sorkin in a 2018 interview at the *Vanity Fair* New Establishment Summit in Los Angeles. As head of WarnerMedia, he described a new nightly cramming ritual: "I'll find something to eat on the way back from the office walking home, and I'll go to the stack [of discs in his apartment] and I'll invest an hour right when I get home eating and going through some of this." Stankey's tone was so devoid of enthusiasm, Sorkin asked, "Are you enjoying this?" His professions of delight rang hollow.

"Not only is [he] not a fan, he really was actively uninterested in content," said one former WarnerMedia executive. "If content is king, that's got to be your number one ethos. And for John, it's all about the platform and the paradigm and the balance sheet."

Casablanca, *Brief Encounter*, and other classics would prosper in the flywheel of WarnerMedia's broader service, Stankey assured analysts, without invoking FilmStruck. "It's a software experience wrapping creative excellence that we're going to [use to] showcase specific brands to help the customer navigate and find the right curated content that they

want," he said. Historically, gaining access to Time Warner content required signing up for a cable TV subscription or buying a movie ticket.
Stankey may have had a tin ear for the urges of film and TV enthusi-
asts and creators, but he recognized that erecting barriers for customers
wasn't as viable in a frictionless, online world. Since the internet and
then streaming had let that genie out of the bottle, traditional entertainment companies had spent years expecting they could coax it back
in. They were starting to pay the price for that decision, as millions
of pay-TV customers began canceling their subscriptions each year, a
trend that ate away at the distribution fees companies had collected for
decades. Movie ticket sales, too, had started to drift down. "When you
have disenfranchised consumers empowered by new technology and
a new generation of creators and companies embrace it," one senior
WarnerMedia executive said, "you're going to lose."

Stankey wasn't about to concede defeat. "It's got to be easily acces-
sible," he said of WarnerMedia's streaming entry. "It's got to be ubiquitous. Over all devices, anywhere that customer wants to go, it's got
to have a great value proposition. It will be a combination of original
content that's unique and special that gives it character, it'll have library
content and, over time, growing third-party partnerships that bring additional content in that help augment those brands."

During the question-and-answer session, UBS analyst John Hodu-
lik asked Stankey if WarnerMedia had the scale to pull off its planned
shift into streaming. He then added a string of follow-up questions,
trying to pack as much as possible into his limited time allotment.
"We've adopted the White House question standards here, so there's
no follow-up questions," Stankey intoned in that way of his that left a
question about whether he was kidding. The line was a nod at Donald
Trump's press-conference squelching of CNN reporter Jim Acosta in
the East Room of the White House a few weeks before the analyst day.
"Hold that microphone away from him," Stephenson half-joked. "There
goes another lawsuit."

After his attempt to be lighthearted, Stankey grew serious, his sonorous baritone as deep as ever. "The short answer is, yes. I think we can play really well," he said. "Think about what's going to happen over the next eighteen to twenty-four months." He went on to outline his expectation for "a pretty substantial structural shift" in the media business. Entrenched companies were rethinking their strategies as streaming became the new priority. Instead of licensing their content to third parties, as they had done for years, reaping hundreds of millions of dollars through sales to Netflix, Amazon, and Hulu, Stankey said companies would start redirecting it to their own platforms. As the competition grew, he argued, WarnerMedia would be in a prime position because of its collection of well-known consumer brands, chief among them HBO.

"Ours isn't the warehouse strategy," he said. "It's going to be the strategy of great value, great depth, and great brands that people know how to navigate to the content they want to in those brands." With decades of customer relationships already in the bank, he went on, "they're going to require a lot less investment than a ground start."

Of the total viewing time on rival services, Stankey added, "seventy-five percent, eighty percent of their total view in tonnage is sitting on a lot of that licensed content. So their pressure is they've got to make this pivot to get people off of viewing content that sits in our library, or the Disney library, and get it onto their own."

In other words, Stankey was arguing, as had his traditional media peers, that content like the Warner Bros.–produced *Friends*, or Disney's Marvel and *Star Wars* movies, or NBCUniversal's *The Office*, were what defined Netflix. Reruns of decades-old syndicated shows topped the charts of the most popular titles. Pulling back those shows, therefore, would tilt the advantage back to traditional media companies. Of course, that view ignored the ten-year head start Netflix, Amazon, and Hulu had in building high-functioning streaming services, which had thrown off a massive quantity of data. Plus, their original programming had earned a place at the table. Shows like *Transparent* on Amazon Prime, *The Handmaid's Tale* on Hulu, and *The Crown* on Netflix had all topped critics' lists and won awards. Acquired shows were nice, but making original shows and movies was the mission.

Netflix had weathered previous instances of high-profile titles acquired from Disney, Fox, and other suppliers leaving, managing to keep growing and raising prices all the while. Co-CEO Sarandos simply shrugged off the idea of a threat, noting, "While many of these movies are popular, they are also widely available on cable and other subscription platforms at the same time as they are on Netflix." Netflix had anticipated years earlier that it would need to scale its original programming efforts after starting off as a home for other studios' shows. As Stankey and his colleagues were addressing Wall Street, Netflix had just reached a long-planned goal of having original titles account for the majority of its total viewing. Household-name sitcoms could come and go—as long as the company continued its strategy to spend upward of $15 billion a year making hundreds of original series and movies, subscribers would find something else to watch. The libraries of Netflix and its established peers were changing, yes, but hardly getting thinner.

On top of the technological and strategic challenges facing Warner-Media, there was also an organizational knot to untie. To drive toward a unified streaming goal, it would have to demolish its collection of silos and cliques that had been famously resistant to the kind of synergy that made many other media companies hum. The as-yet-unnamed streaming service would offer a chance to bring the divisions together. AT&T recognized the cultural currency of *Game of Thrones* and used the HBO show to solidify its message to investors. In a sizzle reel played at the analysts' meeting, a dragon was shown flying over a suburban neighborhood, where family members talked on AT&T mobile phones and returned home to watch TV via AT&T hookups. The dragon was a benign one and did not breathe fire or torch a row of three-bedroom colonials. But its shadow stretched for blocks, making it an ominous choice of corporate mascot.

AT&T's existing customer relationships gave the new streaming service an unusually solid foundation, Stankey and his colleagues insisted. Instead of starting from scratch, as even potent rivals like Apple and Disney would have to do, there were already ten million subscribers to HBO paying for the premium network through AT&T TV and broadband services.

Programming for the new service would need to be similarly broad in scope, transcending the long-honed, targeted approaches of individual networks, chief among them HBO. A strategic notion was emerging, and it was either tantalizing or sacrilegious, depending on where you stood. With the walls coming down between divisions of WarnerMedia, a streaming service with HBO at its center could also feature *Rick and Morty*, *Friends*, and *The Big Bang Theory*. Why keep HBO a network for sophisticates, who tended to be older and only in urban centers? Why not give WarnerMedia's streaming service the same kind of mass appeal as one of the company's comic book movies or an NCAA March Madness basketball telecast?

As Stankey and the other Johns were meeting with Wall Street, a team of marketers was working on a way to tout the mass-audience potency of a signature HBO offering on advertising's biggest stage: the Super Bowl. Ad agency Droga5 had long crafted marketing campaigns for *Game of Thrones*, the most successful original show ever aired on HBO. For the Super Bowl, where ads cost $5.3 million for thirty seconds, they came up with something every bit as jarring as the idea of mashing up *Scooby-Doo* cartoons and laugh-track sitcoms with the home of *The Sopranos*. They would join HBO's prestigious, Emmy-winning, mega-budget series with Bud Light, the beer brand known for bringing the world Spuds MacKenzie.

"What was special about that final season of *Game of Thrones* is that we were in the middle of television transforming into an on-demand binge model where streaming was starting to take over," former HBO marketing head Chris Spadaccini recalled. "We all felt it coming. This was like the end of a chapter of television. *Game of Thrones* was one of the last remaining monocultural events that we knew would be a shared viewing experience around the world, where people would tune in on Sunday night to watch together."

Well before the Super Bowl, in early November, the push to market the final season had begun when Spadaccini got a call from one of the social media specialists at HBO. "You're not going to believe this," the colleague told him, "but the president just posted a *Game of Thrones* meme to Twitter." Sure enough, Trump had issued a warning to Iran by posting a picture of himself looking tough. "Sanctions are coming," the obvious parody of the motto of House Stark, in a *Thrones*–rip-off font, declared. HBO execs knew if they were going to respond, it would need to be quickly. Spadaccini and his colleagues conferred with CEO Richard Plepler on the proper clap-back and decided on the subtweet, "How do you say trademark misuse in Dothraki?" The response got 126,000 likes and was one of the most retweeted ever on the show's official handle, giving the marketing blitz some earned media when the press covered the dueling tweets.

When it came to finalizing the Super Bowl spot that would run in February to tout the show's April premiere, the creative team focused on the show's own out-of-left-field plot twists. They also embraced the idea of *Thrones* being "culture-jacked" and memed on social media. What if the Super Bowl spot were to be an elaborately produced version of such a hijacking where *Thrones* finally got a measure of revenge on a consumer brand? After mulling various options (Coca-Cola's polar bears, for one), the group reached an agreement with Anheuser-Busch, a perennial presence on the Super Bowl broadcast since 1985. The company's successful "Dilly Dilly" run of medieval-themed spots was said to be inspired by the breakout success of *Thrones*, so the match was made. In the 2019 spot (sixty seconds on TV and ninety seconds on YouTube), familiar characters gather at a small outdoor arena for a jousting tournament featuring the blue-clad Bud Knight. The king, the queen, and their subjects are in high spirits, toasting each other with Bud Light bottles, their merriment cut short when the knight is abruptly jabbed off of his horse by his opponent. Only when his foe approaches the prone knight is his identity revealed: Gregor "the Mountain" Clegane, the nearly seven-foot-tall, heavily muscled figure infamous for his bloody exploits on the gory HBO series. In one motion, he reaches down and—just after the camera quickly cuts away—gouges out the knight's eyes and crushes his skull, killing him. (Fans of *Thrones* immediately picked up on the moment as a callback to a Mountain scene from Season 4.) As distraught members of the royal court process what they have seen, a dragon flies overhead and then vengefully breathes fire. The logos of HBO and the show appear in the lower right-hand corner of the screen.

Anheuser-Busch, already nervous about killing off a major spokesman, asked HBO to consider alternate endings to the spot that would allow the Bud Knight to survive. The network adamantly stuck to its guns, enlisting several of the directors and producers who had brought *Game of Thrones* to life in order to have them imbue the spot with authentic touches. The creative team also took pains to shoot down script ideas that might have given away plot points for the upcoming season. All the way through the months-long production and testing process, the beer contingent quailed at the level of violence, asking for it to be toned down. In the end, while the murder occurs offscreen, the sound of the Bud Knight's head crunching was at the pitch of a potato chip campaign. HBO even opted to shoulder more of the cost when the initial plan for forty-five seconds of airtime was expanded to sixty seconds. Because the ad was part of a $20 million marketing campaign for the show's final season, the incremental spending was considered well worth it.

The day after the game, a senior HBO executive in New York beamed when the subject of the ad came up. "Didn't you think that was amazing?!" he marveled. "It's incredible that the secret didn't get out. I thought it was just so clever." Audiences were a bit more divided. Some grumbled about the violent end of the Bud Knight, others sparked to the cheekiness of the spot and got pumped for the show's premiere, and a third group felt confused. The ad finished at number sixteen out of the fifty-eight Super Bowl commercials ranked by *USA Today*'s Ad Meter survey of viewer sentiment.

Brash and expensive-looking, the ad signaled to viewers that HBO was taking some of its boldest swings yet in selling the final season of its biggest commercial draw. To WarnerMedia and AT&T employees, it sent a different message with an ominous implication: HBO was just another product to sell, like the cars and gadgets and tortilla chips hawked during a football game. The network that had insisted for years that it was above the fray, custom-made for cocktail-party conversation, was now eager to elide the difference between itself and light beer. "The company now views content, once the lifeblood of the company, as a commodity," one former longtime staffer observed. "The distinction between an HBO show and a TNT show or something done by Warner Bros. Television for CBS, all those big, mass-market hits—what happened to that?"

Especially in a streaming environment designed to make WarnerMedia more competitive with Netflix, Stankey's flywheel didn't turn differently depending on what programming it was putting online. "If you're driving toward a single direct-to-consumer product," the former executive said, "it doesn't matter if you stay true to the brand promise of any other outlet. It's about the good of the whole. And that can be a tough directive for people to follow if they've committed their professional lives to bringing one particular brand to life."

PART III

Showtime

CHAPTER 12

▶ Touched by Tinker Bell's Wand

If there's one thing the marketing maestros at Disney know, it's how to build anticipation. The studio parked a giant replica of the *Millennium Falcon* spaceship in the middle of Hollywood Boulevard for the 2018 premiere of *Solo: A Star Wars Story*, and re-created Pride Rock to provide a red-carpet backdrop for the star-studded debut of 2019's live-action remake of *The Lion King*. Back in the days of even more lavish promotional budgets, Disney invited some thirty thousand people to the outdoor premiere of the Pixar animated film *Cars* at the Lowe's Motor Speedway in Charlotte, North Carolina, a spectacle that featured a twelve-lap race around the track (with actual NASCAR drivers, like Darrell Waltrip, behind the wheels) and live performances by country artist Brad Paisley and rock-and-roll legend Chuck Berry.

The April 11, 2019, investor day on which Disney was expected to detail plans for its forthcoming streaming service would be no less of an eye-catching affair. Disney chief Iger had maintained a steady drumbeat of promotional plugs for more than a year, using the traditionally staid affairs of quarterly corporate earnings calls to drop news, as he had in November 2018, when he announced the name of the service, Disney+, and talked up new, exclusive content, including a new *Star Wars* series starring Diego Luna as the Rebel spy Cassian Andor, and a Marvel Studios production in which actor Tom Hiddleston would reprise his role as Loki, the god of mischief. Throughout the year, Disney had parceled out details designed to stoke a fan frenzy for the new service, including the buzzy news that *Iron Man* and *Lion King* director Jon Favreau would helm a *Star Wars* series that would become Disney+'s first breakout hit, *The Mandalorian*.

Disney's investor day had a different audience in mind—Wall Street. Iger and the lantern-jawed executive leading the company's direct-to-consumer initiative, Kevin Mayer, needed to convince the investment community that their ambitious, bet–the–Mouse House strategy would position the company for success in the digital future, even if it cost billions of dollars in the short term.

The analyst community had no dearth of questions. Would Disney offer estimates of how many subscribers it hoped to attract or provide financial guidance? How willing would it be to sacrifice near-term earnings in pursuit of future opportunity? After all, the media giant reaped $5 billion to $8 billion a year in fees from licensing its movies and television shows to third parties, according to some estimates.

Some sought clarity about Disney's plans for Hulu, the shining gem at the heart of its $71.3 billion deal for 21st Century Fox's entertainment assets. How would the streaming service, which had gained momentum with the success of *The Handmaid's Tale*, an adaptation of Margaret Atwood's dystopian novel set in a totalitarian future state, fit in within the Happiest Place on Earth?

Mayer described the preparations as akin to mounting a major motion picture—with the stakes arguably even higher. He and his team spent hours in conference rooms, working with the former research director of an investment bank who served as Disney's head of investor relations, Lowell Singer, developing the story line. They crafted a message and Mayer prepared financial forecasts. Scripts would be written and revised, honed to underscore the point that the Disney+ service represented the full manifestation of all the acquisitions it had made over the past dozen years, culminating with the giant Fox deal, the ultimate expression of its strategic thinking about the power of entertainment brands. A walled garden (the tech industry's term for a closed ecosystem) with the most fragrant of flowers.

"We could have a full, robust direct-to-consumer business in our own ecosystem and never have to license a piece of content from anyone else if we didn't want to. We had critical mass at that point with Fox," said Mayer, noting that as other media companies launched streaming services, tending to their own gardens, it would "be harder and harder to license content . . . If everyone's a vertical walled garden, you better have the best walled garden or you're going to be in trouble."

Disney selected Soundstage 2 on its Burbank studio lot as the setting for the investor presentation—a choice rich in history, as it was the place where Jack Webb filmed television's breakthrough police procedural, *Dragnet*. The giant soundstage occasionally was given over to theme park construction projects, including much of the work on the double-decker Mark Twain riverboat that still churns the Rivers of America at Disneyland in Anaheim. It also doubled as the Edwardian London setting of *Mary Poppins*, where Julie Andrews sang her way into the hearts of the Banks family.

Rehearsals began as soon as the stage was constructed. In the last three days before the event, the run-throughs were virtually nonstop, from eight or nine in the morning until ten o'clock at night, with a final dress rehearsal on the morning of the event. The presentation had been polished to a glossy sheen before media analysts and journalists arrived on the Burbank studio lot, to be greeted outside the soundstage by stormtroopers.

"The amount of focus that Disney put on this was incredible," said former Hulu CEO Randy Freer, recalling multiple revisions to his own presentation. "The reality was Bob [Iger] was leading that charge, with Kevin [Mayer] and others. It was very, very curated, very managed, and they did a tremendous job telling the story they wanted to tell."

As this was the first meeting with analysts since it completed its acquisition of Fox's film and television business, Disney sought to emphasize how the breadth of the studios' combined entertainment portfolio would propel it into entertainment's next act, streaming. Actors Anthony Hopkins and Ian McKellen narrated a promotional video that wove footage of Walt himself into a kaleidoscope of movies and TV shows, including clips from *Star Wars*, the Marvel Cinematic Universe, *Toy Story*, and *The Lion King*, as well as Fox blockbusters such as *Titanic*.

"These companies have been entertaining the world at the highest levels, creating an indelible connection with billions of people and a treasure trove of long-lasting valuable content," said Iger, in a dark suit and crisp white dress shirt, as he took the stage. "The Disney+ platform is being built on that foundation, one that no other content or technology company can rival."

Mayer made the business case for embracing streaming—the explosive growth in the number of homes with broadband connectivity, the promise of high-speed 5G wireless access, and the seemingly endless thirst for on-demand content, with the world's viewers watching an improbable 1.2 billion hours of video a day.

"Our aggressive move into this space reflects a fundamental shift in the marketplace and growing consumer demand for streaming services, which is a tremendous opportunity for us given the unparalleled strength of our brands and the quality of our intellectual property," Mayer told investors. "And we're confident in our unique ability to leverage all of our assets to drive long-term growth."

Disney+ was a career-defining moment for Mayer, representing the culmination of the hard-charging executive's tenure at the company. A native of Bethesda, Maryland, he broke into the entertainment business at its bottommost rung: as a movie theater usher. At fifty-eight, he still maintains the powerful physique of his earlier days playing club football for the Massachusetts Institute of Technology, where he earned a degree in mechanical engineering and spent summers in L.A. as an intern for Hughes Aircraft Company. He moved to San Diego and joined a startup specializing in high-frequency microelectronics, along the way earning a master's degree in night courses in electrical engineering at

San Diego State University. While he considered himself in his twenties a "hard-core mechanical engineer," he also had a lot of curiosity about the financial side of things, and he soon wound up at Harvard Business School. He joined Disney's sharp-elbowed strategic planning division in 1993, working alongside other Harvard and Stanford MBAs.

"I have often described [the Disney culture] as a nonstop rugby match," another strat-planning veteran, Meg Whitman, wrote in *The Power of Many*. "I don't think the most obstreperous guest at a Disney park has ever been treated as roughly as executives at Disney treated one another. When I worked there it often seemed like pure testosterone flowed in the drinking fountains."

Mayer rose quickly through the ranks and was promoted to senior vice president of strategic planning in 1998. He left the company in 2000 for an opportunity to become CEO of a media company with a less wholesome image: Playboy Enterprises. That lasted seven months. Mayer did stints at Clear Channel Communications and at LEK Consulting before his friend, Disney chief financial officer Tom Staggs, convinced him to return to Disney in 2005, as Bob Iger assumed the role of chief executive.

As head of Disney's strategic planning group, Mayer earned a reputation for his intelligence and his ability to intuit, in a qualitative and strategic sense, what would be happening five years down the road. He also was known for pushing his staff to work long hours—the *Wall Street Journal* reported that employees in the strategic planning unit would tell new hires which convenience stores nearby sold Red Bull.

"He's extremely demanding. I don't think he would shy away from that description," said former Activision president Nick van Dyk, who worked alongside Mayer for a decade in strategic planning. "He has a really high bar. He demands excellence. You have to look at who he's been managing . . . In corporate strategy, this is made up of former investment bankers. They're used to long hours and high levels of performance. Kevin is no different than any managing director of Goldman Sachs. It's the same demand for professional excellence."

As an engineer by training who'd spent time leading Clear Channel and Playboy's interactive businesses, Mayer could clearly see disruption on the media giant's horizon and began warning about the threat of cord-cutting even before Disney acknowledged it had become a reality. "I was the canary in the coal mine on that for years," he said. "People used to make fun of me, call me 'Dr. Doom,' 'Debbie Downer,' or whatever it was, but I was sure that it was coming and it was just a matter of time."

Recognition of pay TV's tenuous hold on American living rooms dawned as Disney's biggest profit center, ESPN, began losing millions of television subscribers, and with it viewership and ad revenue. The dominant sports network shed an unprecedented twelve million subscribers from its peak of nearly one hundred million in 2011 to eighty-eight million a short seven years later, according to Nielsen data. The losses only confirmed investor fears about changing viewing habits and shrinking demand for traditional pay-TV packages, causing Disney's stock to drop.

Disney began to respond to the rise of direct-to-consumer streaming with its investment in BAMTech and a directive from Iger to have Mayer examine Disney's licensing strategy. Rather than license content to others, why not retain the rights and launch a streaming service? Disney should transition from being a wholesaler of content to a retailer, forging the kind of direct relationships with consumers that it enjoyed in its parks.

Mayer and other division heads formed a working group to explore the ramifications of disrupting old business models while building toward the future. Iger described how Disney devoted its entire annual board retreat at Walt Disney World in Orlando in June 2017 to the matter of disruption—and the company's proposed solution, launching a Netflix competitor.

"We took it to the board and they said not only yes, they said, 'Go faster,'" recalls Mayer.

Iger went public in August 2017 with the company's plan to create an entertainment-based service and another built around ESPN, firing the starting gun for a grueling race to launch. In announcing the decision to investors, he essentially burned the bridges so Disney's army couldn't retreat.

Mayer and his team had spent months painstakingly thinking through the minutest details of the offering, starting with the name. "The first thing we had to decide—were we going to call it Disney or not?" he said. "That became pretty clear, pretty fast, of course we're going to call it Disney." It's one of the world's most recognizable brands. Why squander that advantage?

The team considered and rejected more than a dozen variants of the company moniker before settling on a name that nearly every other media company would emulate: Disney+. More time was invested weighing whether to spell out "plus" or use a symbol. After arriving at a consensus about using a plus sign, there was the question of how to render it.

"The first plus signs all looked like they were the Red Cross, like a medical alert," Mayer recalls. "So, that wasn't good."

The resulting name and logo, with the rounded horizontal arm of the plus symbol curving ever so subtly to touch the arc of a star sweeping above the Disney name, was something Bob Iger personally vetted, choosing from among three options. The mnemonic—a tone that plays anywhere video of the logo appears—was inspired by the snapping sound that an Apple plug makes when it plugs into a wall outlet. Disney+ marketing chief Ricky Strauss said Iger recalled Apple founder Steve Jobs's demonstrating the sound during one of their visits. Iger felt the snap would give the right punctuation to the star's sweep.

The New York–based BAMTech team developed the interface, opting to embrace a format that subscribers would find familiar and easy to navigate, one dominated by a rotating carousel of "hero" images of featured films and series, stacked atop a second row of five tiles, labeled by entertainment brand: Disney, Pixar, Marvel, Star Wars, and National Geographic. Subsequent rows of clickable images offered recommendations, highlighted new offerings, and promoted viewing trends.

"We thought long and hard about whether to do something brand-new and different, and we decided there's enough risk in not getting any licensing revenue, making this huge investment, launching the thing. Do you want to also take a risk in trying a brand-new form of interface that's never been done before?" Mayer said. "And we decided, we didn't want to take that risk, explicitly. We said, 'You know what? There's a state of the art, there's an expectation that people have when they look at things . . . We're not going to change the paradigm.'"

The nearly three-hour-long presentation set the template that other media companies would imitate. One by one, Disney executives appeared onstage to describe the company's distinct online offerings.

The existing ESPN+ service would continue to focus on live events, including popular global sports like soccer, cricket, and rugby; pay-per-view UFC matches; and college sports with passionate fan communities that don't attract a national television audience, such as lacrosse and volleyball. Hulu would serve as the home of edgier adult fare, including FX's hit series *American Horror Story*, *Sons of Anarchy*, and *Justified*. India's Hotstar, which Disney acquired as part of the Fox deal, would give Disney a significant presence in the world's second-largest market, with more than three hundred million monthly users, thanks, in part, to its exclusive online rights to stream Premier League cricket matches.

Streaming services president Michael Paull touted the prowess of BAMTech, the battle-hardened underlying technology that would power Disney+. He said it had been built to handle millions of simultaneous viewers drawn to live sporting events like the *UFC Fight Night: Cejudo vs. Dillashaw*, a mixed martial arts matchup on ESPN+, giving it the capability to ably handle the crush of fantasy fans who flocked to the seventh-season finale of *Game of Thrones* on HBO Now.

The overview of the other streaming services was a warm-up to the main attraction. Mayer, in a tailored suit, returned to the stage to demonstrate the app, which organized content around the company's major entertainment brands. The top of the page would feature new and noteworthy content—be it an animated hit like Pixar's *Coco*, a theatrical film like *Captain Marvel*, or a Disney+ original like *The Mandalorian*. As with other streaming services, it would offer recommendations based on past viewing.

Few in the room needed a refresher course in Disney's entertainment offerings. Still, each of the studio heads spent long minutes describing the original movies and series coming to the service, to augment the massive film library that dates from the first animated feature film, *Snow White and the Seven Dwarfs*, which debuted on December 21, 1937. In the first year, Disney+ would feature more than 7,500 episodes of television, 400 library titles, and 100 recent theatrical film releases, such as *Captain Marvel* and *The Lion King*. Within five years, Disney expected to produce more than 50 original series a year—along with 10 original movies, documentaries, and specials.

The entertainment offerings' quality, at least as much as their quantity, left analysts impressed. The showstopper, though, was the price. Disney announced it would undercut market leader Netflix by offering the subscription service for $6.99 a month. Analysts in the room audibly gasped. It was almost half the price of Netflix's most popular subscription plan.

"So let's add it all up. We have the brands that matter. We have the library content that has been loved for generations, as well as new original content made by many of the same creators, all wrapped in a beautiful package and delivered to consumers at a very reasonable price," said Mayer, like an assured litigator making closing arguments before the jury. "For these reasons, we feel very confident in the success of Disney+."

Disney was so convinced of Disney+'s prospects, it was willing to operate it at a loss for the first few years, forecasting profitability by fiscal 2024.

Chief Financial Officer Christine McCarthy laid out the numbers. She predicted Disney would gain sixty to ninety million subscribers by the end of fiscal 2024, with about one-third of those in the United States. If the forecasts were accurate, Disney would boast more subscribers than the nation's largest cable TV provider, Comcast, though not as many as the dominant Netflix. As it turns out, Disney wildly underestimated the service's appeal.

Disney planned to spend $1 billion in cash on original content in fiscal 2020, with investment doubling by 2024. That figure didn't include the $1.5 billion the streaming service would pay other divisions in 2020 to license movies and series. In addition to the steep costs, Disney would forgo hundreds of millions in revenue it would otherwise receive from third parties like Netflix for licensing its movies and television shows.

"What we're putting forward is an aggressive strategy that's very purposeful because we feel, obviously, the strategy is extremely important to us," Iger said. "And we feel that if we're going to implement it, we've got to be very, very serious and be all-in on it. And that's because we believe that that is the best way for this to succeed."

When asked by one analyst, Iger declined to say whether he believed Disney+ would accelerate the decline of the traditional pay-TV bundle—"We're not going to talk about what we believe the impact of this would have . . . it's not something we'd care to share."

While many aspects of Disney+ were still being worked out, one thing was certain: its rollout would be no stealth event.

Strauss, the stylish studio executive whose interior design of his Sunset Strip home had been featured in *House Beautiful*—and who oversaw the marketing of such blockbuster films as *Black Panther*; *Star Wars: The Force Awakens*; and *Beauty and the Beast*—laid out a sweeping awareness campaign. Disney would tout the service at fan events like the *Star Wars* celebration in Chicago, San Diego Comic-Con, and Disney's own D23 Expo in Anaheim. It would get the word out to its most ardent devotees through its Disneyland and Walt Disney World theme parks, its Disney Cruise Line and Disney retail stores. And it would use the megaphone of its television outlets, like ABC's *Good Morning America*, to broadcast details to some one hundred million U.S. households.

"One of the clear advantages we have in marketing Disney+ is our access to an incredible number of touch points across the Walt Disney Company," said Strauss. "And as you would expect, we plan to leverage this unparalleled reach, engaging our millions of fans and influencers across our brands and around the world."

The investment community got the message, loud and clear. Disney's stock hit a record high, adding as much as $25 billion in market value, for a total of about $235 billion. Netflix, meanwhile, lost as much as $8 billion in market capitalization on news of Disney's cheaper service.

"That was unexpected! Going into the investor day, most investors (us included) were hoping for, at best, some way to help us think about the potential losses of the company's DTC & International segment. Truth be told, most investor days don't live up to the hype and this one had the potential to be disappointing," wrote Michael Nathanson, one of the preeminent media analysts. "Disney had set a high bar of expectations and rose to the challenge."

CHAPTER 13

▶ "I Love That Show and I Think You Will Too"

Apple's product presentations have a familiar, predictable rhythm, not unlike the structure of a Broadway play. The opening act invariably features a short video designed to evoke a warm sentimentality about Apple's products and their place in our lives. The CEO steps onto an empty stage to rousing applause. Then, products are unveiled in ascending order of importance, building toward the finale, the "one last thing" that the late cofounder Steve Jobs made famous. This event, on September 10, 2019, would be no different.

Details of the Apple TV+ streaming service came within the first fifteen minutes of the nearly two-hour-long presentation at the Steve Jobs Theater in Cupertino, wedged between the introduction of a new subscription gaming service, Apple Arcade, and an update of the venerable iPad tablet. The consequential news—namely, the latest iteration of its cash cow the iPhone, the single product that accounts for more than half of the company's revenues—fell at the end of the event.

Clad simply in a black cardigan and black jeans, Cook took the stage to recap Apple's grand ambition for its streaming service: to deliver "stories that help you find inspiration, that are grounded in emotion," he said, hands clasped, preacherlike. "Truly, stories to believe in. Stories with purpose."

Unlike at the star-studded event six months earlier, Cook served as

Apple TV+'s lone pitchman. He touted such premier originals as *For All Mankind*, an alternate telling of the 1960s space race from *Battlestar Galactica*'s Ron Moore; *Dickinson*, an anachronistic period drama in which a teenage Emily Dickinson, played by Hailee Steinfeld, rebels against her father's refusal to let her publish her poetry; and *The Morning Show*, a star-studded drama that, he crowed, *Entertainment Weekly* had declared "fall's most anticipated series."

Cook used the Cupertino stage to screen a trailer for *See*, a post-apocalyptic fantasy starring Jason Momoa and Alfre Woodard that takes place in the distant future, after a deadly virus has decimated human-kind and left the few who survived blind. "I hope you can get a sense of why I love that show and I think you will too," said Cook, after screen-ing a two-minute reel that cut between sweeping, mountainous vistas and scenes of a fur-clad primitive society girding for battle.

Apple's aggressive pricing suggested the seriousness of its ambitions. Apple TV+ would launch in more than one hundred countries on No-vember 1, 2019, and cost $4.99 a month—cheaper than any existing service. Anyone who purchased a new Apple product—iPhone, iPad, Mac, or Apple TV—would receive the first year free, Cook said.

"We can't wait for you to start watching Apple TV+ on November 1 on the Apple TV app across all of your screens. That's Apple TV+," said Cook, efficiently dispensing with Hollywood. "Now let's turn your at-tention to iPad. . . ."

After the debacle of Apple's March event, some of Hollywood's deal-makers had grown cool to Cupertino's overtures, adopting a wait-and-see attitude. Many expressed skepticism about what the service would look like, how it would be delivered.

Eddy Cue—the long-tenured Apple executive whose broad portfo-lio of responsibilities as internet software and services chief includes the Apple TV+, Apple Pay, Apple Music, and iCloud services—granted a rare interview to *GQ* in the summer preceding the launch, in which he described Apple as poised to capitalize on the tectonic shifts altering the television landscape.

"We think there's an opportunity for us, given the changes that we see in technology, to play a part of it," Cue said of the looming television revolution and the coming end times for pay TV. "And the way we do things is we always say we try to be the best, not the most. And we're getting excited about it. The shows we're creating are really, really good."

Apple looked to reprise its triumph in music nearly two decades earlier, a far easier feat in some respects since, unlike in video streaming, the company didn't have to produce the music itself but just improve the delivery system. It helped that the recording industry was in a vulnerable state, having been turned upside down by a Massachusetts teenager who wrote a piece of software called Napster, which made it easy for people to dip into each other's hard drives and share music files. Apple introduced a trio of products to take advantage of the digital disruption caused by the file-sharing service. There was the iTunes software, which it touted as "the world's best and easiest to use jukebox" (and a place to hold all that music, ripped from CDs and downloaded). A new generation of iMacs with CD burners would let users become their own DJs and "rip, mix, burn" their own custom playlists onto discs. And, finally, the groundbreaking iPod portable music player would put "1,000 songs in your pocket."

By 2003, with long-secure CD sales in the midst of an alarming free fall, the major music labels agreed to let Steve Jobs sell their music online for ninety-nine cents a track through the new iTunes Music Store. Cue was the hard-nosed negotiator behind those deals—someone who spoke with the authority of Jobs's appointed deputy and who leveraged the industry's desperation to create a legitimate source from which to buy music online.

"To use a recording studio analogy, the reality is at the time Steve was producer, and Eddy was engineer, and between them they both made beautiful things. And it's quite a music-centric analogy, but Eddy would mic everything up and get everything prepared, if not do the bulk of the heavy lifting," said Universal Music Group chairman Lucian

Grainge, who recalled negotiations with Jobs and Cue while overseeing Universal's UK division. "When Steve was in the meeting, everybody was quiet and there was deference before Steve. But let me be very clear, other than the fact that [Eddy's] my friend, the reality is he's someone that you can trust, he's someone that's got integrity, and he's someone that you can do business with."

Others in the music industry described Cue as "quietly dispassionate" in leveraging Apple's clout. Ted Cohen, former head of digital distribution at EMI Music, which is now a division of Universal, said Cue agreed to terms that Apple never lived up to—like sharing anonymized purchasing data. When challenged, Cue said the label could always bring a breach of contract suit—and Apple would simply stop selling EMI's music while the dispute played out in court.

"He wasn't an asshole to work with, he was actually pleasant at times," said Cohen. "It was all the broken promises but none of the broken legs."

Finesse would be required to win over the film and television world.

Cue talked about applying Apple's meticulous approach to craft to the realm of video programming. He noted its painstaking re-creation of NASA's Manned Spacecraft Center (more commonly known as Mission Control) in period space-race show *For All Mankind*. "We worked a lot with the best people in the business to create a show that has a great deal of attention to detail," Cue told *GQ*, noting the show used the actual control panel—not a replica. "We were able to get a lot of the original stuff. We didn't create fake ones," he said. "We actually got the original stuff."

But would Apple TV+ have the right stuff?

Some wondered how the service would manage to attract subscribers, given the paucity of its offerings. It planned to launch with a handful of original series but no library of familiar movies and television shows to provide comfort-food viewing in between the helpings of haute cuisine. Studio executives wondered why Cue didn't tap Apple's massive $200 billion cash reserve to acquire Sony Pictures Entertainment, which had been fielding offers on and off for years. The studio that's home to such film franchises as *Spider-Man*, *Men in Black*, *Ghostbusters*, and *Jumanji*, and such hit television series as *Better Call Saul*, *Breaking Bad*, *The Crown*, *The Blacklist*, and *Outlander*, would have instantly addressed the lack of a library.

Still, limited as its initial foray seemed to be, the tech giant had resources to burn. So, Apple TV+ became a regular stop for pitch meetings for many—even if they knew that working for Apple came with strings attached.

Van Amburg and Erlicht worked to tamp down the trade's perception that they were averse to darker, more challenging material. The duo would tell agents that while Apple wouldn't green-light a film like *Natural Born Killers*, in which Woody Harrelson and Juliette Lewis portray two young, attractive serial killers who become tabloid-TV antiheroes, violence was acceptable, so long as it offered the viewer something redemptive.

While the duo brought to Apple a sparkling résumé with hits like *Breaking Bad*, one former Sony executive who was their colleague notes that their new roles were quite a bit different from being production executives. "On their stuff, they were sellers. They didn't have to really refine or address all of the aspects of a show—audience segmentation, determining the tone, using the show as a way to acquire customers, that kind of thing," the executive said. "When you're Apple, now all of a sudden, you're the network. You're the one who's supposed to be giving notes. That takes an adjustment."

Along with the success stories, Van Amburg and Erlicht had also shepherded shows like *Powers*, a superhero riff with vague similarities to Amazon's *The Boys*. FX had rejected it at pilot stage, so Sony wound up finding an unlikely home for it: the PlayStation video game console. At the time, the gaming division was dabbling with TV, adding a pay-TV package, Vue, and experimenting with original programming. *Powers*, an $80 million production, quickly ran out of juice, ending after its sparsely viewed second season.

As the new heads of Apple TV+ established their brand, agents detected an inherent buoyancy to the projects they bought, starting with its marquee launch title, *The Morning Show*. "The messaging is: 'It's Americana.' These are two actresses people love . . . Their presence is evocative of a certain feeling," said one agent who requested anonymity to maintain an ongoing business relationship with Apple. "Even if the show is darker, they're not—and that's a choice."

Netflix, by contrast, made its mark with *House of Cards*, the political thriller whose jarring opening scene depicts the central character, South Carolina representative Frank Underwood, played by Kevin Spacey, strangling a neighbor's dog after it's been hit by a car. "Moments like this require someone who will act, who will do the unpleasant thing, the necessary thing," says Underwood, staring unsettlingly into the camera.

Agents described Apple's sensitivity about certain creative choices that could tarnish the pristine consumer brand and alienate customers, such as negative depictions of religion.

The talent community was alive with stories about Apple's excessive meddling with projects and copious notes providing feedback on scripts. Some interpreted the heavy-handedness as anxiety about producing a polished, highly curated product—even if it likely repelled some showrunners. Jay Carson, a former political strategist who served as an advisor and supervising producer on Netflix's *House of Cards*, exited *The Morning Show* amid "creative differences." Writer and producer Bryan Fuller left Steven Spielberg's *Amazing Stories* over clashing visions for the anthology series. He envisioned a show akin to Netflix's *Black Mirror*, while Amblin Television and Apple were looking for family-friendly fare, *Variety* reported. "Never have so many notes been given on a single television show," said one source on the receiving end of the criticism.

One writer-producer with a show under development at Apple says there's pressure to deliver excellence, a mark that would be difficult to hit in the absence of any Apple TV+ shows to watch prior to launch. Apple's executives fretted about potential overlap of creative concepts, though the company's culture of secrecy would make it difficult to discern whether a central character would bump up against another project in development. The level of secrecy goes beyond the industry's norm about keeping mum about shows in the works.

"Even if you're working with a writer that's on another Apple show, that writer better not tell you what show they're working on—which is so strange because that certainly doesn't happen elsewhere," says the writer-producer, who has found a way to adapt to the tech giant's distinct culture. "It just becomes a joke. 'Well, on that show that you can't tell me about, do you still have time to talk to us at two o'clock or are you on that show that you can't talk to us about?'"

Apple scored a coup in January 2020, when it announced a deal with longtime HBO chief Richard Plepler, the executive who helped make the premium network an original programming powerhouse, amassing 160 Emmys across his twenty-seven-year tenure. His production company, Eden Productions, signed a five-year deal to make movies and television shows for Apple TV+. Plepler initially met with Van Amburg and Erlicht to explore the possibility of bringing his boutique shop to Apple. The HBO veteran had long admired their work, especially two series that he felt would have been at home at his own network, *The Crown* and *Breaking Bad*, suggesting that they shared a sensibility about quality and excellence in programming. With their support, he met with Cue at Allen & Co.'s annual summer gathering of tech and media titans in Sun Valley and discussed the possibility of making documentary films and series for Apple.

Over lunch two weeks later, at the Mark Restaurant on New York City's Upper East Side, which is run by the chef Jean-Georges Vongerichten, the Apple executive signaled his desire to formalize the relationship. That fall, Cue, Van Amburg, and Erlicht met at Apple's Manhattan town house to begin structuring a deal. "Apple just felt the most embryonic and I felt maybe I could make a small contribution to what I know is going to be a very successful service, working with people I respect and trust," said Plepler.

Cue and Plepler had forged a relationship back in 2015, when HBO debuted its stand-alone streaming service, HBO Now, in the iTunes store. Back then, Plepler was confronted with a problem. HBO's most popular show, *Game of Thrones*, ranked as the most pirated TV show in the world. Viewers were unwilling to pay for an expensive cable television package to "legally" watch the show, so they downloaded it instead. Legally or otherwise, viewers were flocking to internet streaming by the millions.

Plepler reached out, via an intermediary, to the Apple media boss with a proposition: would Apple want to sell HBO's service in its App Store? Behind the scenes, a flurry of cloak-and-dagger negotiations by his executive team secured Plepler a spot on the premier stage in Silicon Valley: an Apple product launch event. The San Francisco event was so monumental, Plepler kept a framed copy of his speech on the wall of his HBO office until he vacated.

The Plepler partnership, announced on January 2, 2020, helped Apple burnish a reputation as a boutique purveyor of content.

The anthology series *Little America* debuted later that same month to critical raves. The series, developed by *The Office* veteran Lee Eisenberg and the husband-and-wife writing team behind *The Big Sick*, Kumail Nanjiani and Emily V. Gordon, offered uplifting vignettes of the immigrant experience. One vignette centered on a Nigerian student who discovers his sense of self while embracing Oklahoma's cowboy culture, providing an antidote to the toxic political rhetoric of the Trump administration.

Eisenberg said the show seemed a natural fit for the Apple brand, which is global, optimistic, and aspirational. He found his interactions with the Apple TV+ executives to be constructive, not stifling (though some might have found his numerous phone calls with Apple's Erlicht, debating the chyrons and images used at the conclusion of each episode, to cross into obsessive terrain).

"I've had the experience of notes that feel like, 'Did you get past page four?!'" says Eisenberg of other shows. The feedback from Apple wasn't like that. "The attention to detail, the midnight emails, it never felt like a pain. It always felt like, 'Oh, we have partners on this that are as passionate about it as we are.'"

The collaboration has been fruitful enough that Eisenberg and Apple struck a multiyear deal to create television and digital media projects under a new banner, Piece of Work Entertainment. In February, Apple announced its next project with Eisenberg, a limited series based on the Wondery podcast *WeCrashed: The Rise and Fall of WeWork*.

The new service seemed poised to prove its Hollywood mettle with a civil rights drama starring Samuel L. Jackson and Anthony Mackie. *The Banker* was scheduled to premiere at the American Film Institute's annual festival in Los Angeles when Apple abruptly withdrew it, an unusual move on the festival circuit. Allegations that the son of one of the film's central figures had committed sexual abuse forced the company's hand. (Bernard Garrett Jr. denied the allegations but was dropped as one of the film's co-producers.) After conducting a review, Apple concluded it could release the film in a few theaters and on its streaming service. It came and went quickly.

Controversy sparked again when Oprah Winfrey withdrew from a documentary film by Academy Award–nominated filmmakers Amy Ziering and Kirby Dick two weeks before the film was set to premiere at the Sundance Film Festival. *On the Record*, which gave voice to a music executive who came forward to accuse hip-hop mogul Russell Simmons of sexual assault, was later picked up by HBO Max, where the co-directors' series *Allen v. Farrow* streamed in 2021. "I have decided that I will no longer be executive producer," Oprah wrote in a statement to several industry trades. "And it will not air on Apple TV+."

CHAPTER 14

▶ Quibi Vadis?

Those inclined to question Quibi's long-term viability found more fuel for their skepticism in February 2020, when a commercial for the streaming service aired during the Super Bowl matchup between the San Francisco 49ers and the Kansas City Chiefs.

Most Super Bowl ad time is bought months in advance. But Quibi's entry took shape just a couple of weeks before kickoff. Someone had broached the idea during the Sundance Film Festival in late January 2020, where founder Jeffrey Katzenberg and CEO Meg Whitman hosted a VIP cocktail hour. They spent the evening pitching the virtues of short-form mobile content—handing out phones and headphones for attendees to screen footage of *Survive*, in which Sophie Turner (*Game of Thrones*) and Corey Hawkins (*BlacKkKlansman*) portray the lone survivors of a plane crash on a remote, snow-covered mountain. Once the crowd dissipated, a small clutch of executives was chatting when the subject of a splashy Super Bowl debut came up—and Katzenberg immediately embraced the suggestion.

"By the time we were driving to the airport to go home that night, we were buying a Super Bowl ad," recalled one former executive. "It was like, 'Really?'"

It was a promotional stunt pulled straight from the Hollywood playbook—at least the one created in the twentieth century. To build anticipation for an upcoming movie, drop a trailer during the most-watched television broadcast of the year. But it ignored the advice of Quibi's own marketing team, which knew of Gen Z's (and young adults') well-documented indifference to televised sports. The campy, hastily produced commercial, featuring four masked bank robbers frantically hailing their getaway car, whose driver was amusing himself watching one of Quibi's short videos, amounted to an expensive misfire.

"Five million dollars—basically going to the trash. We were still three months before launch. It was stupid and we all said, 'We shouldn't do this,'" recalled one marketing executive, whose presentations about reaching young digital natives where they lived had been dismissed. "Then, we did it again with the Oscars—ten million dollars thrown into the trash. We were looking at the numbers with Meg and saying, 'This is doing nothing.'"

A lack of traction was glaringly apparent upon Quibi's April 6, 2020, debut, though the extent to which COVID-19 should be blamed would be debated. There was obvious peril in launching an on-the-go mobile video service as the nation was sheltering in place. Katzenberg held fast to his original theory, though, believing eighteen- to thirty-four-year-olds would eagerly seek out a few moments of diversion from the bleak news of the deadly virus's relentless spread.

"Here is a moment in time when, collectively, all of us are stressed out, anxious, depressed, threatened. Life as we know it has just been turned upside down and inside out," said Katzenberg, summoning a reality distortion field that was every bit as potent as Steve Jobs's. "Here comes something that's new, it's unique, it's different. As you know, the entire goal of our enterprise is to inform and to entertain and inspire."

Whitman had planned a $400 million "rolling thunder" marketing campaign to grab the attention of a distracted world, kicking off Quibi's launch with a glitzy, star-studded Hollywood red-carpet event, with one hundred or so celebrities parading before the world's entertainment press.

The eye-catching spectacle would have given ignition to a service that needed to distinguish itself in a crowded space dominated by such globally recognized brands as Netflix, Amazon, and Disney. But concerns about the rapidly spreading coronavirus nixed the event, unwinding a year's worth of planning and leaving Whitman to ponder how to virtually simulate celebrity sizzle.

As strategically placed clocks counted down the days, hours, minutes, and seconds to launch in Quibi's modern Los Angeles workspace, Whitman set to work on Plan B. "The good thing" about having to pivot, she said in a March 2020 interview, "is we're a digital company, right? So we have lots of ideas about how we could have a red carpet event—but just online."

Quibi's launch ultimately was a muted affair, with the service announcing a ninety-day free trial to entice subscribers. In an ominous sign, downloads of the app peaked during the week of launch, at 1.5 million, then fell off by 57 percent the following week, according to data from researcher Sensor Tower.

Social media lit up with criticism. Some expressed frustration at the inability to capture and share screenshots on social media. "They are totally cutting themselves out of meme culture," observed Grace Watkins, founder and CEO of Click Management, a company that works with gaming and internet influencers. Others complained about being forced to watch Quibi's films and shows on the smallest screen in the house, the mobile phone. By this point in technology's evolution, it was oblivious to how consumers wanted to view content—anywhere, anytime, and on any device.

Quibi added a screenshot feature in an effort to generate viral lift for its programming. Alas, social media conversations can take a vicious turn, as was the case with Sam Raimi's retelling of an old campfire story about a man who covets his wife's golden arm and steals it from her after she dies (with vengeful, beyond-the-grave consequences). In the Quibi take for the anthology series *50 States of Fright*, Emmy Award winner Rachel Brosnahan is the one with the unhealthy obsession with the prosthetic. She is diagnosed with "pulmonary gold disease" but refuses to consent to an amputation. On her deathbed, she mutters a line that would reverberate across the Twitterverse, "When I die, bury me with my golden arm."

The most searing critiques were reserved for the quality of the shows. Even though the service launched with an abundance of titles—fifty at launch—and enough celebrities to fill the *Vanity Fair* Hollywood Issue, it lacked a single breakout hit.

"What's on-screen just isn't worth a full two eyeballs," wrote Spencer Kornhaber in his review for the *Atlantic*.

Quibi barely managed to achieve launch velocity before it found itself in court, facing a patent infringement suit brought by an interactive video company, Eko. The New York–based firm accused Quibi's employees of misappropriation of trade secrets in creating its breakthrough Turnstyle feature. Katzenberg agreed in September 2021 to turn over Quibi's video-flipping Turnstyle technology to Eko to settle the suit that continued long after the mobile video service had shut down.

Even before Quibi's eventual demise, the postmortems arrived in a flood of hot takes, heaped with schadenfreude at the $1.75 billion stumble by two accomplished executives, Whitman and Katzenberg. As *Wired* magazine tartly noted: "Laughing at Quibi is way more fun than watching Quibi."

Quibi struggled to hang on to users once the ninety-day trial period lapsed. Sensor Tower estimated a mere 8 percent of users opted to subscribe, though Quibi pointed to the more favorable 27 percent conversion rate cited by another independent measurement firm, Antenna. At that rate, it would fall short of internal forecasts of seven million paying subscribers in its first year. The entire business case, according to one insider, was premised on Quibi matching the weekly subscriber gains of Spotify, Netflix, or Disney+ in its first year. "We all knew that . . . hitting those numbers was extremely difficult," said the source.

Quibi was finding success in niches. Maurice Harris's talk show, *Centerpiece*, in which he would interview Black creatives and interpret their personalities into floral installations, attracted the attention of cultural tastemakers like Lena Waithe. But in Katzenberg's eyes, it wasn't performing.

"We took all that money from advertisers, we raised all this money, we had to have the biggest possible number," said one of Quibi's former creative executives. "As opposed to . . . the riches can be in the niches. Get ten of those shows, and now what are we talking about? *Now* you've got a cool platform."

The service offering "quick bites" of content became an easy punch line. During a virtual version of Disney-ABC's annual upfront presentation to advertisers in June 2020, late-night talk show host Jimmy Kimmel deadpanned: "Here I am, standing here like a damn fool with nobody watching. I feel like every show on Quibi right now."

Within three months of the mobile video service's launch, Hollywood insiders had written off Quibi for dead, the streaming equivalent of the star-studded cinematic dud *Cats*.

In retrospect, the missteps were easy to see, starting with the decision to launch a mobile service when the coronavirus had eliminated the "in between" moments that Quibi had hoped to fill with short bursts of entertainment. Perhaps Quibi was simply less compelling than the social media apps, games, and other diversions on the phone.

"I'd argue the problem isn't that those moments have disappeared, it's that they were already spoken for," wrote Doug Clinton of the Minneapolis research firm Loup Ventures.

The fatal flaw is that Quibi was built around a particular use case—consumers' desire to watch video on their smartphones—not a business model. But one-third of consumers already do that, using their existing Netflix, Hulu, or Amazon Prime subscriptions, according to a 2015 survey by Pew Research. Quibi's chief competition turned out to be the pause button.

"Quibi is what we used to refer to, in the movie business, as a feathered fish," said one senior Hollywood executive, who requested anonymity to maintain a long-established business relationship with

Katzenberg. "It's not Netflix, where you can watch and watch and watch. It's not TikTok. It feels unfortunately like it was designed by someone who wasn't of the generation or generations that you thought you were attracting for Quibi."

The extravagantly well-funded startup whose founder bragged it would reimagine entertainment for the mobile era had instead delivered the app equivalent of New Coke: a vigorously marketed product that no one wanted. Quibi's hobbled launch during the early, fearful months of the COVID-19 pandemic foreshadowed its collapse, a mere seven months later. On its first day, it reached number 3 in Apple's App Store, but it quickly tumbled out of the ranking of top ten app installs, sinking to number 284 by mid-June.

Katzenberg initially sought to blame the underwhelming debut on external forces, telling the *New York Times* in one particularly damaging interview, "I attribute everything that has gone wrong to the coronavirus." A few weeks later, he said the slow start provided the equivalent of a beta period, allowing the company to take stock and regroup after hitting the "brick wall" of COVID-19.

But in the midst of a nationwide lockdown, viewers were devouring hours of programming in marathon binge sessions on their living room TVs to fill the seemingly endless expanse of time, not seeking out movies and TV shows in "snackable" form.

The roots of Quibi's problems went deeper, though, to its founding premise. Katzenberg would frequently point to Dan Brown's mega-selling novel, *The Da Vinci Code*, with its 105 breezy chapters, as validating his idea of delivering quick bursts of premium entertainment to fill spare moments of the day. "When I asked about it, he said, 'I want [my readers] to have a fantastic reading experience that I have designed to be satisfying at every step along the way and convenient to what is now a more fragmented and segmented time schedule that people have,'" Katzenberg said in April 2019. "If you've got ten minutes, read a chapter or two. Got an hour? Keep going."

Quibi's all-star lineup failed to produce shows that succeeded in pulling attention from the spontaneous, goofy, and surprisingly intimate videos on TikTok. Amateur social media influencer Nathan "Doggface" Apodaca drew a bigger crowd grinding his skateboard down Highway 20 in Idaho Falls, sipping cranberry juice while listening to Fleetwood Mac's "Dreams."

But it isn't as if Katzenberg wasn't warned. He surrounded himself with young development executives who cautioned Quibi was squandering its money on talent that the audience didn't care about. (One source of irritation was Reese Witherspoon's reported $6 million payday to narrate a nature show, *Fierce Queens*.) "There were fights all the time," noted one insider, who added, "There wasn't a lot of humility from Jeffrey in trying to understand really the audience that we were going after."

"Jeffrey's ego got the best of him," said one veteran television executive, who said Katzenberg failed to test out the concept with the target audience. That resulted in flawed programming choices. The younger population is playing games, chatting, watching YouTube videos, or engaging with social platforms on their phones, not looking for long-form content, chopped up in chapters. "The initial concept was problematic, and their inability to listen or hear who that audience was," the executive said. "And then, even if they had a shot at working, the pandemic just killed them."

Quibi marked a stunning misstep for the Hollywood mogul whose previous startup, DreamWorks, needed time to warm up but soon produced Oscar winners like *American Beauty*, *Gladiator*, and *Shrek*. Katzenberg failed to green-light a single hit among Quibi's fifty launch shows.

"In six months, it's going to be gone," producer Jason Blum presciently observed in an interview conducted in early October 2020, days ahead of the official announcement that it would cease operations. "It's just one of the most amazing flameouts. It's the WeWork of entertainment."

Over the summer months, Whitman scrambled to adjust course.

She examined the data and proposed different tactics, like launching a free version of the service in Australia and New Zealand, and reversed its phone-only approach so users could watch shows on the living room TV—a feature that users requested but that put it in direct competition with other streaming services. She looked for ways to reduce Quibi's cash burn to buy more time to iterate.

"Jeffrey wanted to literally go big or go home, to double down on spending more money in marketing," said the former marketing executive. "With Meg, we were trying to extend the runway of this company. Jeffrey's decision was to burn it in a summer push, with another hundred million dollars in marketing."

In September 2020, Katzenberg and Whitman began looking for a buyer. The *Wall Street Journal* reported Quibi contemplated a variety of other options, including raising more money and going public through a merger with a special-purpose acquisition company. There were no takers. Katzenberg and Whitman announced on October 22, 2020, that they would shut down the service on December 1, 2020, and return as much of its remaining cash as possible to its investors.

"Quibi was a big idea and there was no one who wanted to make a success of it more than we did," Katzenberg and Whitman said in an open letter to employees and investors. "Our failure was not for the lack of trying; we've considered and exhausted every option available to us."

Katzenberg and Whitman sought to explain the failure, something neither one had tasted all that often. Fleeting setbacks, sure—a bomb at the box office, a delayed product launch—but never an outright belly flop from such heights.

Quibi failed "likely for one of two reasons: because the idea itself wasn't strong enough to justify a stand-alone streaming service or because of our timing," the executives said. "Unfortunately, we will never know but we suspect it's been a combination of the two."

During an emotional video call with employees, Katzenberg managed to work in one last plug by encouraging Quibi staffers to listen to

"Get Back Up Again," a song from the DreamWorks Animation film *Trolls*, to lift their spirits.

Quibi's epic fizzle had echoes of an earlier unsuccessful venture, Pop.com, a partnership that DreamWorks and Ron Howard's Imagine Entertainment formed in 2000. As with Quibi, Pop sought to recruit top Hollywood talent to create original short-form content for the pre-YouTube web. Despite reaching agreements with big names like Will Smith, Julia Roberts, Eddie Murphy, and Steve Martin, Pop went bust when it was unable to find a buyer at a $200 million valuation.

"We literally did not have a business plan," Katzenberg said of Pop in an interview prior to Quibi's launch. "It was, 'If you make it they will come and we'll figure out how to make money from it.'"

CHAPTER 15

▶ "If You Want to Grab People's Attention, You Have to Tease"

In the fall of 2019, when NBCUniversal named its streaming service Peacock, the reaction, to put it kindly, was rather mixed. "The name is a play on NBC's multicolored logo, but it also sounds like an idea that was left on the *30 Rock* cutting room floor," wrote Miles Surrey in the Ringer. "Just imagine the conversation you'd have with a friend who isn't literate in all things pertaining to the streaming wars. 'I tried Peacock last month, it's been amazing so far!' you'd beam, before your friend gave you a weird look and said, 'Dude, is that another one of those elitist non-dairy milks?'"

Even supporters of the name noted that some potential customers might think of the title of a saucy Katy Perry pop song rather than the industry shorthand for NBC. Partisans did note one clear plus: NBC-Universal didn't just tack a "+" onto its name, as Disney and Apple (and BET and ESPN and Samsung) had done, one after the other. NBC considered hundreds of possibilities before landing on Peacock, including another fowl contender, Roost, which was discarded for trademark reasons, according to one well-placed source who feared backlash: "I could just see some of the nasty press against the term." Still, securing the

Peacock web address required last-minute negotiations with a Hawaiian author by the same name, Everett Peacock. "We were extraordinarily lucky," said Bonnie Hammer, who led Peacock until a few months before its launch. "It came down to the eleventh hour."

Inside the company, most executives took comfort in research supporting their instinct that a more subtle nod to NBC's past would be better than overtly leading with one network name. It would enable them to treat this as much more than another TV Everywhere simulacrum, and also bolster their pitches to advertisers by adding an entirely new brand to the mix. There would also be freedom on the programming front, given that many shows on Peacock would intentionally fall well outside of the family-friendly zone of NBC mainstays like *This Is Us* or *The Good Place*. Edgy originals, as Netflix and Amazon Prime and Hulu had all demonstrated, were an attention-grabbing tool for acquiring new streaming customers. One such show planned for Peacock was a scripted take on the only-in-L.A. story of Angelyne. The quixotic, buxom pop culture figure became a sensation in the 1980s by putting up self-styled Barbie-esque billboards and driving a pink Corvette across the city. She starred as herself before the days when reality TV made that an actual profession. Played by Emmy Rossum in prosthetic cleavage, pink bikini top, and platinum-blond bouffant hairdo, the show's title character observed in a show trailer, "If you want to grab people's attention, you have to tease."

The Angelyne series was championed by Hammer, who had been appointed as the head of Peacock at the start of 2019. The veteran cable television executive had spent the first part of the year establishing the service's original content strategy, seeking to replicate her many successful branding and programming efforts for NBCU's cable networks. In addition to edgier series, there would be plenty of coloring inside the lines, with reboots of *Punky Brewster* and *Saved by the Bell*, which are instantly recognizable to viewers, to tap into nostalgia and rekindle interest in NBCU's library. "Timely and timeless," is how she expressed the brand positioning, a broad enough canvas to encompass the network's live news and sports broadcasts, its Universal Pictures films, and its cable channels. Along with the Angelyne project, another ambitious swing was an effects-heavy adaptation of Aldous Huxley's *Brave New World* starring Alden Ehrenreich and Demi Moore. "Reboot or original, it's about creating great content that draws viewers in," said Hammer. "People can tune in and watch multiple episodes of an existing NBCU TV series and then have something new, fresh, but familiar with its reboot. Then, on the other side, we deliver original shows and event series that are big and noisy . . . to help attract new subscribers."

Peacock's exact premiere date in 2020 had not been set, but the goal would be to leverage the Summer Olympics in Tokyo for a massive promotional push. As Disney and Apple neared the launch of their streaming services, the pressure intensified inside NBCUniversal, and by October Hammer was passing the Peacock baton to Matt Strauss. She told colleagues she felt relieved to return to a more familiar role as head of NBCUniversal Content Studios. "He was the perfect person to bring over once the framework was started, once the idea, the branding, the name, were in place," Hammer said. "Somebody who could technically and innately understand how to launch a digital service." While Steve Burke respected Hammer, the leader of Peacock needed a combination of digital and TV savvy. Programming, Hammer's main specialty, would still be important, but Peacock needed to hit the mark in terms of its user interface, treatment of advertising, distribution scheme, and marriage of traditional with high-tech qualities. Strauss found himself at an executive retreat held at Brian Roberts's summer home in Martha's Vineyard, a mansion overlooking a chain of smaller islands in Vineyard Sound where the cable magnate had previously hosted guests like his seasonal neighbors the Obamas. Strauss outlined his strategy for leveraging Comcast's Xfinity cable and internet service to support Peacock.

"A few weeks later, I was having dinner with my family—it was a Thursday—and I got a call from Steve and essentially he asked if I would consider actually coming to NBC and running Peacock," recalled

Strauss. "To me, that was one of the most awesome challenges that I can think of doing."

Strauss didn't hesitate. Three days later, he packed his bags and moved temporarily to New York from his home in Cherry Hill, New Jersey. His wife drove him up the New Jersey Turnpike and he checked into a hotel for three months to oversee the launch. True to his life-long ambition to improve the TV experience, Strauss had the conviction that streaming, too, could be better. During the eighteen-month period when Comcast and NBCUniversal had secretly developed Peacock, Strauss had had a seat at the table, advising on how it should run through Comcast's Xfinity X1 systems. He had long ago pinpointed the opportunity for NBCUniversal in the crowded streaming marketplace. "I feel like I had this really unique perspective and understanding of this behavior [at Comcast]," he reflected later. "I had access to a lot of data and I had access to understanding how people were interacting with different products and services."

Because of that, Peacock would "zig where others zag," in Burke's phrase. "TV tends to be very dynamic," Strauss observed. "It's current. It's social. Many streaming services feel more like a casino. There's no sense of time or place."

Peacock, by contrast, would start to display moving video as soon as the app was launched, to emulate the experience of turning on the TV. "It's really meant to tap into that pulse," Strauss said, as a "destination where you can come to it every single day and know that not only is it being updated and changing but it's incredibly timely. It's current to what's going on in the world." Social media has that mood-ring customization down pretty well, he added, but "you don't see it as much in streaming."

At Strauss's direction, a large team started ramping up its efforts to produce a January 2020 investor event that would position Peacock to the press and to Wall Street. Sitting inside famed Studio 8H at 30 Rock, home of *Saturday Night Live*, the audience would not be an easy mark. It was saturated with streaming messages from similar events hosted by Apple, Disney, and WarnerMedia, not to mention a mushrooming number of streaming pitches to advertisers and ongoing news from Netflix. Fatigue was a distinct risk. A deliberate choice was made to keep the Peacock presentation moving briskly and emphasize the entertainment quotient. The speaker lineup was liberally sprinkled with stars, including Tina Fey, Jimmy Fallon, and Seth Meyers, as well as recognizable NBCUniversal on-air personalities like Savannah Guthrie, Lester Holt, and Mike Tirico. Few speakers took more than five minutes onstage, though of course there would be substantive discussion of financial and subscription projections.

Burke didn't dwell on bygone eras, but right from the top he gestured at radio, alluding to the studio's origins as the home of the NBC Symphony Orchestra and conductor Arturo Toscanini in the 1930s and '40s. "Some of the most important events in media history have happened right here in this building and right here in this room," Burke said. "From the golden era of radio to the first TV commercial to the first color broadcast—they all happened in this building, in this room, and because of NBC."

While NBCUniversal ran a portfolio of digital brands and dabbled in Snapchat, the trappings and tone of the event did not exactly scream "high tech." After exiting the wood-paneled elevators and walking down hallways lined by framed black-and-white photos of *SNL* and *Kraft Television Theatre*, attendees took their seats in the very womb of show business. Peacock might have been a twenty-first-century streaming venture, the presentation seemed to say, but it was on the same comfortable continuum as what had emanated from NBC for decades.

Tonight Show house band the Roots warmed up the crowd eager to see who would traverse the shiny-floored, catwalk-like stage. True to his straight-ahead style, Burke delivered words that many in the audience were glad to hear. Speaking next to a series of bright yellow and blue bar charts, he embraced the skepticism around Netflix and the sense that high-end subscription services were oversaturating the market. Netflix had its boosters, of course. But many investors and journalists considered it a profligate, unsustainable company heading toward a meltdown as soon as its subscriber numbers plateaued. Netflix, for better or worse, had only a single product and, at least as the 2020s began, no major franchises capable of driving consumer products, video games, and other revenue streams.

NBCUniversal, by contrast, was a media heavyweight owned by a parent company with a massive broadband operation and the largest U.S. cable TV provider. Peacock, despite its out-of-the-box name, was not going for anything fancy. "Ad-supported business has been a proven business model for decades," Burke said. The 250 linear TV networks selling ads commanded 92 percent of all viewers, with ad-free networks like HBO and Showtime left to the remaining 8 percent, he noted. NBC, CBS, and ABC had minted money for decades with an exclusively ad-based business model. Why ditch that all of a sudden? "Networks put shows on the air hoping to attract, say, twenty million viewers, and when they did, they made money on advertising," Burke continued. "This is what Peacock is going to aim to do. And in some ways, we're creating the equivalent of a twenty-first-century broadcast business delivered on the internet." That strategy seemed to be working for Hulu and a host of others, after all. It didn't have to be Netflix or bust.

Hammer's programming instincts were legendary and vastly successful, though she took a different path from HBO, FX, AMC, and other networks ushering in TV's prestige era at the dawn of the twenty-first century. At USA, once known mainly for repeats, tennis, and the tawdry detective series *Silk Stalkings*, Hammer oversaw a dramatic leap into original programming. One key aspect of USA's breakthrough was what came to be known as its "blue-sky" strategy, which yielded more inviting shows like *Burn Notice*, *White Collar*, *Monk*, and *Suits*. With the exception of a much darker USA hit, *Mr. Robot*, most of the network's series followed conventional genre lines, delivering satisfying, closed-end episodes, in contrast to the serialized storytelling favored by HBO, FX, and early streaming efforts. They also underscored their appeal as "comfort food" viewing by shooting in seductive, sunny locations. As she once explained to the *New York Times*, her programming "makes you feel good rather than shut it off and you're in some dark place, depressed." Unscripted fare had also prospered on Hammer's watch, with E! creating a mint-making, culture-changing phenomenon with *Keeping Up with the Kardashians* and its many offshoots.

Other speakers hailed NBC's fabled comedy and drama lineups, Telemundo's Spanish-language shows (a potential weapon given the over-indexing in streaming of U.S. Hispanic viewers), and top-shelf sports programming. In all, seven thousand five hundred hours of film and TV titles would be included in the basic tier, which would be offered for free. Peacock Premium would boost that level to fifteen thousand hours and offer wrinkles like next-day streams of new prime-time series from NBC and other networks, or late-night shows from Jimmy Fallon and Seth Meyers starting at eight P.M. Linda Yaccarino, head of advertising sales for NBCUniversal, highlighted a number of offerings designed to lessen the impact of commercials, which frustrated viewers had been ducking for years. Total ad time would be no more than five minutes per hour of programming, about one-third what linear packs in, and "frequency capping" promised to prevent repetition of the same ads, long a bugaboo.

Strauss detailed the experience of Peacock—a presentation he had been born in Oyster Bay, Long Island, to deliver—including the plan to offer a selection of linear channels. In addition to being able to pull up selections on demand, viewers could also browse a few dozen live, linear channels in a cable-like environment, complete with an on-screen programming guide. Some of the channels would be built on core NBCUniversal properties like the *Today* show, the Olympics, and *SNL*, but others would come from outside suppliers like the Bob Ross Channel (yes, that happy-little-tree-painting network actually exists). A "trending" tab would offer two-to-four-minute clips from NBC News or highlights from E! or NBC Sports. (After the event, Strauss said the company saw that offering free streaming networks, as Roku, Amazon Fire, Pluto TV, and others had started to do successfully, was a key element of the strategy. "We didn't call ourselves NBC Plus, and by doing that, I believe we have permission to be an aggregator," he said. In other words: a cable company.)

Because of Peacock's advertising focus, its pricing was perhaps the most intriguing part of the investor day. Its basic tier would be free, no matter where you accessed it. The higher level, Peacock Premium, would be offered at no cost to existing Comcast customers and $5 a month for others. Those wanting a completely ad-free version could pay another $5 on top of that. Peacock would be offered initially to Comcast subscribers on April 15, with the full nationwide launch on July 15, a date designed to maximize the promotional benefit of the 2020 Tokyo Olympics, which Burke liked to call the "afterburner." Price was one reason NBCUniversal believed it would have thirty to thirty-five million active users by 2024, becoming profitable by that time. Projecting users, rather than subscribers, had a sly logic to it. Comcast subscribers would be given Peacock automatically, so if they simply tapped on the app once, they would be counted as a user, a different bar to clear than that for subscription services bent on complicated free trials and conversions.

The ninety-minute presentation glided to a conclusion with a Q & A session with analysts. True to its mission, it had not overstayed its welcome, offering an ample selection of meaty statistics, razzle-dazzle looks at new shows, and insight into company strategy. Asked by one analyst about how Peacock would handle distribution given that many pay-TV operators are already paying for NBC and its other networks, Burke expressed confidence. He said most operators besides Comcast (and Cox Cable, a smaller one announced as a launch partner) would also be drawn to the free price point. "If you look at it as a cable executive or a satellite executive, you're getting a product that's worth $5 or $6 for free for all of your customers," he said. "So I would anticipate the vast majority of people will carry it." Two entities that did not announce deals with Peacock ahead of its launch were major gatekeepers Roku and Amazon Fire TV, which together reach into more than one hundred million U.S. households.

Strauss, after the investor day, said expanding carriage would be a key goal throughout the launch phase of Peacock. But he also thought of the service itself as a distributor—something that could not be said of any of the new arrivals in 2019 or 2020.

"In many ways what I wanted to do with Peacock was to re-create the cable bundle," Strauss said. With live, linear channels, trending content, and a wealth of on-demand film and TV titles, "that feels a lot like television—and that was the whole point."

Strauss said he had "no ambition of trying to compete with Netflix or Disney+." Even the binary that had stuck in most people's minds was a false one, he added. "It's not one or the other. It's not linear, it's not on demand—it's both. It's about tapping into the right content for the right user at the right time and it's about giving them choices. Again, I really believe that's the secret sauce here, and if I can do that right, and if I can create an aggregation platform, I think that if you fast-forward a few years, I've created the next evolution of the cable bundle."

As the house lights came back up inside Studio 8H and the Roots struck up an exit jam, the crowd headed to another 30 Rock jewel, on the sixty-fifth floor: the Rainbow Room. The lavish, historic space saw relieved NBCUniversal executives let off steam, along with talent. *Law & Order* producer Dick Wolf gave *Mr. Robot*'s Christian Slater a hug. Jamie Dornan, who shot to fame in *Fifty Shades of Grey* and was starring in Peacock's *Dr. Death*, greeted Dulé Hill, who was reprising his role on USA's *Psych* in a feature movie sequel. Nattily dressed entourages pointed at each other and smiled. As guests spilled into the space, which had been a cabaret, hosted the Tony Awards, and served as home base for world-class bartender Dale DeGroff, there was little hint that anything involving streaming or technology had just happened downstairs. Instead, it felt like a high-end premiere party, Hollywood's longtime forte. Drinks flowed freely and the city lights twinkled outside for miles in every direction.

Attendees who were not part of the red-carpet scene partook of the buffet dinner and sized up what they had just seen. Two analysts availing themselves of the free sushi expressed admiration for the Peacock plan. "It's smart," one said. "Why not take advantage of what you have? They're sitting on this unbelievable ad-sales machine. This is a new way to put it to use." Wall Street generally took that view. The event did not result in a Disney-like bump in the stock price, but a wave of guardedly positive reactions displayed a general sentiment of "Aha—so *that's* what they're up to." Gregory Williams of Cowen expressed some reservations. For one thing, he wrote in a note to his clients, "the clip roll at the beginning of the presentation didn't seem as compelling (to us, anyway) as what we saw from either Disney or Warner/HBO during their respective analyst presentations." A more material issue, he said, would be the profit outlook. "We weren't totally sold on the notion that Peacock is going to revolutionize the ad market," he wrote. Dan Ives, an analyst with Wedbush Securities, was more starstruck, calling the launch "an impressive event, with stars like Seth Meyers, Lester Holt, Jimmy Fallon and Tina Fey," in a message to his clients. "It is poised to successfully jump right into the mix with Netflix, Apple and Disney" and will "clearly disrupt the leader, Netflix, and its subscriber trajectory in this streaming battle over the coming years," he said.

Strauss wore a look of satisfaction at the party, gamely posing for pictures and taking overdue sips of water. The work was far from over, but this had been a major step toward letting everyone inside the thinking behind Peacock, which represented a unique new species in the streaming chase. The idea that he was out to disrupt Netflix was never accurate, he said. He credited the streaming giant with stimulating viewer demand for premium programming, but that wasn't the bar he was trying to clear. When he looked at the streaming field, he didn't see a glut or a big red leader to follow. He saw a large gap to be filled by his hybrid model, a product sustained by ads but still offering viewers things they couldn't get over the air. Peacock would not ruffle any feathers. It would not threaten to disrupt Comcast's lucrative pay-TV business, it would merely augment it. "People have confused Netflix as a replacement for television," he said. "Netflix is not a replacement for television. Netflix is an added ingredient. People love Netflix, but many people love Netflix on top of all the other choices that they want to have access to because people have a love affair with video and they always have. They're just content carnivores. They want more."

CHAPTER 16

● The IQ Test

The sales pitch began the moment visitors passed through the studio gate. After boarding golf carts for a ninety-second ride to Stage 21 on the Warner Bros. lot in Burbank, they saw and heard the case for the latest streaming service preparing to hit the market. Instead of a press release or a TV ad, this come-on by WarnerMedia came via experiential marketing. It aimed to immerse Wall Street analysts and members of the press in the company's storied past and its vision for the digitized future.

As a montage of swooning film music poured out of the cart's speaker system, the driver/tour guide spoke into her headset, offering brisk, scripted notes on the procession of soundstages as they passed. This was no ordinary cluster of beige buildings at the foot of the Verdugo Mountains, the tour implied. This was a place of show-business legend. Productions on the lot, the guide noted, have included "amazing classics like *Bonnie and Clyde*, starring Warren Beatty and Faye Dunaway, and some of our greatest TV shows, including the spy comedy *Chuck*, which filmed on your left-hand side on Soundstage 10, and the hit millennial TV show *Pretty Little Liars*."

Barely pausing for breath, the guide kept up her name-checks of titles and stars, affecting the well-scrubbed, chipper tone of an infomercial. "Coming up ahead is Soundstage 14, which is home to where the phrase 'Here's looking at you, kid' was coined, which came from the movie *Casablanca*, starring Humphrey Bogart and Ingrid Bergman. In 1942, it won the Best Picture Academy Award," she said. "Up ahead you'll see the soundstage where some of our great TV shows were made, including *The Big Bang Theory*, *The West Wing*, and, of course, the unforgettable *Friends*, which is celebrating its twenty-fifth anniversary."

Just before the cart reached the final stop (the very place where *National Lampoon's Christmas Vacation* was filmed, the guide noted) came the clincher. "All of these TV shows and movies . . . will be among the ten thousand hours of programming" on WarnerMedia's new streaming outlet, she said. "Please watch your head while exiting. Enjoy the show!"

The autumn sun slipped behind the mountains as the golf carts emptied and about a hundred attendees started to fill seats. Risers were set up in a semicircle occupying half of the soundstage space. Communications staffers and employees at the company's outside PR firm hovered nearby as the press arrived. Publicists filled empty seats before showtime, giving the impression of a packed house while also enabling them to keep an eye on reactions. The walls, floors, and chairs were all a uniform shade of black, so as to help focus attention on the sizzle reels, trailers, and other visuals to be shown on the oversized screen. Event planners had gone to school on Disney's investor day, which not only wowed the industry and consumers watching online but boosted the company's stock price more than 10 percent in a single day. WarnerMedia hired the same vendors for the day's equipment, cut trailers to a similar length. This final Tuesday in October had been declared as WarnerMedia Day, and the unveiling had some of the trappings of a holiday—as well as some of the familial angst.

As soon as the lights dimmed, a trailer lit up the screen and the familiar, resonant baritone of Morgan Freeman filled the air, discernible but nearly overwhelmed by a lush, insistent musical score. Just as he had done with penguins and Visa cards and the *CBS Evening News*, Freeman, with his sonorous tone, had a knack for turning clumsily written scripts into something that felt important, even sublime. His going rate for these voice sessions ran into the millions of dollars. Gravitas doesn't come cheap.

The screen showed a swirl of images and sounds linking AT&T's nineteenth-century telephone and telegraph origins with later advances in wireless, broadband, and the internet. "The spark" from the company's decades of innovation, Freeman intoned, "has spread to change our lives forever, connecting us instantaneously from the stars high above. Today, that spark has continued to spread, transforming not only our communication but our knowledge, entertainment, and emotions." The trailer hit every note—a century of film and TV heritage at Warner Bros.; Ted Turner's CNN and Turner Broadcasting blazing a trail in the 1970s; HBO, transforming the medium of TV. Members of the audience could have been forgiven for feeling like they were still getting the golf-cart tour, only with colorful visuals and seat-rumbling, cinema-quality sound.

"When the next revolution began, in our own living rooms," Freeman went on, "the most successful innovators understood how the rules had changed and how many opportunities had been born." The reference was to the mass adoption of television in the 1950s, but the contemporary nod was impossible to miss. Streaming was the next industry crossroads. WarnerMedia believed it had the institutional fortitude to bend change to its will, creating cultural artifacts comparable to those that had come before.

After the five-minute trailer ran its course, the main presentation got under way, and a good-sized crowd (including thousands of company employees) watched via webcast. WarnerMedia CEO John Stankey strode onstage, ready to deliver a new business-school metaphor for what he and the company were building. Out went the flywheel, in came . . . the virtuous cycle. "We've created a vertically integrated company that will allow us to benefit from a virtuous cycle of development and growth," Stankey said, wearing his signature entertainment-mode ensemble of navy suit and light blue dress shirt, its top button unbuttoned to signal that he was on leave from Dallas. He expanded on the concept of the virtuous cycle: "When you take our beloved, high-quality premium content and add innovative features to provide a superior user experience, it promotes subscriber engagement. The customer insights we gain from this engagement will inform our content and product decisions and enhance targeting to lead to a better experience and even more engagement. HBO Max, with its brand promise and on-demand content for everyone, will be the lead product in our drive to establish an initial customer relationship in most U.S. households."

Advertising, through AT&T's Xandr unit (rebranded in 2018 under that flip shorthand as a tribute to—who else?—Alexander Graham Bell), would be the glue. Xandr's technology would make HBO Max's algorithms more sophisticated, its eventual ad messages more precisely targeted. Stankey, known for his directness, sought to level with the investors and media in the room. "In the era of Amazon, Apple, Google, and Netflix, scale is no longer defined by distribution to one-quarter of U.S. consumers," he said, in reference to HBO's rarefied, if limited, reach. "It's a global game." Some HBO staffers watching the presentation online flashed back on the similarly unsparing message Stankey had delivered during his infamous town hall with Richard Plepler.

Stankey stressed one key differentiator: WarnerMedia was not starting from scratch. HBO already had ten million subscribers within the AT&T footprint, across satellite, cable, wireless, and existing streaming service HBO Now. The new service would cost them nothing extra to sample, and who doesn't like a free upgrade? "On day one, we'll provide a frictionless opportunity for these HBO subscribers to sign up and get HBO Max immediately," he said. "We expect that this alone will create word-of-mouth marketing, momentum, and buzz right out of the gate." By this logic, hitting the company's goal of fifty million U.S. subscribers by 2025 seemed well within reach. Including Latin America and Europe, the target was seventy-five to ninety million. The number was slightly more aggressive than Disney's projection of sixty to ninety million in five years. One major hurdle that would not come to light until well after the presentation was the reality of long-term distribution deals for HBO in several key territories, like the UK, Italy, and Germany. HBO Max would not be able to launch there until at least 2025.

AS A DOZEN EXECUTIVES FOLLOWED STANKEY to present aspects of HBO Max—its look and feel, programming, economics, and features—the carefully choreographed event hummed along. There were no tech glitches or fumbles with the teleprompter. But there's an old saying, recently popularized by actor Michael Caine: "Be like a duck," he recalled his mother telling him. "Remain calm on the surface and paddle like hell underneath."

Many webbed feet at WarnerMedia were spinning madly underwater. Numerous participants recalled an anxious atmosphere in the days leading up to the event. Scripts were rewritten countless times, often by the speakers themselves, up to the last minute. Trailers were continuously tweaked and recut. While revisions are routine, many of those involved say it went above and beyond the usual level of angst. The pressure to justify AT&T's $85 billion acquisition of Time Warner and articulate not just a streaming service but an entire media and digital ecosystem was immense. Disney had set a high bar. WarnerMedia, with its long-delayed merger with AT&T finally taking effect, was forced to play catch-up. Unlike Disney Investor Day, which had a stable management team and a well-articulated brand identity, WarnerMedia Day was the product of dueling corporate identities. The newly configured company had an array of new faces in control and little experience in the direct-to-consumer technology arena.

Two major figures who found themselves in the same foxhole were longtime industry colleagues Kevin Reilly and Bob Greenblatt. Reilly, a rakish, sharp-witted Long Island native, had a steady climb to the top of the television business. Having made his way to Los Angeles after Cornell University, he did stints as a freelance producer and Universal Pictures publicist before getting hired as a creative executive by industry legend Brandon Tartikoff. At age thirty-two, Tartikoff had become the youngest entertainment chief in TV history, and Reilly had a front-row seat during a historic decade. He turned NBC's prime-time lineup into the gold standard throughout the 1980s, green-lighting shows like *The Cosby Show*, *Cheers*, *Family Ties*, *Miami Vice*, and *Seinfeld*. Reilly took note of the way Tartikoff dealt with talent, charmed the press, and out-maneuvered opposition forces in the corporate suite. He then moved on to senior executive posts at Brillstein-Grey, FX, NBC, and Fox, championing such shows as *The Sopranos*, *The Office*, *30 Rock*, and *Glee*, before arriving at Turner Entertainment in 2014 to turn around TBS and TNT, two established, widely distributed networks that were creatively moribund. (For years, the biggest ratings generator on TBS was reruns of *The Big Bang Theory*.) Possessed of good taste and a long list of talent relationships, Reilly quickly injected new life into both shops, hiring Samantha Bee to do a late-night talk show and green-lighting buzzy shows like *Animal Kingdom* and *Search Party*. In late 2018, he was promoted to chief content officer of HBO Max, while retaining oversight of the cable networks.

Having had preliminary conversations with Stankey about leading HBO Max, Reilly was stunned when a publicist came to his office in the squat brown-brick office building in Burbank in March 2019 to share the news that Bob Greenblatt had been hired as chairman of Warner-Media Entertainment, reporting to Stankey. The building was outside the gated confines of the studio, physically and symbolically (people driving by generally knew it as the building with a Claim Jumper chain restaurant on the ground floor), and now Reilly felt equally on the outside looking in. Reilly had not heard a peep about it, but now Greenblatt was his boss. The surprise announcement was emblematic of Stankey's leadership of WarnerMedia. The executive, with his incomprehensible business-school jargon—"He could make ordering breakfast sound like a math equation," observed one executive—was closed off from the senior staff who turned to him for direction. "I've sent John emails proactively, just going, 'Well, haven't heard from you in a while, so thought

I'd share some thoughts on how I might go about this.' Thinking maybe I would engage him," recalled the executive. "Not even a response, not even a 'Thanks for the input, I'll get back to you.' It would just go off into the vacuum. I'd heard this from others too, who were in similar situations where they would just say, 'I don't know anything. Do you? I can't seem to get any feedback from this guy.'"

In just seven months, Greenblatt and Reilly would appear onstage together, making their streaming pitch. The two executives had known each other for three decades and had traveled parallel routes through the broadcast network development trenches. Greenblatt, who grew up in Rockford, Illinois, had arrived at WarnerMedia after turning around NBC's fortunes as its chairman. He also had executive runs at Showtime and Fox, and as a producer, he shepherded TV series like *Six Feet Under* and Tony Award–winning Broadway shows like *Dear Evan Hansen* and *9 to 5*. Greenblatt wore his reddish-brown hair closely cropped and his passion on his sleeve. One of his early pet projects at NBC had a glittery pedigree, with Steven Spielberg among its producers, but it soon became a punch line: *Smash*. The insider-y look at the making of a Broadway musical, described by BuzzFeed as "TV's biggest train wreck," lasted just two seasons. Some network suits are operational wonks or finance sharpies. Greenblatt put most of his focus on programming, and he relished an extravaganza. One of his signature programming moves at NBC was introducing an annual live musical to the network's lineup, which helped bring the world new spins on *Peter Pan* and *The Sound of Music*. Christopher Walken as Captain Hook and Carrie Underwood as Maria von Trapp were casting maneuvers aimed at enticing casual viewers to tune in. At least for a few years, they did.

Compared with the treadmill of catering to advertisers and broad audiences, with ratings in secular decline and the zeitgeist overwhelmingly favoring cable and streaming, wrapping himself in the high-thread-count cloth of HBO felt right. In the months between his exit from NBC and his entrance at WarnerMedia, Greenblatt had envisioned taking over HBO before ending up with a far bigger job. He felt ready to trade the flyover country of *Sunday Night Football* and *The Voice* for shows with resonance among coastal influencers. At NBC, he had agitated in vain to get the company to commit to streaming. At Warner-Media, the mission to stream couldn't have been more clear.

Reilly said there was never any overt friction with Greenblatt, whom he had known for decades, hung around with at conferences and the up-fronts, and would meet for yearly dinners. But he concedes, "I knew Bob for twenty years, and respected him, but I wasn't super psyched to have him be my boss, to be honest." It was a job Reilly had been promised. During the scramble to prepare for the investor day, as Greenblatt personally rewrote his remarks multiple times, Reilly told him they could be fixed later. "You're fixing it now," Greenblatt snapped at him, according to one observer. "If you don't want to be here, you can leave." As Reilly saw it, the task of getting WarnerMedia Day off the ground was a galvanizing process for the larger team. The presentation of the service "brought out the producer in Bob, in a positive way." Of course, as HBO Max was in its formative stages, as Reilly recalled, "he could have been spending a lot more time understanding the strategy and where we were headed and what decisions we should be making." Instead, Greenblatt's obsession became granular, down to every color choice and music cue.

Settling on the name HBO Max had not been an easy process. From the moment AT&T had proposed taking over Time Warner, it recognized HBO as the crown jewel. For its thirty-four million U.S. subscribers, and millions more internationally, the brand was a well-established draw, its three letters promising prestige. Warner Bros. was itself a storied brand, of course, and Turner also had decent-sized roots and a namesake in Ted Turner, who was one of media's foremost pioneers. But in terms of a consumer-facing brand name, focus-group research repeatedly showed the benefits of leading with HBO. The name was universally disdained by HBO employees and many others at the company, who worried about the potential for brand dilution. AT&T leadership clung to that research from the moment it hit the inbox.

There was one catch to leaning into the HBO brand, though: there were already two streaming services in the market with "HBO" in their names. HBO Go enabled subscribers paying for the network to stream its content online. HBO Now was a stand-alone version of HBO available to those interested in getting it outside of the pay-TV bundle. Calling the new streaming service HBO Max risked confusing consumers. A countless series of meetings were consumed by the question. Many WarnerMedia staffers argued the ultimate destruction of the HBO brand would be the result of the process.

Branding was proving to be a challenge beyond the name. The studio lot's iconic white water tower, which had borne the studio's royal-blue "WB" logo for decades, had a new look for WarnerMedia Day. It was festooned with the purple-hued logo for HBO Max. The logo had been refreshed not long before being plastered all over the lot. Three months before the event, in July 2019, the first version of it drew jeers when it debuted publicly, creating a hiccup months before the service went live. That version's mash-up of the classic Avant Garde Gothic HBO logo (created in 1975 by Bemis Balkind, the same design firm behind the ESPN and CNN logos) and a round-edged, lowercase "max" was perplexing from the first glance. Exacerbating the problem was the way the last of the lowercase letters was elongated in a distracting, exaggerated way. The effect was not unlike the jaunty exclamation points and waggish punctuation attached to startup names from Yahoo! to Del.icio.us. Design firm Trollbäck+Company, one of dozens of vendors hired to get HBO Max off the ground, was called upon to make a quick logo change, a highly unusual move in consumer marketing, given that untold "impressions" from the first try at the logo could linger. The revamp made all three letters a uniform size and left the "HBO" part alone, implementing a blue-and-violet gradient color scheme. The firm said its goal was to give the new streaming service a "friendly personality," with the colors emphasizing its "vibrant spectrum of content." *Hollywood Reporter* TV critic Tim Goodman, assessing the July reveal of HBO Max's look and details, called its typeface "ugly" and wondered, "'What did the letter X ever do wrong to WarnerMedia (or the designer)?'"

The logo misfire was a glimpse at how hard those duck feet continued to paddle. The pressure was starting to mount. Just three days after WarnerMedia Day, Apple TV+ would light up, free for the first year for anyone with a new Apple device. Disney+ would debut less than two weeks after that, with a six-month free trial for Verizon customers. It was increasingly looking like HBO Max would be the last one into the pool.

Technology was another reason for concern. Designing a full-blown, direct-to-consumer streaming service reconciling content from divisions long operated autonomously, with capabilities for advertising and live broadcasts down the line, would be tricky on such a short timeline. And, as WarnerMedia's chief technology officer Jeremy Legg knew full well, viewers would not tolerate glitches. When servers crashed in 2014 during the fourth season premiere of *Game of Thrones* streamed on HBO Go, it sparked social media backlash. In 2020, the stakes would be much higher, and the engineering outfit that had brought HBO Go and HBO Now to life—BAMTech—had been acquired by Disney for its own streaming effort, so it wouldn't play a role in HBO Max. This new service was meant to be the future, not a supplement. CEO Randall Stephenson had already proclaimed HBO Max as "the workhorse" of AT&T.

"Traditional television service, while largely maligned as it relates to the consumer experience, works really well from a technical perspective," Legg said. "You turn the TV on, the video plays. It's very rare that television service goes down. And that's because the infrastructure is owned." Streaming, on the other hand, could never be owned by any one company. It operates on a managed network, with a range of participants. Bandwidth and cloud infrastructure for streaming have to be bought, and the price rises with demand. Plus, "every point along the delivery chain is owned by someone else, and the technologies are often different," Legg said. A single service would need to operate seamlessly at large scale, across dozens of networks and distribution points. And unlike Netflix, which had thousands of engineers working on a single app, WarnerMedia's more modest tech forces were also tasked with handling live broadcasts and other projects related to the company's linear networks.

The only way to manage through the crush of deadlines in the short term was to delay the launch. Instead of rolling out an early version of the service in the fourth quarter of 2019, with the official debut in early 2020, HBO Max was now ticketed for spring 2020.

Any of the challenges facing WarnerMedia in 2019—lining up streaming technology, creating a name and logo for the streaming service, settling on content strategy—paled next to the massive restructuring that had overhauled the company months earlier. The team standing inside Stage 21 looked a lot different from the one that had started the year. A reorganization of epic proportions had reshaped WarnerMedia, breaking down the barriers between its HBO, Warner Bros., and Turner divisions—which Bewkes had deliberately kept separate, to provide him with more options for an eventual sale. Hundreds of employees exited, including dozens of senior executives with centuries of combined experience. Richard Plepler, the twenty-seven-year veteran of HBO who rose from publicist to CEO and was considered the architect of its creative renaissance, as well as a powerhouse in New York media, entertainment, and political circles, departed eight months after AT&T finalized its acquisition of Time Warner. David Levy, who spent thirty-two years at Turner, rising from junior sales associate to president and building its estimable portfolio of valuable sports rights, left on the same day. Dozens of others, each carrying with them intimate knowledge of how prestige media brands were built, were cut loose.

AT&T had promised Wall Street it would achieve $2 billion in cost savings. But most of the focus was supposed to be on back-office and administrative functions, not the creative executives who had been the public faces of the company for years. Time Warner veterans felt the plunge into streaming could work, but only under certain conditions. "Let us say yes to things we want to say yes to," one of the alums said. "Improve the data we get on our viewing. Let's add some programming that matters." Instead, the executive continued, "they blew the whole fucking thing up."

As the pink slips were still flying (and staffers with at least ten years of service took buyouts), Chief Financial Officer John Stephens took the stage at a Wall Street investment conference. He insisted that the company was not looking to play the heavy. It was surveying every nook and cranny of its $500 billion in assets—real estate, land, minority investments, digital assets—for things it could shed to pay down debt. "We wanted to protect the culture," Stephens said of WarnerMedia as he somehow kept a straight face. "A finance bean-counter from a telephone company doesn't want to go in and spoil what is a tremendously good asset."

Far from being protected, the culture of WarnerMedia was being loaded into a corporate Cuisinart and pureed into something unrecognizable. It wasn't that longtime staffers all yearned for the status quo. One CNN executive described Time Warner before AT&T as "almost like a government bureaucracy," with a lot of workers in a comfortable form of stasis. "We're a company that sucks at systems, and so we are so rooted in relationships and who knows who." But AT&T was making a dizzying series of changes that threatened to fry the circuit board. Activist investment firm Elliott Management, after acquiring a $3 billion stake in AT&T, launched an attack on the company, arguing it needed to cut DirecTV loose and jettison top management, including Stankey. On the day before WarnerMedia Day, the parties announced a truce. The leadership team, Elliott agreed, deserved a chance to get HBO Max off the ground and make other moves to turn things around.

The personification of the new overseers at AT&T trying to put their stamp on the company was a DirecTV veteran named Brad Bentley. The executive, who'd spent much of his fifteen-year run at the satellite TV operator working in sales and marketing, had worked with Stankey on rolling out the internet-delivered TV bundle DirecTV Now (later known as AT&T TV Now) in 2016. In overseeing the DirecTV Now event, which was held just weeks after AT&T announced its offer to acquire Time Warner, he made sure it delivered one head-turning reveal. DirecTV Now customers could get HBO as part of their package for just $5 a month. The promotional rate, an unheard-of discount from the typical $15 price, meant AT&T would book a loss on each subscriber, but it was designed to show the value it would bring consumers as the owner of Time Warner. (Federal antitrust regulators would cite AT&T's bundling of HBO for DirecTV customers in the antitrust lawsuit they filed in 2017 to try to block the deal.)

In 2015, AT&T had spent $49 billion to acquire DirecTV, becoming the number one pay-TV provider in the U.S. with twenty-six million subscribers across satellite and its existing U-verse cable systems. Immediately after the ink dried on the transaction, though, cord-cutting started hitting DirecTV hard, and between 2015 and 2019 it lost about 20 percent of its customers. Stankey and AT&T CEO Randall Stephenson did not deny the traditional business was eroding but said DirecTV's customer relationships would be invaluable as TV migrated online. Enter DirecTV Now, which was among several "skinny bundle" services crowding the market. Once thought of as fleet successors to traditional pay-TV operators, with no annual contract and a leaner, cheaper offering of channels, the skinny bundles soon got fat, adding channels and hiking prices. DirecTV Now had gained subscribers for several consecutive quarters after launching. But just two years later, with HBO Max waiting in the wings, the product Bentley and Stankey had ushered into the world was already fading from the scene. Today, the AT&T–DirecTV deal has been pilloried by most investors and Wall Street analysts. Craig Moffett, a veteran analyst with MoffettNathanson, has called the unit that houses DirecTV a "cancer" on AT&T.

Warner Bros., Turner Broadcasting, and HBO for decades had operated independently. Now, stripped of layers of employees and suddenly needing to crack the streaming code, the workforce intermingled, but with a mix of camaraderie and anxiety. Asked to describe these meetings, participants return to a single word: "weird." There was "weird body language," as one put it, especially among the HBO rank and file, which had the most to lose. Every conversation with an HBO staffer revealed a bone-deep suspicion that what they were devoting long hours to was a pastiche. Scott Galloway, a marketing professor at NYU, spoke for many when he flagged the high degree of brand-perception risk of the venture. "AT&T purchased Time Warner in the hopes that phone service and content would yield a peanut butter and chocolate combination," he said. "Instead, AT&T is junking up Time Warner's luxury product, HBO, and turning it into HBO Max. This is the equivalent of Hermès selling JanSport alongside Birkin bags."

Just after the Time Warner deal closed in 2018, Bentley was given significantly broader entertainment oversight as executive vice president and general manager of direct-to-consumer operations for WarnerMedia. According to the accounts of numerous current and former employees, Bentley cut a quixotic figure when interacting with the entertainment teams, many of whom had decades of seniority. His style would end up achieving something unlikely: bringing Reilly and Greenblatt into complete sync in considering him the biggest obstacle standing in the way of HBO Max's success.

Bentley, like the rest of the AT&T brass, had embraced the language of streaming, particularly the notion of moving toward direct-to-consumer operations. "'You've just got to get out of the wholesale business in the next four years and you'll be able to attract DTC subscribers,'" one former senior executive recalls his saying. The executive's reply: "But there's *not* a one-to-one relationship. We're bundled." Multiple meetings were devoted to figuring out ways to promote the last season of *Game of Thrones* from the TBS telecasts of the NCAA Final Four basketball tournament, a step beyond the Bud Light Super Bowl ad. And Bentley, who had created the first direct sales operation at DirecTV, had another hard sell: putting ads on HBO. Bentley felt the network's prestige air was an untapped resource, an Arctic National Wildlife Refuge just waiting to be drilled. He was reminded that the founding premise of HBO was that it was a premium network, running everything commercial-free. Legally, having signed countless talent deals affirming its ad-free environment, it couldn't insert ads even if it wanted to. Bentley stuck to his guns, leaning on his ad-sales background to oversee the creation of business plans for the ad-supported version of HBO Max, which he believed would enable the service to start to recoup its losses.

Bentley ultimately failed WarnerMedia's version of the Netflix keeper test, leaving the company a few months before WarnerMedia Day. He is now president of a Southern California renewable energy firm called Inspire. While Bentley's exit eased some of the friction in the organization, the two-headed structure for HBO Max still proved unwieldy.

FOR REILLY AND GREENBLATT, INTRODUCING CLIPS and reeling off the programming planned for HBO Max on WarnerMedia Day drew on well-developed sets of muscles. Being a successful TV executive meant constant promotion, at the annual upfronts for advertisers and twice-yearly gatherings of the Television Critics Association. The art and science of these pitches was hooking the audience with enough elements—stars, creators, concept—and a smidgen of footage, with scarcity leaving them wanting more. In the social media age, the goal was online buzz. WarnerMedia Day generated a good amount of that, thanks to the dozens of original shows and movies announced that day. Stankey's virtuous cycle depended on a product offering far deeper than that of HBO.

The slate was headed by a special reuniting the cast of *Friends*, which was planned as the marquee launch title. The Warner Bros.–produced sitcom had been a popular streaming draw on Netflix for years before WarnerMedia wrested it away in a $425 million, five-year deal. Other major gets included the library of the longtime Disney affiliate Studio Ghibli, whose animated features included *My Neighbor Totoro* and *Spirited Away*. *South Park*, another mainstay of animation from another company's stable, ViacomCBS network Comedy Central, was acquired for more than $500 million. Titles were drawn from more than a dozen WarnerMedia brands—films from Warner Bros. and Turner Classic Movies; series from TNT, TBS, Adult Swim, and Cartoon Network; anime from Crunchyroll.

Reilly and Greenblatt's remarks gestured at the potential of streaming but they were rooted in the era of television's supremacy. Reilly, for example, made an impassioned argument for releasing episodes one at a time, instead of the all-at-once binge drops of Netflix. "We like creating cultural impact and nurturing maximum IP value from our IP," Reilly said. "Our creators also see the difference in rolling out shows gradually and letting them breathe. HBO hits like *Succession* and *Chernobyl* became part of the zeitgeist with a weekly release schedule rather than fading quickly after a binge and burn. We know people love to binge, and on HBO Max, you can binge previous seasons and library content to your heart's desire."

As head of HBO Max Originals, Sarah Aubrey, a Reilly lieutenant at TNT and TBS, was able to ignore the strictures of linear TV and fully focus on streaming. Before landing at WarnerMedia in 2015, Aubrey was a producer, first on indie films like *Lars and the Real Girl* and *Bad Santa* and then as a partner with Peter Berg, where she produced *Friday Night Lights* and the HBO series *The Leftovers*.

As a producer-turned-suit, she said she had reconciled herself to the role played by algorithms. "We call it 'Gut-Data-Gut,'" she said in an interview prior to WarnerMedia Day. "You can really love something but then you need to see if the data can support it and help you understand what audiences to go to." Discussing her producing days, she said, "I used to hate data. Data used to be something that would do nothing but cost us our marketing budget. You'd go into a test screening and they'd say, 'Congratulations, you scored one hundred!' Or they'd say, 'Well, this wasn't so great,' or 'This could be better.'"

One of the biggest coups for WarnerMedia on the eve of its investor pitch was signing an exclusive deal with film and TV producer and director J. J. Abrams. The deal was a huge validation for an old-line media company, as was a major renewal with TV powerhouse Greg Berlanti (who made a brief appearance via video at WarnerMedia Day). Abrams, known for rebooting both the *Star Wars* and *Star Trek* film franchises, also had created TV hits like *Lost* and *Alias*. After taking meetings with a range of suitors for a year, he had turned down an offer from Apple said to be worth about twice as much. Some of his peers on the top of the A-list had been scooped up by Netflix, and tech companies were constantly on the lookout for talent they could hook from the traditional pool. Apple held enormous appeal for Bad Robot, the company Abrams runs with his wife, Katie McGrath, given their interest in developing the company into a consumer brand. But Apple also lacked theatrical distribution, something Abrams considered to be table stakes. WarnerMedia would shift Abrams's film pipeline to Warner Bros. Pictures from Paramount and unify it with Warner Bros. Television, where he had been set up since 2006.

In showcasing Bad Robot, WarnerMedia took a decidedly different tack than Disney had on its investor day six months earlier. Disney, looking to show its potential to leverage major Hollywood talent in pursuit of streaming, welcomed director and producer Jon Favreau, who appeared in jeans, sneakers, and an untucked shirt. His delivery was the exact opposite of his casual outfit: crisply on message. The director and producer revealed footage from *The Mandalorian* as well as his feature remake of *The Lion King*, which would end up on Disney+ down the road.

Abrams, a creative potentate of equal stature to Favreau, was dressed similarly and is accustomed to hitting his marks and delivering what is called for on a corporate occasion—as he had onstage in Cupertino, bantering warmly with Sara Bareilles about the forthcoming Apple TV+ romantic comedy *Little Voice*. Unlike Favreau, though, he had no projects to discuss. *Demimonde*, a sci-fi drama Abrams had created for HBO, was the only title he mentioned by name, and it was in a very uncertain state after parting ways with its original showrunner. Abrams turned on the charm but offered only quips and platitudes. "I stand before you today clearly underdressed," he wanly joked before heaping praise on the executive suite. John Stankey, he said, "blew [Bad Robot] away with his vision, his ambition for what AT&T could do as the parent company of this extraordinary studio," but he added, "He makes me call him Mr. Stankey." (Zing!) While he concluded by saying "anything is possible" for WarnerMedia, Abrams conceded, "It's too early to go into specifics," adding that Bad Robot was "in talks with HBO Max about some projects that I cannot wait for the world to see."

Far from a lean-forward moment that proved HBO Max would bring maximum firepower to the streaming fight, the segment elicited shrugs—if it even registered at all.

"Everybody was like, 'J. J. will do what J. J. will do,'" recalled one of the executives who had orchestrated the event. Abrams, one of the most powerful creative forces in the industry, looked like he had ambled through Studio 21 on his way to the gym.

Once the last sizzle reel had played, a key moment fell to Tony Goncalves, who oversaw many of the product and distribution details about HBO Max. Goncalves also handled the big reveal: the price and release date of HBO Max. The price was $14.99 a month—on par with expectations, though higher numbers had been considered internally—and the release date would be May 2020. It was official: HBO Max would be the last and one of the most expensive of the new streaming services coming to market, and $2 more than the most popular version of Netflix. John Stephens, chief financial officer of AT&T, then offered five-year projections for its growth and said the break-even point would come in 2024, after $4 billion had been invested. "What you've seen here today, I don't think is like anything else," AT&T CEO Randall Stephenson said, closing the official program. "This is not Netflix. This is not Disney. This is uniquely HBO Max."

The house lights came up and it was time for the Q & A period with analysts. By and large, they were favorably impressed. While AT&T stock barely budged the next day, most of them expressed upbeat reactions in the room and their reports to clients would reflect that optimism. There may not have been the gasp-inducing moment of Disney's $7 price reveal, but it seemed that WarnerMedia was very much a viable streaming contender. In Reilly's estimation, "It was a successful day, but not Disney."

The nagging question of brand confusion became an unavoidable one: it already ran two other HBO-branded streaming services and was about to launch a third. "How do you explain *that* to the consumer?" one senior executive had wondered before the investor day. "I don't think that challenge really hit us until we were well down the road with this." Colby Synesael, an analyst with Cowen, also was puzzled by that after the two-hour presentation. He asked a two-part question: the first concerned pay-TV operators' response to HBO Max, the second part zeroed in on the existential dilemma. "What's going to happen to traditional HBO and HBO Now?" he asked. "It seems like with you giving your affiliates access to HBO Max, those, over time, will have lesser value."

Stankey asked Goncalves to assess the state of negotiations before he handled the latter part of the question, about potential brand confusion. Having had a solid minute to reflect on his answer to the potential for HBO brand confusion, Stankey proceeded to give the kind of blunt, almost bruising answer that had become his calling card. "I look at it as a degree of an IQ test," he said, his serious expression never wavering. "Why wouldn't you want twice the content for the same price?" As he continued talking, his words became more wonky by the second. "It will be that [HBO] product standing alone, as well as that product co-resident in the Max offer, whichever way the customer chooses to get it," he said. "We'll make all the right decisions internally about ultimately re-platforming Go and Now onto the same technology platform, and we'll skin them and we'll have the ability to render strictly HBO content on the same technology platform so we're not maintaining two or three different technology sets to deal with that, but that's our approach to it."

A small ripple passed through the audience, a barely perceptible murmur as attendees took the full measure of Stankey's response. Though he is often described as sardonic and much funnier than he can come off in public appearances, he had just delivered a pitch to customers that sounded more like a taunt. By this reasoning, it wasn't up to WarnerMedia to minimize confusion and articulate the reason to sign up for HBO Max—even to existing customers who already paid for regular HBO. It was a test the customer would simply have to be smart enough to pass. Which raises the question: What if they fail?

Executives onstage with Stankey managed to project a calm exterior, but internally many winced. One later said George C. Scott could have played Stankey in the movie version of the HBO Max saga. "He is so convinced he is right, he has this military style about him. The language and the communication are just so inscrutable." WarnerMedia staffers watching the webcast could hardly believe this was their leader's stated view of customer relations. After Jeff Bewkes's infamous comparison of Netflix with the Albanian army, Stankey's comment would become one of the most oft-quoted lines about the streaming business.

"There's an expression I've heard used about surgeons, military leaders, and in the business world: 'often wrong, never in doubt,'" one former senior WarnerMedia executive said. "I think that holds true of John."

PART IV

The Incumbent Responds

CHAPTER 17

▶ Netflix Bets on Itself

The solitary figure of Reed Hastings appeared for a Zoom interview from his son's childhood bedroom, the early-morning light barely illuminating the unadorned loft space that had become his familiar backdrop on the company's pandemic-era earnings calls. It was a far cry from Netflix's dynamic Sunset Boulevard offices in Los Angeles, with its video wall, trophy case, and constant hum of activity. This tableau's royal-blue bedspread, wood accents, and lone landscape photograph on one wall resembled a low-fi version of *MTV Cribs*, as Recode's senior data reporter Rani Molla quipped on social media.

It was nonetheless a fitting setting for Netflix's cofounder, whose streaming service revolutionized home entertainment. The Silicon Valley entrepreneur, once dismissed as a Hollywood also-ran, had vanquished home video colossus Blockbuster; popularized whatever-you-want, whenever-you-want viewing (and, in the process, rendered prime-time network TV schedules irrelevant); and ignited the "streaming wars." On this July morning, Hastings seemed unperturbed about the forces of Hollywood allied against Netflix, seeking to knock it off its streaming throne.

"What people forget is, it's always been intense competition," said the unflappable Hastings. "I mean, Amazon did streaming at the same time we did in 2007, so we've been competing with Amazon for thirteen years."

Numerous accounts from people doing business with the company, though, suggest Netflix perceived a heightened competitive threat. One creator and showrunner behind a top Netflix title said Disney's entry, in particular, triggered a restlessness in the atmosphere and sparked a frenzy to spend lavishly to secure top talent.

While the atmosphere changed, though, there was plenty of reason for Hastings to feel confident. As the global pandemic darkened movie theaters, silenced concerts and festivals, and hobbled professional sports, Netflix had only gained momentum, emerging as the entertainment choice of preference for a home-bound, bored world seeking an escape. Its shows had entered the zeitgeist, whether with a lurid obsession like *Tiger King: Murder, Mayhem and Madness*; a goofy reality show based on the game the Floor Is Lava; or an adrenaline-filled action flick such as Chris Hemsworth's *Extraction*. It also had laid claim to prestige TV, eclipsing HBO to rack up a record 160 Emmy Award nominations in 2020, and asserted itself at the Oscars, supported by lavishly financed awards campaigns.

The depth of Netflix's protective moat would be revealed as subscribers flocked to the service for entertainment refuge, as the unseen virus spread across the globe. Netflix added as many customers in the first six months of 2020 as in all of 2019, though that torrid growth rate leveled off by the summer of 2020. Sales rose 25 percent and earnings jumped 73 percent in the first nine months of the year. As most streaming rivals, save for Disney, struggled to find their footing in this new environment, Netflix was firmly ensconced. It was rooted in the television firmament. For millions of consumers, Netflix had become synonymous with TV. As he had for more than two decades, Hastings continued touting the culture of innovation that had allowed Netflix to triumph over larger, more entrenched competitors like Blockbuster. "I'm also confident that it will help us serve our members best now, and find ways of serving our members better than HBO does, or better than Disney does," Hastings said. "Because they've got so much internal process around things that it slows them down."

The future wasn't so clear in the summer of 2017, when Netflix found itself with a red-envelope-colored target on its back, as Disney, the company responsible for reshaping the modern entertainment landscape, announced it would launch a competing service.

When Disney chairman and CEO Bob Iger told investors he planned to pull the company's blockbuster films from Netflix and reserve them for the 2019 launch of its own on-demand service, one prominent media analyst, John Janedis, predicted a coming sea change, as other media companies followed suit. Netflix's stock, which had been on a roll, took an immediate hit. But inside the streamer, the news that electrified Wall Street hardly caused a ripple. The response was: Disney, what took you so long?

"The feeling at Netflix was that these entries were inevitable and the more the merrier because internet TV is better than linear TV," said one former executive. "The launch of new streaming services was always seen as likelier to put the final nail in the cable coffin than hurt Netflix . . . and that seems to be the case."

That's not to say Netflix failed to respond. Less than a week after Disney's announcement, the streaming giant said it had signed ABC's most prolific showrunner, Shonda Rhimes, the creator of such hit shows as *Grey's Anatomy* and *Scandal* and executive producer of *How to Get Away with Murder*, to a multiyear, nine-figure deal that two sources say exceeded $150 million.

Netflix had been courting Rhimes since the fall of 2016, even though she had a year left on her ABC contract. She had spent her entire career, up to that point, maintaining a grueling schedule of producing twenty-four episodes of *Grey's Anatomy* every season, structuring the narratives around commercial breaks. She was ready to try something new.

"There were things she wanted to say, stories she wanted to tell and bring into the world, that just existed better on a platform that was more fluid and not as limited," said her agent, Chris Silbermann.

Rhimes and Silbermann met with Sarandos for breakfast at Republique, a modern French eatery housed in a two-story Spanish-style building with soaring arches, a courtyard with a fountain, and a nostalgic connection to old Hollywood. It had been built in the late 1920s as a business investment for Charlie Chaplin. Silbermann described it as just a casual meeting to see how everyone would get along. The deal terms, which Disney declined to match, were hammered out later, he said.

"He understood what I was looking for—the opportunity to build a vibrant new storytelling home for writers with the unique creative freedom and instantaneous global reach provided by Netflix's singular sense of innovation," Rhimes said, referring to Sarandos, as the Netflix deal was announced.

Sarandos informed his longtime content collaborator, Cindy Holland, about his desire to reach an overall deal with Rhimes. She had known that this day would inevitably come, as the television studios that had locked top creators into long-term deals grew resistant to their showrunners' selling projects to a competitor like Netflix.

"There are going to be four to five really big global players, and there's only so much talent that is proven to be globally successful, so there's going to be a fight for resources," Holland said. "There were good reasons to do it. *Grey's Anatomy* had been very successful on a second-run basis on Netflix. 'We can do that,'" she remembered telling Sarandos, adding, "'That means you're going to tip the first domino and you're going to start a very big war for talent.'"

The headline-grabbing talent deal signaled a shift in strategy for Netflix, which had aggressively ramped up its spending of billions of dollars on original content with the expectation that media companies would eventually withdraw their movies and television shows from Netflix to bolster their own services.

Speaking at a UBS investor conference in New York in 2018, Sarandos said Netflix had set out to "wean" itself of its dependency on third-party suppliers and cultivate its own content and creative relationships. Its ambitions had expanded year by year since it entered the original content arena in 2012, across more genres and regions of the world. By 2018, Netflix was spending billions to stock its library, but soon would see some of its most popular titles leave because rivals refused to license them anymore. The company began programming for an array of tastes, augmenting its scripted fare with twenty reality shows, including a refurbished version of the popular fashion makeover show *Queer Eye*. It green-lit an eclectic slate of original series, from the futuristic *Altered Carbon*, to the controversial teen suicide drama *13 Reasons Why*, to a fourth season of the resurrected dysfunctional-family sitcom *Arrested Development*. As Netflix's content flowed onto millions of screens around the world, it invested deeply in local-language production to attract subscribers from Darfur to Kuala Lumpur.

Netflix discovered its shows effortlessly traveled the borderless world of the internet, propelled by local-language dubbing and its recommendation engine. The German time-travel series *Dark*, the postapocalyptic Danish series *The Rain*, India's crime thriller *Sacred Games*, and France's action mystery *Lupin* would find audiences well beyond their countries of origin. Meanwhile, veteran studio executive Scott Stuber launched Netflix's pursuit of a Best Picture Oscar with *Roma*, director Alfonso Cuarón's sumptuous black-and-white portrait of a domestic worker set in 1970s Mexico City. "We keep investing more in programming, but we're also getting more users and more hours of usage from our existing users," said Sarandos, explaining Netflix's content strategy. "Meaning there's a lot more growth." Netflix began scrutinizing individual shows for their cost relative to global subscriber acquisition. Hollywood producers, who for decades had made an enviable living by running the gauntlet of getting shows on the air or online, suddenly had to contemplate their material's appeal to India or other large global populations.

Its pursuit of top talent intensified in the wake of the deal with Rhimes. If Hollywood refused to license Netflix its popular films and TV reruns, the streaming service would simply lay claim to the most coveted creators, offering extravagant sums to develop movies and series exclusively for the streaming platform. It's the same approach Netflix uses when recruiting programmers or entertainment executives: identify the "rock stars" and pay them more than competitors would. The resulting bidding war heightened the studios' resentment of Netflix, as it forced rivals to pay more to keep top creators from defecting.

Netflix wasted no time securing the industry's boldfaced names. In February 2018, it struck a five-year, $300 million deal with Ryan Murphy, the producer of such hits as *American Horror Story, Pose, Nip/Tuck,* and *Glee*. Five months later, it signed Kenya Barris to a three-year contract worth roughly $100 million. The creator of the ABC hit *Black-ish*, the first broadcast TV comedy in years to feature a Black family, had run into conflict with the network over its refusal to air an episode that dealt with the controversy over athletes' kneeling to protest police brutality during performances of the national anthem.

When pressed about this sort of drunken-sailor spending at *Vanity Fair*'s 2018 New Establishment Summit in Beverly Hills, Sarandos shifted from new age studio executive to quant. He said the agreements with Murphy and Rhimes, as with any other content deal, were informed by years of viewing data. Netflix has been carrying Murphy's shows since *Nip/Tuck* started airing on FX, and audiences are reliably drawn to the shows' sexy, darkly funny sensibility.

"So we have a long history with Ryan and I think we've sized that deal to his proportionate value," said Sarandos, adding that the service could validate the spending through subscriber gains. "Is Ryan enhancing the Netflix subscription? Is that a reason—having access to those shows—is that a reason why I join Netflix? And that's incredibly valuable if it is."

The same is true of Rhimes, whose long-running medical drama *Grey's Anatomy* is one of the most-watched shows on Netflix. The showrunner would later validate Sarandos's bet with *Bridgerton*, a period romance that became one of the streamer's biggest series ever. Within a month of its Christmas Day 2020 premiere, it had reached eighty-two million households around the world. That made it, for a time, the company's most successful original series.

In a less heralded move, Netflix began filling the children's programming void that Disney's planned withdrawal would create. It struck a deal with Glen Keane, a veteran Disney animator who brought to life such popular contemporary characters as Ariel in *The Little Mermaid* and the Beast in *Beauty and the Beast*. Keane agreed to direct *Over the Moon*, an animated musical film about a girl who builds a rocket ship and blasts off in hopes of meeting a moon goddess. Children's programming is a critical component of subscriber retention, as any parent might attest.

"The more members of a household that use a service like Netflix, the less likely they'd be to cancel," explains Andy Yeatman, Netflix's former director of kids' and family content. "As an adult, as a parent, I'll get into a show. I might not use a service in between seasons of that show. But if my children are using the service, I'm very unlikely to cancel. That's why you're seeing a focus on kids and family."

Netflix did its best to hang on to popular network reruns for as long as it could, as it furiously stocked its library with originals. In December 2018, it paid an enormous sum, $100 million, to keep *Friends* for another year—reportedly triple what it had previously paid to bring Ross, Rachel, Joey, Monica, and Chandler to subscribers' living rooms. It was only a matter of time before these enduring favorites would disappear.

"Some of the incumbents should expect that their libraries are going to become a lot thinner," WarnerMedia chief executive John Stankey suggested in remarks to investors, without identifying Netflix by name.

NBCUniversal reclaimed the rights to all nine seasons of *The Office*, with the entire staff of Dunder Mifflin packing up to move home to the network's streaming service, Peacock, in January 2021. WarnerMedia outbid Netflix for the rights to *Friends*, paying a reported $425 million over five years to secure the streaming rights for HBO Max in time for its launch on May 27, 2020. Netflix scored one victory: winning the bidding war for another popular network sitcom, *Seinfeld*, from Sony Pictures Television. The following year, in 2021, it signed a five-year deal with the studio for exclusive U.S. rights to Sony's films once they leave theaters and on-demand services.

Hastings shrugged off the loss of popular reruns, telling investors,

"We're ready for it, anticipating it, and in fact we are eager to have more and more of our money to be able to do spectacular new titles."

While maintaining a calm exterior, veteran tech entrepreneur Jim Lanzone says his friend Reed Hastings is likely living the credo of all Silicon Valley entrepreneurs. It was perhaps best captured by the late Intel CEO Andy Grove's most famous slogan: "Only the paranoid survive," which became the title of his bestselling book describing his management philosophy.

"He's never going to take his competition lightly," said Lanzone. "Until the day he leaves his company, he will be pushing them as if tomorrow could be their last day."

As Netflix crossed the two-hundred-million-subscriber mark, Hastings celebrated the milestone in the same way he'd observed earlier mileposts of one million and one hundred million customers—with a steak dinner ordered from Denny's. But at Netflix there would be no resting on its laurels. A month before the culture-defining drama *The Queen's Gambit* debuted on the service, becoming Netflix's most-watched limited scripted series, Netflix ousted Holland. The move stunned Hollywood and even some of the company's suppliers. The creator of one of the most successful shows on Netflix described Holland's exit as "shocking," but added that even the most fruitful partnerships in entertainment run their course. Perhaps it shouldn't have come as a surprise. In Hastings's book, *No Rules Rules*, he relays a number of reflections from staffers about the company's evolution, often as detailed through the company's famously candid 360 evaluations. One such critique, shared by Sarandos, hinted at friction between the original architects of Netflix's programming strategy. "Your 'old married couple' disagreements with Cindy are not the best role model of exec interchange," Larry Tanz, vice president of content, wrote to Sarandos. "There should be more listening and understanding on both your parts."

In Holland's place, the company named as the new head of global television Bela Bajaria. The executive had seen a meteoric rise over her four years at the company, starting out with unscripted and licensed programming before moving to local-language originals. She set about reorganizing the TV troops. Many veterans departed along with Holland, sensing change in the winds. Bajaria recruited or promoted people she had worked closely with for years, but that often meant showrunners with great track records were having to reckon with a new management regime and an adjusted strategy.

Bajaria had championed shows with a more mainstream sensibility, such as the stalker thriller *You* (among several shows cannily plucked from cable and broadcast networks and turned into hits by Netflix) and the reboot of *Queer Eye*. Her background in unscripted shows tied her to the wildfire success of reality shows at Netflix just three years after they were added to the programming mix. (Reed Hastings readily admits he was wrong to initially object to entering the reality game.) These series, which cost dramatically less than *The Crown* and its ilk, in many ways had come to define the service by 2020. Every couple of weeks, the streaming giant seemed to strike gold (based on limited available numbers) with new takes on dating shows (*Love Is Blind*), competition (*Floor Is Lava*), cooking (*Nailed It!*), real estate (*Selling Sunset*), and home decorating (*Tidying Up with Marie Kondo*). Many of the unscripted shows deviated from the binge model the company had introduced, with individual episodes being fed to viewers one at a time, just like in the old TV days.

The reorganization, another embarrassingly public demonstration of Netflix's dispassionate "keeper test," reflected the streaming giant's efforts to create more broadly appealing shows. In her eighteen-year tenure, Holland had put Netflix on the map as a maker of high-quality original series, but Netflix's culture had no room for sentimentality. "We've always said it's a team, not family," said Hastings. "I'm trying to do what I see is the right thing for the company, and that they've signed up for that performance orientation. So, people whose primary drive is job security, they don't come to Netflix." Asked months later about the circumstances of her exit, in her first interview since leaving, Holland declined to address the topic.

"They basically did an analysis of all of their programming and saw that their international scripted and their unscripted programming, which was delivering huge for them, is just tremendously more cost-effective," said one Hollywood dealmaker. That meant Bajaria, for the moment, was the keeper. There would still be bumps, however. The pace of Netflix's subscriber growth slowed by the spring of 2021, which the company blamed on pandemic-related production delays that resulted in fewer big shows. The quarterly financials failed to impress Wall Street, and investors punished the stock. As with previous rough patches, though, this one proved to be short-lived. By the autumn, shares had passed $600, establishing yet another all-time high.

PART V

Meeting the Public

CHAPTER 18

▶ Liftoff

By the time Kevin Mayer went to bed at two A.M. on launch day, he was feeling exuberant. The Disney+ service, which had consumed his life for more than a year, was attracting hundreds of thousands of people who raced to sign up as soon as the service went live at midnight on November 12, 2019. It was on track to surpass his wildest expectations. Mayer sent a message to Disney CEO Bob Iger, saying the service might reach two million subscribers on its first day. The boss's response: "That's awesome." Disney's bold bet on the future was paying off.

Mayer slept for a few hours, woke up, and glanced at his phone. The screen was filled with missed-call messages, the caller's name in bold letters: Bob Iger. Bob Iger. Bob Iger.

"What's going on?" Mayer wondered, now fully awake. He looked at the app and realized the service was down. "And I was like, 'Oh my God, how could this be happening?'"

Mayer called the BAMTech team in New York, knowing that Disney streaming president Michael Paull and chief technologist Joe Inzerillo had planned to work through the night to midwife the Disney+ birth. They confirmed his worst fears: the system was down and people were unable to sign up. They initially suspected the e-commerce system, which the BAMTech team had repeatedly tested and for which it had built backup systems as a fail-safe against a technical malfunction.

"We talked a lot about redundancy, and a lot about failovers, so if something goes down, you go to the next system. We really simplified our login procedures . . . to make sure that wasn't a big bottleneck," said Mayer. "So, we thought we were in pretty good shape."

Paull talked confidently about the lessons BAMTech had learned about system overloads and crashes, drawing from the embarrassing 2016 outage during the highly anticipated "Battle of the Bastards" episode of *Game of Thrones* on HBO Now, which it powered.

"Fortunately, we've had the experience with *Game of Thrones*, we've had the experience of ESPN+ with the big pay-per-view events that we're doing with UFC exclusively on our platform," he told the Verge. "We're getting big bursts. We've built capabilities to sustain that, both in terms of processing the transactions that all come in—in a very, very short period of time—as well as the streams."

Within a matter of hours, the BAMTech team offered Mayer a preliminary diagnosis: a flaw in Amazon Web Services' real-time customer analytics software. Mayer urged Inzerillo to fix it, adding, "This is not good." Word leaked out to the press that a "third-party vendor" was to blame.

"At midnight, the system was humming along fine. Everyone was going through as many checks as possible. Clearly, everyone was streaming the first episode of *Mandalorian*, it was all on point," said one West Coast–based tech executive. "Little did we know it was going to be a *Game of Thrones*–style [event] where people were calling in sick . . . So the moment the East Coast came online, it was a tsunami of traffic, just an absolute ton of traffic. It just overwhelmed the front end."

Mayer contacted Amazon CEO Andy Jassy—who at the time headed the company's cloud computing business, which powers a number of streaming services, including Netflix—to ask what had gone wrong. Jassy offered to take the fall for the Disney glitch but said the real problem was with Disney's own app. BAMTech had hacked Amazon Web Services' search function to deliver movie and TV recommendations—not an intended use. Inzerillo developed a manual work-around that got the service up and running within a matter of hours and kept the

Disney+ app functioning until BAMTech offered an updated version of the app weeks later. About one-third of people who had trouble getting through the front door couldn't remember their passwords, a problem Disney helped create by requiring consumers to use the same login as when they bought theme park tickets, booked travel through the Disney Vacation Club, or shopped its online stores, said the tech executive. Since these are occasional activities, memory lapses were inevitable.

Mayer publicly exonerated AWS at the Code Media conference in Hollywood a week later, attributing the problem to the app's architecture. "If something's your fault, damn it, you take responsibility for it," Mayer said. "I'm a very strong believer in that."

Disney had been stoking anticipation for the service for months, taking advantage of the media's seemingly insatiable interest in all things Disney to generate exhaustive coverage about the forthcoming service. The marketing kicked off with Disney's biennial fan event, D23, held within walking distance of Disneyland in Anaheim, California. A two-plus-hour showcase in August 2019 highlighted the original films and series coming to the Disney+ service—with fan favorites putting in appearances, including Ewan McGregor, who would reprise his role as the Jedi master Obi-Wan Kenobi in a forthcoming *Star Wars* series; Anna Kendrick and Billy Eichner, starring in a holiday comedy, *Noelle*; Kristen Bell touting her unscripted high school musical series, *Encore!*; and Jeff Goldblum affording a peek at his quirky new self-titled National Geographic series, *The World According to Jeff Goldblum*.

The promotional drumbeat continued across the Disney empire. *Dancing with the Stars* host Tom Bergeron talked up the streaming service during one Disney-themed episode of ABC's long-running competition show. Buses wrapped in Disney+ ads ferried guests to and from Walt Disney World in Orlando, Florida. Disney Store employees wore lanyards emblazoned with QR codes, enabling shoppers to scan them with their phones and start instantly downloading the Disney+ app.

With anticipation this high, there was a high risk of backlash. Users who had rushed to download Disney+, some of them gladly submitting their credit cards nearly three months before the service became available, encountered an error message on day one. It featured two characters from the Disney animated film *Wreck-It Ralph*, with text reading, "Unable to connect to Disney+."

"My wife and I both took a vacation day off work to stream @disney plus but so far we're stuck with this error code for the last hour," tweeted Dan Brooks, a librarian and sci-fi and fantasy fan in Cary, North Carolina. "Who else is seeing this?"

While launch glitches are hardly unheard-of in the tech realm—the hotly anticipated online version of the popular *Grand Theft Auto V* video game in 2013 was similarly marred by error messages, game freezes, and other problems—it nonetheless served to underscore criticisms about the company's lack of technical experience.

"Six hours! 6 damn hours on hold," tweeted Mike Calkins, a self-described baseball fanatic and beer lover in Southern California, who posted a screen grab of his extended Live Chat wait. "I could have driven to San Francisco by now. This is the worst. Keep up the good work of wasting my time. #DisneyPlusfail."

With media coverage of the Disney+ launch focusing on the technical failure on the first morning, Disney decided to reclaim the narrative. The following day it announced the service had signed up ten million customers on the first day—a massive consumer response that exceeded even the rosiest analyst projections.

"Honestly, that was way beyond anything we ever contemplated," said Mayer.

Disney+ maintained its frenetic growth over the first year, signing up more than 73.7 million subscribers, which put it at the high end of the range the company had predicted it would reach within five years. The debut set an impossibly high bar for the other nascent streaming services to clear, especially after COVID-19 gripped the country and paralyzed the industry in March 2020. A year later, in March 2021, Disney+ surpassed one hundred million subscribers around the world.

Apple had preceded the Disney+ launch by nearly two weeks, but being first out of the gate didn't guarantee a successful entry. Its initial slate of shows elicited a decidedly mixed critical reaction. The *New York Times'* James Poniewozik called its marquee title, *The Morning Show*, a kludge, "something assembled in a cleanroom out of good-show parts from incompatible suppliers." The headline of his review urged viewers: "Wait for the Upgrade."

See came in for a similar critical drubbing. "Care was taken in the hiring of performers and consultants to make the presentation of blindness convincing," wrote the *New York Times'* Mike Hale. "But no one seems to have done the more difficult, and boring, work of really thinking through how to make the premise convincing onscreen."

One critical standout was *Dickinson*, which the *New Yorker* called "absurd but sincere, pop but abstruse," a work that cross-pollinated literary history with adolescent fantasy in a way that reviewer Troy Patterson found compelling. When the show had its world premiere at the Tribeca TV Festival, star Hailee Steinfeld, also a platinum-selling pop star, highlighted the musical core of the show and, by implication, Apple's streaming advantage. Tracks from Billie Eilish, Lizzo, A$AP Rocky, and others on the soundtrack are a clear commercial hook for Gen Z and millennial viewers. Steinfeld herself recorded a new song, which was featured in the series and on iTunes, allowing cross-promotion between the Apple streaming platforms and signaling a strategic focus on overall subscriptions to various services, not just Apple TV+. "For me, what's really special is working on this with Apple and Apple Music," Steinfeld said. The global potential of the show thanks to Apple's reach was driven home for Steinfeld when she was stopped by a girl in a shopping mall in Manila in the Philippines. Steinfeld asked her name and the girl replied by quoting a famous Emily Dickinson line: "I'm nobody, who are you?"

Still, the generally tepid early reviews, together with a lack of compelling library content, translated to a slow start. Apple remained mum about how many of its customers opted to give the service a try. One respected technology analyst, Toni Sacconaghi, estimated that fewer than

10 percent of those who purchased a new Apple device over the holiday quarter took advantage of the year-free promotion—roughly ten million people.

The Bernstein analyst wasn't prepared to write off Apple TV+ as a failure—after all, Apple has one of the most powerful distribution channels in the world, in the form of 1.5 billion devices. Perhaps, Sacconaghi posited, the service had failed to resonate simply because of its limited offerings.

Apple's marketing wizards set to work behind the scenes to position the service as worthy of the pristine Apple brand. It targeted a group of influencers known to be swayed by elaborate promotional campaigns, or dinner and a movie (screening)—the Hollywood Foreign Press Association, the ninety-member group that awards the Golden Globes. Whatever Apple did worked. *The Morning Show* received a trio of nominations in 2020—one for best television drama and two for best actress, Aniston and Witherspoon.

More than any wining and dining or awards campaigning, the global pandemic changed Apple's fortunes. As the lights went dark in the nation's theaters, anxious film studios began seeking out other forms of distribution that could bring in revenue during the box-office drought. Film studios became distressed sellers, angling for a buck. The cash-flush Apple was happy to oblige, though it would do so opportunistically, and with care not to overpay.

"They try to get movies for less money than others," said one Hollywood dealmaker. "Actually, because they're Apple, there's an ego that's attached to that."

Take Sony Pictures' World War II sea epic *Greyhound*, starring Tom Hanks as a U.S. Navy captain leading his first convoy of ships through a portion of the Atlantic Ocean that was swarming with Nazi U-boats. Sony financed the film for about $30 million and planned to release it into theaters on June 19, to roughly coincide with the seventy-fifth anniversary of Germany's surrender. But uncertainty about when theaters would open and whether the studio could find a new release date in an increasingly crowded 2021 film slate, promoted its sale to Apple for $70 million, a bargain price that came with the added promise of an aggressive marketing campaign.

While the lack of big-screen distribution was an undeniable loss, one of the film's backers, Jason Cloth, found the arrangement rewarding. Apple saw a 10 to 15 percent increase in subscribers. Cloth more than recouped his investment. Although *Greyhound* might have brought in $150 million in box office, according to pre-release projections, it was unclear when the World War II epic could have found its way to the screen. Even after exhibitors fully reopened, they would likely focus more on mega-budget franchises and tentpoles, leaving midpriced films like *Greyhound* in limbo.

"I'm not sure Sony was happy to sell *Greyhound* to Apple," said Cloth, the Toronto-based financier who also invested in another Apple project, *The Morning Show*. "But the times are unique. As a temporary strategy, I think it worked well for all involved."

Seeing the Hanks film move the needle, Apple filled its slate with other large-scale works and paid a Sundance-record $25 million in January 2021 to acquire buzzy festival breakout *CODA*. Months after launching with a mixed-bag slate, Apple started to hit the target with films like the documentary *Boys State*, the Spike Jonze–directed *Beastie Boys Story*, and animated musical series *Central Park*. Apple TV+ and its executives seemed to be finding their footing. At the Emmy Awards presentation in September 2020, it received the validation its executives had been craving. *The Morning Show*'s Billy Crudup received the supporting actor award for his portrayal of the scheming network news president on the service's marquee show. Though another series that debuted in the summer of 2020, *Ted Lasso*, a fish-out-of-water comedy about an American college football coach who is hired to manage a fictional Premier League soccer team in England, would crystalize the essence of Apple TV+, with its warmth, unflagging optimism, and critical acclaim. It won seven Emmy Awards, including the prize for the year's outstanding comedy series.

NBCUNIVERSAL'S PEACOCK WAS THE NEXT STREAMING service to roll up to the launchpad with its radically different premise but also far deeper resources than a startup like Quibi. As the rest of the market chased Netflix, Peacock sought to capitalize on the market Hulu had abandoned in 2016, one as old as broadcast television itself—free, ad-supported streaming. Seeking to give Peacock a boost, corporate parent Comcast offered a preview version of the service to its Xfinity X1 and Flex customers on April 15, 2020, with a broader nationwide rollout on July 15. The summer debut had been timed to coincide with NBC's exclusive U.S. broadcast of the 2020 Summer Olympic Games in Tokyo, though the cornerstone launch programming crumbled beneath it in March, when the International Olympic Committee postponed the games until July 2021 because of the pandemic.

"When we targeted April 15th as the launch date we knew we had our work cut out for us," Strauss and NBCUniversal CEO Jeff Shell wrote in a joint email to staff. "But we never imagined we would be faced with the challenges that this global pandemic has created."

The nationwide stay-at-home orders, however, created what NBCU recognized as a once-in-a-century opportunity for media companies, as Nielsen reported a 60 percent spike in streaming across the country. Strauss and Shell hoped to meet this demand by throwing open its film and television vaults.

Peacock would offer 7,500 hours of movies and television shows— including dramas like *Downton Abbey* and *Law & Order: Criminal Intent*; comedies like *Parks & Recreation* and *30 Rock*; popular films like *Jurassic Park*, *The Bourne Identity*, and *The Matrix*; and the current season of reality shows like *Undercover Boss*. For an extra $4.99 a month, subscribers would get twice as much to watch, including current primetime shows such as *Law & Order: SVU* and the trilogy of Chicago-based dramas, *Chicago P.D.*, *Chicago Fire*, and *Chicago Med*; comedies like

Saturday Night Live and late-night talk shows, including *The Tonight Show with Jimmy Fallon*; Spanish-language programs from NBC-owned Telemundo; and a broader selection of films, including *Shrek*, *Ted*, and *Forgetting Sarah Marshall*.

NBCUniversal reserved its original series for the nationwide launch of Peacock, though critics were largely unimpressed by its marquee show, *Brave New World*, adapted from Aldous Huxley's novel. It originally had been developed for NBCU's Syfy channel and then for the USA Network, giving it what one reviewer termed an "off the rack" quality. It somehow managed to feel dull and unsexy, despite the backdrop of a hedonistic future society where people are slaves to pleasure, noted the *New York Times*.

Strauss and Shell did their best to tamp down expectations. They labeled the phased 2020 launch of Peacock merely the "runway to 2021," when the service would gain access to reruns of the NBC comedy *The Office*, which was a perennial favorite on Netflix, ramp up its production of originals, and air the postponed Olympic Games.

The results reflected this cautious positioning. Peacock's ad-supported streaming service had attracted ten million sign-ups in its first three months. Sign-ups weren't the same thing as active users, and for months there was a significant gap between how many people signed up and who was actually watching.

IN MAY 2020, IT WOULD BE HBO Max's turn to run the coronavirus gauntlet.

Much as Quibi had done, WarnerMedia planned a lavish promotional campaign to introduce its new service. Appearances of talent were booked at the South by Southwest festival in Texas and the Met Gala in New York. A three-month television ad blitz was due to start with the first whistle of the March Madness college basketball tournament on sister cable network TBS. COVID-19 only compounded the internal issues at WarnerMedia, which was managing an intensely challenging period of restructuring, austerity measures, and establishing a unified culture after fiefdoms had ruled for decades.

"We lost a huge launch platform with the NCAA basketball tournament," Bob Greenblatt, chairman of WarnerMedia Entertainment and its direct-to-consumer business, said in an interview on the eve of the launch. "When those shut down, or were taken away, that was four or five hundred hours of programming that we were going to heavily advertise in." The NBA, similarly, disappeared before mounting a "bubble" return in July 2020. In a typical year, the NBA playoffs, from April to June, offer prime TV advertising real estate, a good amount of it on WarnerMedia network TNT.

For a moment, it looked like the deadly virus threatened to derail more than HBO Max's marketing efforts. As production after production shuttered in March, Greenblatt and his team discussed whether they could realistically complete the technical work on the HBO Max platform by the end of May, with everyone working from their kitchen tables at home. "With a one hundred percent remote workforce, it's hard to know if things are actually getting done," said WarnerMedia chief technology officer Jeremy Legg a few weeks before the launch. "It's not that I think nothing's getting done. But two engineers can't stand up at a whiteboard and figure out a problem." Testing the product across devices is a similar challenge, he added.

"We did talk about 'Should we delay' when the shutdown happened in March," Greenblatt conceded. "But none of us wanted to, because we were late to the party."

The opportunity to reach an effectively captive audience seeking a way to pass the time while in quarantine couldn't be ignored, especially after AT&T had invested more than $85 billion to acquire Time Warner and capitalize on the rise of streaming. Of the five new streaming entrants, HBO Max was the only one whose launch was delayed.

The technical team completed the project virtually, working, as Greenblatt said, "twenty-four/seven." Production work on the Max Originals was not so easy to replicate on a Zoom call. HBO Max launched with a mere six original series, including *Love Life*, a romantic comedy anthology series starring Anna Kendrick; *On the Record*, the documentary about sexual violence in the music business, told through the account of one of Russell Simmons's accusers; and *The Not-Too-Late Show with Elmo*, where celebrity guests join the Muppet in telling a joke or singing a song. The widely anticipated *Friends* reunion, which chief content officer Kevin Reilly knew would serve as a beacon to attract subscribers, much as *The Mandalorian* did for Disney+, was postponed. Even though Reilly sought to assure the cast that the production could be done safely, the stars felt that a buoyant reunion, during a pandemic that had separated so many people from their elderly family members, would send the wrong message.

"It's like we had literally just made our way to the starting block and then we've got cold water thrown on us," said Reilly. "The world had cold water thrown on it, but for our new product launch it was terrible timing."

Love Life, which became the flagship HBO Max show at launch, was a step down in terms of sparkle from the *Friends* reunion special. Its star, Kendrick, emerged as the unofficial poster child of the 2019–20 streaming/pandemic period, with shows on Quibi, HBO Max, and Facebook Watch. She also had a voice part in DreamWorks Animation's *Trolls World Tour*, which skipped its planned theatrical run for a precedent-setting video-on-demand release. Kendrick put in a brief appearance at the premiere for the *Sex and the City*–adjacent *Love Life*, which was held virtually due to COVID-19. "Attendees" of the event could go to an "after-party," featuring separate "rooms," including a club DJ and a relationship expert dispensing free advice. Paul Feig, one of the producers of the show and director of films like *Bridesmaids*, held court in one room, serving cocktails from his home bar and wearing a red smoking jacket. "I think my screen froze again," Feig said, trying to stay upbeat but cracking self-deprecating jokes about the event, which was the exact opposite of the electrifying premiere parties that had long been HBO's signature. "It's a whole new technology, my friends. Blame COVID. As if it could get any worse." Feig's patter never stopped. "Am I going to drink another Manhattan? I may," he said. "It's a pandemic!"

Even HBO itself, the namesake and anchor of the new streaming service, had entered a fallow period. The finale of *Game of Thrones*, which drew 19.3 million TV viewers and set a record for the nearly fifty-year-old premium cable network, had aired a year ago. The third season of the futuristic *Westworld* wrapped up in early May, just before the streaming launch, and the next big-budget drama, *Perry Mason*, starring Matthew Rhys in the title role, would arrive almost a month later.

That left HBO Max with no choice but to lean heavily on Warner Bros.' film and television library, and acquisitions from third parties, such as Studio Ghibli. It won exclusive streaming rights to the current season of *Doctor Who*, the long-running sci-fi time-travel series, through an agreement with BBC Studios, which also brought HBO Max a total of seven hundred episodes of such popular British shows as *The Office*, the original cubicle-farm comedy starring Ricky Gervais, and the psychological crime drama *Luther*, starring Idris Elba.

"There's a lot of other stuff in this mix that we think is extraordinary," said Greenblatt in the run-up to launch. "And hopefully we'll be back into production sooner than later." Another senior executive, though, said the optimistic sentiment about the strength of the library was too widely held. What they needed was original programming that would compel people to subscribe, or for current HBO subscribers to activate their HBO Max privileges. "People kept saying, 'Where's your *Mandalorian*? Where's your *Mandalorian*?'" the executive remembers. "And I think that we were a bit overconfident that our *library* was our *Mandalorian*. And that just didn't prove to be true, because ultimately people may respect that library, and they may watch it. It may help with engagement and retention, but it's not going to get people excited to stop what they're doing in the middle of a pandemic and sign up for your service."

WarnerMedia would learn a lesson that Netflix groks at a molecular level: shiny objects, in the form of fresh content, attract subscribers.

HBO Max's social media campaign sought to underscore the breadth of the service's offerings through minute-long promotional videos, like one titled "HBO Max/We've Got the Lolz," which used decade-old internet slang in an unfortunate attempt to appear hip. It featured quick cuts from popular television sitcoms like *The Fresh Prince of Bel-Air*, *Friends*, *South Park*, and *The Big Bang Theory* and films such as *Crazy Rich Asians*, *Ocean's Eleven*, and *The Lego Movie*.

Billboards and social media messages featured the slogan "Where HBO Meets So Much More," indicating that subscribers would get the regular HBO offerings as well as thousands of additional hours of film and TV. The slogan elicited some eye rolls among media mavens, especially when it was attached to one punny message noting that *The Sopranos*, *Friends*, and *The Big Bang Theory* all had the same streaming home. "From Bada . . . to Bing . . . to Bang," read one cringeworthy tagline. Peter Naylor, former head of ad sales at Hulu who is now at Snapchat parent Snap Inc., retweeted a *Fast Company* reaction to the WarnerMedia ad. The tweet's text didn't mince words: "HBO Max is a branding disaster, and this ad proves it."

HBO Max executives put the best face on the May 27, 2020, launch—even though the app wasn't available on the Roku or Amazon platforms because of an impasse over consumer data.

"We launched a product, I think seamlessly, and we put an incredible volume of great stories in front of consumers," Tony Goncalves, chief executive of AT&T's Otter Media division, with responsibility for the HBO Max streaming service, told the Verge. "The passion and engagement that we're seeing around the content offering is incredible. All in all, we had a great day yesterday." AT&T CEO John Stankey went even further, hyping the rollout as "flawless" during an earnings call with Wall Street analysts.

The numbers did not quite back up the buoyant official assessments. AT&T reported in July 2020 that HBO Max had signed up around 4.1 million customers in the month since its launch—a number that one knowledgeable source said WarnerMedia executives vigorously objected to disclosing. The high-stakes gambit had fallen well short of the Disney+ debut. About one million of the total number represented true direct-to-consumer subscribers, who came in the front door and paid $15 a month. The more unsettling statistic was the 3.1 million subscribers who had authenticated their HBO subscriptions via AT&T wireless or pay TV, less than one-third of the total existing subscribers to HBO in the company's footprint.

"HBO Max, supposedly the salvation of an otherwise hemorrhaging WarnerMedia segment, has gotten off to a rather inauspicious start," observed veteran telecommunications analyst Craig Moffett.

More than a dozen current and former employees closely involved with the launch confirmed in interviews that the service had "laid an egg," in one insider's damning view. Another believed the general-entertainment approach of packing fifteen thousand hours in led to an unfocused offering. "If we were guilty of one thing, it's that we just threw too much stuff at the wall programming-wise to see what stuck," the person said. Some of the "classics" hadn't aged particularly well. *Gone with the Wind* got entangled in the racial equity movement sparked by George Floyd's murder by a Minneapolis police officer. Filmmaker John Ridley penned an op-ed in the *Los Angeles Times* calling on HBO Max to hit pause on the film, which romanticizes the Confederacy. "It is a film that glorifies the antebellum south," he wrote. "It is a film that, when it is not ignoring the horrors of slavery, pauses only to perpetuate some of the most painful stereotypes of people of color." The service did not yank the film but added a companion piece of programming intended to provide context, a 2019 panel of film historians discussing the film's legacy and educational value at the TCM Classic Film Festival, an event programmed by WarnerMedia's Turner Classic Movies network. Had WarnerMedia not been so heavily compartmentalized, with Turner, HBO, and Warner Bros. all in different cities pursuing different agendas, more consideration might have been given about how to reckon with the complicated legacy of *Gone with the Wind* in 2020.

HBO Max suffered from a thousand cuts—some of them self-inflicted. It had cultivated a confusing brand identity, with four different products called HBO in the market. "I think that was something that we should have moved faster on, which is the retiring of HBO Now and HBO Go as brand names," WarnerMedia CEO Jason Kilar later conceded.

The verdict on the launch came swiftly, in the form of a massive reorganization three months later at WarnerMedia that swept out two of the programming executives most associated with HBO Max—Greenblatt and Reilly. Kilar, in a memo to staff, framed the shakeup as part of an effort to streamline the entertainment company and focus its efforts on its direct-to-consumer operations. "It wasn't a performance management issue. It wasn't in response to HBO Max," he asserted. "I felt that if we really want to set ourselves up for the next, say, decade of truly doing great work on behalf of customers, I just thought it made more sense to have one content group, as opposed to two."

Kilar placed a single executive, Warner Bros. studio chief Ann Sarnoff, whom he described as selfless, focused, and "a great system-level thinker," in charge of how film and television content would be distributed across the company's various platforms. He elevated a trusted lieutenant, Andy Forssell, who was one of the earliest executives to join Kilar at Hulu shortly after it was formed in 2007, to lead a newly created HBO Max operating unit.

The scrambling of the org chart, which dismissed the very executives Stankey had installed just a year earlier, required Kilar to seek the AT&T chief's buy-in. A few days after the changes, AT&T CFO John Stephens, appearing at an investor conference, insisted that the "refocusing" of the company was "not because we needed to adjust anything, but rather because we're striving to get even better than the launch was."

AT&T likely chose Kilar precisely because of his track record as an unsentimental disruptor. Stephenson and Stankey originally approached Kilar about the WarnerMedia job in 2019, after coming to rely on his advice as a member of its Technical Advisory Council, where he served alongside such luminaries as billionaire entrepreneur Mark Cuban, who cofounded the pioneering streaming service Broadcast.com; Ray Ozzie, Microsoft's chief software architect; and Marc Andreessen, the Netscape founder turned venture capitalist. "It's a once-in-a-lifetime opportunity and I thought that I would absolutely regret not getting in that sandbox, doing things that I think are going to matter for customers," said Kilar.

Entertainment industry veteran Peter Chernin helped set the stage for Kilar's Hollywood revival. The former Fox executive had sought out his friend AT&T CEO Randall Stephenson to partner in a bid to acquire Hulu in 2013—an endeavor the telecom executive enthusiastically joined, seeing mobile video as the future of the company. Stephenson's deputy, John Stankey, would serve as the point person on the venture, and over months of intense dealmaking, the entertainment ingénue and the media veteran forged a close bond. Chernin, in turn, served as a conduit to Hulu's lightning-rod strategist. "John wanted to get my thoughts on Hulu," recalled Kilar, "and so he reached out to me and introduced himself, and Peter connected us."

Kilar expressed confidence that the strength of WarnerMedia's intellectual property and its economic heft would propel HBO Max into the digital future and help it compete successfully with entrenched players like Netflix. "Companies like WarnerMedia and Disney are blessed with deep libraries of beloved franchises and intellectual property that are meaningful and will play important roles in this epic adventure," Kilar told us via email. "The ones that attain the level of success needed to thrive long term will be those (plural) that are world class at storytelling (based on new and existing intellectual property), technology and product. Said another way, the ones that delight the customer again and again, night after night, will define the future of entertainment."

CHAPTER 19

▶ In Space,
No One Can Hear
You Stream

Tom Hanks got up early on a July morning to plug a movie on the *Today* show. In related news, the sun also rose in the east.

Hanks has acted in nearly sixty films and produced dozens more, giving him an innate understanding of the promotional game. Unlike other A-list movie stars, he is famously un-divalike by all accounts, an unfailingly affable fixture in popular culture across generations. He was a natural choice to host *Saturday Night Live* as it returned to the air, remotely, with COVID-19 on the rise in April 2020. A month before that, his revelation that he and his wife, Rita Wilson, had tested positive for the coronavirus was one of the biggest early shocks of the pandemic's initial sweep across the globe. (Both made a complete recovery.)

Throughout his ascent through the Hollywood ranks, Hanks has remained a traditionalist. An unabashed history lover, he cherishes the heritage of motion pictures. Morgan Freeman may get more voiceover work, but ideologically Hanks is well suited to delivering the kind of rhapsody to filmmaking that Freeman did on WarnerMedia Day. Accepting the American Film Institute's annual Life Achievement Award, he paid a lengthy tribute to the act of communion with other moviegoers. "Let's go to the movies!" he urged the crowd, extolling the joys of sitting in a theater transfixed by "this amalgam of light and sound and literature we call the cinema."

It stood out, then, during the *Today* segment, when Hanks lavished a suspicious amount of praise on Apple. The tech company was releasing his latest film, *Greyhound*, after acquiring it from Sony Pictures. Movies turned out to play a crucial role in the streaming race of 2020 and 2021. Streaming in the popular imagination is defined by series. *House of Cards. The Marvelous Mrs. Maisel. The Handmaid's Tale.* Episodes of what used to be called television delivered in binge-y chunks with cinematic flair and few if any commercials. Movies, though, have ended up being an increasingly important weapon in streaming services' arsenals. For Netflix, Apple, and Amazon Prime Video, they represent a new way to disrupt the entertainment industry status quo. For media companies like Disney and WarnerMedia, they offer a ray of hope in a crumbling traditional marketplace. Series get more expensive, and therefore less profitable, the longer they stay alive—one reason why very few of them make it past a third season on streaming platforms. Movies are singular opportunities to gain new subscribers, explore new genres, and work with influential talent—at a fixed cost.

Asked by host Hoda Kotb if he felt "a little bummed" that the film wouldn't play in theaters, Hanks replied, "I'm actually thrilled that Apple TV is making it possible for everybody to see it." Noting that the film's release date on July 10 was the day after his sixty-fourth birthday, he said, "This is a magnificent gift that's come to us because of Apple." With theaters shuttered in most of the country and large swaths of the world due to the coronavirus, he said, "Apple television has saved the day," and added that it was a "benevolent streaming service in every way." Had the company not swooped in to buy the fact-based World War II submarine thriller, Hanks said, it "would have languished in a vault."

Emphasizing the film's global accessibility, Hanks touted the modest monthly subscription price of Apple TV+, though he didn't have it committed to memory. He looked away from the camera and called out, "How much does Apple TV cost? Staff? What is it, five bucks?" Turning back, he gushed to Kotb, "It's a cheap, it's a cheap—" He regrouped and continued, "It's a *magnificent* deal, and we are going to be able to fill up the screens and the living rooms and the beanbag chairs of the world all in one fell shot."

The Hanks who appeared on TV from a book-lined room in his home sounded a lot different from the one captured in an article published by the *Guardian* a day earlier. In that story, he called it "heart-breaking" that there would be no theatrical release of the film, which he adapted from C. S. Forester's 1955 novel, *The Good Shepherd*. "I don't mean to make angry my Apple overlords, but there is a difference in picture and sound quality that goes along with" the change of venue, he said. Even the circumstances of the interview were lamentable, Hanks said. "The cruel whip masters at Apple" had decided the background of the video interview with the *Guardian* needed to be a blank wall, he explained. That way, his interlocutor would be unable to snoop around and draw conclusions from the books on his shelves. Standing in front of a blank void, Hanks said he felt like he was in "a witness protection program. But here I am, bowing to the needs of Apple TV."

Apple immediately did damage control, telling other members of the press that Hanks had been misquoted. The star's trademark sardonic wit had been misinterpreted by writer Hadley Freeman as sincere complaining, the company insisted. The *Guardian* stood by its story, which remained unchanged on its website. Then, on *Today*, Hanks seemed to channel Apple CEO Tim Cook. On the eve of the Apple TV+ launch, Cook raved to Wall Street analysts that its $5 price point was "amazing," as was the offer of twelve months of free service to anyone buying an Apple device. "It's a gift to our users," he said, "and from a business point of view, we're really proud of the content, we'd like as many people as possible to view it."

There is a succinct, if uncomfortable, explanation for why an A-list actor with two Oscars on his mantel and the freedom to make films anywhere would so readily adjust his tone: money. With traditional studios starved of revenue from movies, television advertising, and theme parks, Apple floored the accelerator. It claimed historical action-drama *Emancipation*, starring Will Smith and directed by Antoine Fuqua, and director Martin Scorsese's reunion with Leonardo DiCaprio, *Killers of the Flower Moon*. The prices of both dwarfed the $70 million paid for *Greyhound*, with the former reported to be around $120 million and the latter in the $200 million range. Hanks himself would end up returning to his "Apple overlords" in 2021 with *Finch*, a pickup of a sci-fi drama originally intended as a Universal Pictures release.

In addition to Apple, other entrants in the streaming derby used original films as subscriber bait. Disney has been the most aggressive in mobilizing films for streaming, shifting *Hamilton*, *Mulan*, and Pixar's *Soul* to Disney+ in 2020. (*Mulan* deserves its own business-school case study, as it pioneered a new strategy dubbed "Premier Access," which made the title available for $29.99 only to subscribers of Disney+, a double-dip no other company had dared attempt.) HBO Max, a month after launching, added whimsical Seth Rogen comedy *An American Pickle* and waterslide documentary *Class Action Park*. Peacock mostly positioned itself as the future home of new movies from its corporate sibling Universal Pictures, though after theatrical and home entertainment release.

Disdained by statesmen like Steven Spielberg as "TV movies," films released by streaming services don't reach the public in the same way as traditional studio titles. Theatrical engagements are largely window dressing, with the true goal being gaining or retaining subscribers, as opposed to the revenue godhead of the box office. Even without a meaningful presence in theaters—or perhaps because of it—films delivered via streaming, especially those with recognizable stars, can move the subscriber needle. "Consumers understand the value proposition of new movie watching, compared with TV series," Netflix co-CEO Ted Sarandos said at an investor conference in 2019. "In New York, that's a hundred-dollar night out."

Because of its DNA as a company, Netflix set the bar for releasing original movies via streaming, turning the thrilling stutter steps of *Wax, or the Discovery of Television Among the Bees* into a commercial reality. Film titles on DVD shaped its earliest algorithms and its identity as a startup. Two decades after its launch, movies still made up about one-third of total viewing despite all the binge releases and talk of living in a new golden age of television.

In 2006, Netflix formed a division headed by Sarandos called Red Envelope for the acquisition and release of independent films. It became a fixture at film festivals and bought 126 films during its two-year run, mostly partnering with established distributors like IFC, Samuel Goldwyn, and Magnolia Pictures. It championed a few minor hits, now mostly forgotten, like *Sherrybaby, No End in Sight,* and *2 Days in Paris.* Netflix came to realize that Red Envelope was more of a marginal participant, not the central disruptor the company preferred to be. After the company's 2007 launch of its streaming service, it was on a trajectory to becoming an aggressive aggregator of films and rocket fuel for independent filmmakers. Why help operate the Tilt-a-Whirl and the ring toss when you could own the whole amusement park? "The one thing we learned this year is that there's no shortage of produced movies and there's no shortage of money for viable projects," Sarandos said in 2008 when the company shuttered Red Envelope.

As it moved on to stocking its virtual shelves and throwing its weight behind streaming, the company retained its rapacious appetite for films, even without Red Envelope. Joe Amodei, who runs independent distributor Virgil Films and has known Sarandos since his days in the video business, recalls bringing his friend a binder of one hundred film titles. "I'll take them all," Sarandos said. Cindy Holland, who was Sarandos's first hire, joked that the process of acquiring DVD film titles at scale was like "shoveling coal in the side door of the house." On an earnings call in October 2020, Sarandos recalled ordering as many as eight hundred titles at once, though he soon came to realize that bulking up wasn't effective. "Nobody watched any of them," Sarandos said. "It's really not a chase for how many titles, but are these the titles you can't live without?"

Cut to 2014. Netflix had survived the Qwikster debacle and its streaming operation was prospering—and not just on volume. Original shows were transforming Netflix's brand and market position, and original films, the company determined, could feel like major events for subscribers. Just as it had with original series, Netflix would mine its own catalog for audience trends and viewership patterns. That process was second nature for Sarandos, who had started connecting the movie dots for a living in 1982, as an eighteen-year-old video store clerk in Arizona making recommendations to customers.

Long before his Netflix tenure, Sarandos had taken note of the trajectory of Adam Sandler. Once he was ensconced at Netflix, Sarandos had data to prove the comedian's appeal to subscribers. After graduating from *Saturday Night Live*, Sandler had starred in a string of hit comedies, like *The Wedding Singer*, *The Waterboy*, and *Big Daddy*. After a fast start in the 1990s and early 2000s, he hit a much bumpier patch and his commercial profile was taking on a Jerry Lewis–like dimension, with overseas grosses eclipsing those in the U.S. Critics sneered at Sandler, and in some corners of popular culture he personified all that was cringeworthy and unfunny. "I have occasionally bristled at the recommendations of Netflix," wrote Tom Vanderbilt in his book *You May Also Like*, which explores how companies gauge and manipulate consumer preferences. "*An Adam Sandler film? Are you kidding me?*" On a less personal note, Vanderbilt wisely observed, "Netflix had always sensed this gap between people's aspirations and their behavior." Indeed, that sentence might as well be embroidered on sofa pillows in the company's famous lobby. Netflix knows that people aren't always in the mood for filet mignon when they're looking for a film to watch. Sometimes, a juicy cheeseburger hits the spot.

That dynamic helps explain why, where studios saw waning bankability in Sandler outings like *Jack and Jill* and *That's My Boy*, Netflix recognized upside. In 2014, Sarandos offered Sandler and his company,

Happy Madison, the first film production deal in Netflix history. Netflix would finance and release four movies from Sandler, at his usual budget levels at the time, around $40 million to $80 million. There would be no theatrical runs, and Netflix would own the rights in perpetuity. Even though Sandler was not hot (he was still years away from his lead role in *Uncut Gems*, which finally silenced many haters), the economics of the deal were striking. Typically, stars and filmmakers have "quotes" as well as back-end participation—in most cases, they get a healthy up-front payment and then, if the film breaks out and does well in theaters, online, and in other "ancillary" windows, they get a cut of those proceeds. In certain cases—as with Joaquin Phoenix in *Joker* or Keanu Reeves in *The Matrix*, for example—stars have earned tens of millions of dollars, several times their up-front rate. For years, there had been downward pressure on star salaries, even for stars not on a cold streak like Sandler. Financiers and studios increasingly preferred to back-load talent deals, allowing for more money to be spent on special effects or household-name intellectual properties. Netflix instead negotiates a single up-front "buyout." Scott Stuber, the former Universal executive who came to Netflix to oversee its film operation in 2017, described the company's approach this way: "If we make a film, we pay in success," based on an analysis of past film performance and the budget of the new work. In other words, with no gross points to hand out and no back-end obligations, Netflix has kept the buyouts high as it has elbowed its way into the game.

Sandler, who would be guaranteed in the range of $200 million to make four films for Netflix, released a gleeful statement whose humor hasn't aged particularly well. "When these fine people came to me with an offer to make four movies for them, I immediately said 'yes' for one reason and one reason only . . . Netflix rhymes with Wet Chicks," Sandler said. "Let the streaming begin!"

From those unorthodox beginnings, Netflix has grown into a so-phisticated movie engine producing what Chief Financial Officer Spencer Neumann has called "creative excellence at scale." What qualifies as "excellence" is subjective, of course. The company has put out a number of acclaimed original films and has championed international work like *Atlantics* from Senegal, as well as U.S. standouts like Spike Lee, David Fincher, Jane Campion, and the Coen brothers. But it also distributes a steady stream of Sandlerian crowd-pleasers and teen rom-coms like *The Kissing Booth*. It spends at a level comparable with the budgets of major studios and will soon surpass them. That means it can readily mount the kinds of blockbusters that Stuber oversaw for Universal Pictures. The slate has included *6 Underground*, starring Ryan Reynolds and directed by Michael Bay (known for franchises like *Transformers* and *Bad Boys*), and *The Old Guard*, a graphic-novel-based action movie with Charlize Theron that has spawned a sequel. In 2021, it announced plans for one major movie release per week, with stars like Gal Gadot, Dwayne "the Rock" Johnson, and dozens more.

Amazon, meanwhile, pursued a strategy in its motion picture business that differed significantly from that of its longtime rival, Netflix. Instead of trying to bend the talent community and traditional business to its model, it sought a deliberately blended approach.

The company's initial game plan was to acquire completed films and collaborate with other distributors to release them. Along with *Manchester by the Sea*, films like *The Big Sick*, *Cold War*, and *The Salesman* prospered, collecting Oscar nominations and one Best Picture win (*The Salesman* for best foreign-language film). Established distributors handled the blocking and tackling of getting them out to theaters. But Amazon provided the muscle, in terms of marketing resources and its potent warehouse of content, where the films could be bought, rented, and eventually streamed for free by Amazon Prime members. It was a modern update of Netflix's Red Envelope experiment, only the marketplace had matured to the point where films that worked could generate significant revenue. *Manchester* pulled in $79 million around the world. Not exactly life-changing, especially for a company worth $1.5 trillion, but the start of a sustainable business.

Bob Berney spearheaded marketing and distribution for Amazon's film division from 2015 to 2019. Theaters were in his blood. After a successful early career in art house exhibition, he segued to distribution and marketing, shepherding some of the biggest cinematic phenomena of the twenty-first century, films like *Pan's Labyrinth*, *Whale Rider*, *Y Tu Mamá También*, and *Memento*. Two films he marketed became among the most profitable independent films ever released: *The Passion of the Christ* and *My Big Fat Greek Wedding*, which together grossed more than $850 million.

Working with other execs with traditional backgrounds, among them indie film veteran Ted Hope, Berney tried to carve out a path for Amazon in which it would marry its tech muscle and resources with old-fashioned cinematic tastemaking. It worked well for a time, but then the hot streak cooled. The company paid lavish sums to acquire festival titles like *Late Night* and *Brittany Runs a Marathon*, which fizzled in commercial release but performed well in streaming, the company said. Even before the coronavirus pandemic made specialty theatrical releases a major question mark, Amazon began to adjust course and started to favor bigger, splashier titles that could make waves even without theaters. *Annette*, a not-entirely-coherent musical directed by an auteur's auteur, Leos Carax, which starred Adam Driver and Marianne Cotillard and had opened the 2021 Cannes Film Festival, was acquired for North America by Amazon Studios. The company floated it in a few theaters for two weeks before routing it to streaming—a dramatically tighter turnaround than in Berney's era.

Amazon has continued to write some big checks, of course, but increasingly for mass-audience fare that doesn't require careful nurturing or one-of-a-kind campaigns. In 2020, it acquired Sacha Baron Cohen's *Borat* sequel and *Coming 2 America*, a big-budget Eddie Murphy movie set up at Paramount. *Borat Subsequent Moviefilm* was seen by "tens of millions" of Prime Video members, the company trumpeted with characteristic opacity. *Coming 2 America* finished atop Nielsen's U.S. streaming chart in its opening week, with 1.4 billion minutes of total viewing. (If each Prime household watched the whole film once, that would be about thirteen million U.S. homes.) Similar dents in the Nielsen chart were made by Chris Evans's futuristic action movie *The Tomorrow War* and *Tom Clancy's Without Remorse*, a thriller starring Michael B. Jordan.

TWO FILMMAKERS WHO DIDN'T EMBRACE STREAMING for the money are Joe and Anthony Russo. They directed one of the highest-grossing movies ever released, *Avengers: Endgame*, in 2019, as well as several other Marvel movies released by Disney. Because they know their way around a spectacle, the brothers' project *The Gray Man* in 2020 became the most expensive movie ever green-lit by Netflix to that point, at more than $200 million. The brothers' rise to the top of the entertainment business had been a methodical, quintessentially American one. Born into a family of Italian immigrants who had settled in one of the steel mill towns of northeastern Ohio, they returned home to Cleveland, where their father was a prominent lawyer, judge, and Democratic Party official, to attend graduate school at Case Western Reserve University. They scraped together financing for their independent film debut, *Pieces*, inspired by the story of Robert Rodriguez's making of the breakout hit *El Mariachi* for a shockingly modest $7,000. Their second film, *Welcome to Collinwood*, screened at the Cannes Film Festival and got them a series of jobs in television, producing and directing shows like *Arrested Development* and *Community*.

Relations remained good with Disney, but by 2016 the Russos launched an independent production company, AGBO, to capitalize on the opportunities streaming afforded filmmakers. The amount of the budget and the extent of the spectacle were less important than global scope and currency with young audiences. That prompted the Russos to set up deals with Netflix, Apple, and Quibi. In an interview, the brothers came off as informed and passionate, idealistic but pragmatic.

"I've got four kids," Joe Russo said, "and while I have an intense, emotional connection to a movie theater, and seeing stories told on a giant screen with a collection of strangers in a dark room, my kids do not have that same connection. They have more expedient ways to receive narrative, and ways that are more convenient for them that they've grown up with. They're happy to watch content on a phone, they're happy to watch it on a computer, they're happy to watch it on an airplane, they're happy to watch it on a television. It does not need to be in a theatrical setting." As deep as Russo's connection is with theaters, he also recognizes a practical challenge for an audience awash in creative abundance. "We are receiving too much content for people to frequent the theater regularly. There's a new show or movie to watch just about every three days, and no one is going to spend that kind of money, time, or energy to go to the theater to consume content. So there has to be another delivery system."

The brothers had thought about exploring the potential of streaming as a new delivery system while making their first *Avengers* movie. They suggested to Chris Hemsworth, who played Thor in the Marvel Cinematic Universe, that they team on a movie that would be designed from the ground up as global entertainment. The result was the action movie *Extraction*, which stars Hemsworth as a black-market mercenary recruited to break an Indian drug lord's son out of a Bangladeshi prison. The global feel and universal action plot of the film propelled it to ninety-nine million views within the first four weeks it was on Netflix, still a record for the most-watched film on the platform.

"Hollywood is very myopic, and it has a domestic-driven sensibility to it that is incorrect," Joe Russo said. Apple, with 1.65 billion phones, laptops, and tablets around the world, and Apple TV+ in more than one hundred countries, as of 2021, offered a similarly global environment for another Russo project, *Cherry*, a film about an army veteran who resorts to robbing banks to support his opioid addiction. "We brought it to a range of streamers, and Apple was the most passionate about the film. They felt like they really got it, that they really appreciated it," Anthony Russo said. "If COVID never happened, we would have done the same thing, but probably leaning on theatrical distributors; we would have brought it to a range of theatrical distributors, in the exact same manner, and seen who was most passionate about it."

While they're attached to produce a live-action *Hercules* remake for Disney, the Russos' other projects are all at streaming services. "Disney represented the epitome. It was the Cadillac of how you run a traditional media studio," Joe Russo said. "Netflix is the Cadillac of how you run a future studio, and again, looking at the pandemic, where all of Netflix's assets are digital or in a cloud, and Disney's were all brick and mortar, and have to do with humans traveling to destinations over the large part of their revenue, it crippled them. So, I think that Netflix is a model for how a future studio should operate, and you don't need as many brick-and-mortar assets to achieve market dominance."

PART VI

Navigating the Recovery

CHAPTER 20

⏵ To Everything (Churn, Churn, Churn)

Disneyland's nickname, the Happiest Place on Earth, came to feel like a sick joke during 2020. About twenty-eight thousand Disney parks employees lost their jobs, and the park in Anaheim, California, remained shuttered for the longest stretch in its sixty-five-year history. The extended closure stood in sharp contrast with the situation at Disney parks in Florida, Paris, Tokyo, and around the world, all of which had managed to reopen, albeit with capacity limits. The financial toll was severe. Long the most lucrative part of Disney's sprawling entertainment empire, the parks division suffered a $6.8 billion drop in operating income in fiscal 2020 as the company overall recorded its worst financial year in decades.

At long last, in January 2021, signs of life returned in Anaheim. The park's mouse-eared gates did not swing open, welcoming guests back to Sleeping Beauty Castle and Space Mountain. Instead, Disneyland had converted its massive parking lot into a coronavirus vaccine site, aiming to deliver ten thousand doses a day. Authorities in Orange County described the Disney initiative as a key element of what they billed Operation Independence, a push to get the area functioning more normally again by July Fourth. "The end of COVID-19 is in sight," declared Dr. Clayton Chau, director of the county's health care agency.

Inside the Walt Disney Company, the executive team had not been feeling a shared sense of mission with public officials. In fact, they felt betrayed. Frustrations reached a boiling point in the fall of 2020, as California governor Gavin Newsom refused to ease health restrictions that would allow Disneyland and other theme parks to reopen. He said there was "no hurry" to do so. Disney objected, releasing a statement from the head of public safety for its parks division that said the company "absolutely rejected" the governor's stance. Executive chairman Bob Iger also quit the state's economic recovery task force in protest.

Nearly every corner of the house that Walt built was afflicted by the once-in-a-century plague. The film studio postponed release of such highly anticipated films as Marvel's *Black Widow*, Steven Spielberg's modern interpretation of *West Side Story*, and Kenneth Branagh's *Death on the Nile*, as theaters remained shuttered. ESPN eliminated five hundred jobs— about 10 percent of its workforce—through a combination of layoffs and attrition as the pandemic truncated its lineup of NBA, Major League Baseball, and other sports programming.

The company's new chief executive, Bob Chapek, had barely enough time to settle into his new role before being thrust into crisis management. "About three days after I started the job I had to close about eighty percent of the business other than TV networks," he told a group of students at his alma mater, Indiana University. Chapek had achieved the pinnacle of his twenty-seven-year career at Disney, quietly demonstrating the business acumen he had sharpened during executive stints in the less glamorous corners of the Magic Kingdom, like home entertainment and consumer products, at a moment of uncertainty and peril. "I could have gone into a fetal position and hoped that it ended," he confided to the students, but of course that would have served neither the company's employees nor Wall Street. "They wanted leadership and decisiveness."

It was easy to recognize the lone bright spot against this backdrop of desolation and loss. The streaming business, which wasn't supposed to produce a profit for five years, had kept the entire company afloat.

After being forced to lay off twenty-eight thousand employees, Chapek would throw the prodigious resources of the company's film, television, and animation studios behind Disney+. "Part of it was bailing out the boat so the boat didn't sink," Chapek explained.

Like Walt Disney before him, Chapek grew up in the Midwest and considered himself a bit of an outsider. "Coming from Hammond, [Indiana,] the first thing you consider when thinking about a career is not necessarily working for Disney in Hollywood," he told the *Times of Northwest Indiana* in a 2006 interview. "On the other hand, somebody has to do that job and why not me?" He arrived on the Burbank studio lot in 1993, an emissary from the world of consumer packaged goods. His experience to that point was working at ketchup-maker Heinz and at the J. Walter Thompson ad agency, As an ad man, Chapek's calling card was an Easy Spirit "Looks Like a Pump, Feels Like a Sneaker" commercial that depicted women playing basketball in "comfortable" heels. Those years did little to prepare him for the fragile egos he'd encounter at Walt Disney Studios and the broader industry.

Chapek brought an unsentimental consumer-products sensibility to the studio's home entertainment business, sparking fierce internal opposition when he proposed Disney create home video sequels to its popular animated films in response to consumer demand. That put him in conflict with animation powerhouses like *The Lion King* producer Don Hahn, who viewed the direct-to-video proposal as a creative affront (Pixar Animation cofounder John Lasseter later criticized the direct-to-video sequels as "virtually unwatchable"). "In the early days, he had to learn that the business isn't all about money," said one former studio executive. "He had to change the mindset of the creatives at the studio." Chapek ultimately prevailed, and the resulting home video releases, like *The Return of Jafar*, would never garner Oscar attention, but they were remarkably lucrative. Disney sold fifteen million copies of that *Aladdin* spin-off and brought in $300 million in revenue. Another of Chapek's ideas, which came to be known as the Disney Vault strategy, created artificial demand for home video releases of Disney's animated films by restricting sales to a limited time. His business innovations captured Iger's notice as the money flowed in.

As Chapek rose through the corporate ranks, overseeing consumer products and, later, the theme parks, executives would be struck by his business chops, even if he lacked the charisma of the other Bob—Iger. "He's very disciplined, very organized. Trains run on time at the parks," said one former Disney television executive. "He's impressive from an operational standpoint." As he did in home entertainment, Chapek introduced new ways for the parks unit to boost its profits even though costs for customers kept climbing. In 2021, the company even tacked on a $15 fee to a longtime free line-skipping system, FastPass, a move that riled up even the most avid Disney acolytes. As one business partner jokes, "I don't believe he's ever had to overpay for a roller coaster." The Indiana native with a degree in microbiology and an MBA from Michigan State University made his mark as a sharp-penciled cost cutter with a singular focus on the bottom line. His frugality won him an advocate in one of Disney's major shareholders, former Marvel Entertainment emeritus CEO Isaac "Ike" Perlmutter, who had himself been known to fish paper clips out of the trash.

As the weight of the pandemic crushed film and television production, Chapek would draw upon his knowledge of how films are distributed in non-theatrical windows to keep fresh content flowing to Disney+. The company initially compressed the traditional ninety-day wait between a film's exclusive theatrical run and its later availability in the home to bring Pixar's *Onward* and Disney's *Frozen II* to the streaming service months earlier than expected. Then Disney diverted a trio of theatrical releases directly to Disney+, infusing the service with marquee films when there was little new to watch.

Hamilton, a filmed version of Lin-Manuel Miranda's hit Broadway musical about one of the nation's Founding Fathers, debuted on July 4, 2020, fueling a spike in downloads—though Disney never disclosed precise numbers. *Mulan*, a lavish $200 million live-action remake of the

1998 animated classic, reached homes on Labor Day weekend 2020, followed by Pixar's *Soul*, which debuted on Christmas Day.

The exhibition community interpreted the announcements as a clear signal of Disney's shifting priorities, though *Mulan* would reveal the limits of online distribution when it came to big-budget tentpole films. Disney charged a $30 premium to Disney+ subscribers who wanted to watch Mulan in their homes. "We see this as an opportunity to bring this incredible film to a broad audience currently unable to go to movie theaters," Chapek told investors. With half of the nation's theaters closed, it was the ideal time for Disney to experiment with premium video on demand, an alternate distribution strategy studios and exhibitors have fought over for years. The technology worked, though *Mulan* failed to reap blockbuster returns. The film brought in an estimated $60 million to $90 million in its first twelve days of on-demand streaming, according to researcher 7Park Data—well off from the $191.8 million opening weekend for another remake of a classic Disney animated film, *The Lion King*. Box office was similarly anemic. Chinese audiences rejected this westernized adaptation of the 1,500-year-old poem "The Ballad of Mulan," which recast the central figure as a feminist hero. *Variety* reported it opened to a disappointing $23 million in ticket sales.

As Chapek sought to project a calm, composed demeanor, anxiety bubbled just below the surface. One executive producer of a Disney+ series said it is difficult to overestimate the pandemic's effects. "When there are cost overruns, as much as they say, 'We'll pay for it,' everyone knows that things are really different right now," the producer said. One new source of anxiety is COVID insurance, which is impossible to secure given the level of risk, even in less hard-hit areas of the world. If production had to shut down, as many had to in the middle months of 2020, Disney was forced to just eat the cost of lost production days, which could stretch into the millions of dollars. "Everybody at the company is really stressed," the producer added. "You just feel it in every interaction, that they were hit worse than anybody."

Austerity was a fact of life for the Chapek-led Disney during the pandemic, but the CEO's way with spreadsheets—and apparent lack of interest in cozying up to talent—wound up miring the company in a scandal that exploded the summer of 2021. Eager to continue to press its Premier Access release strategy, which put films in theaters but at the same time as on Disney+ for a $29.99 upcharge, the company alienated the star of *Black Widow*, Scarlett Johansson. The star sued the company for disregarding her contract, which depended on a full-scale theatrical release. Because Disney favored streaming—and would control a higher percentage of the revenue, compared with theaters—the company had effectively cost her millions of dollars, she argued.

As time passed, the optics for Disney got steadily worse. First, it released a sharp-clawed statement, saying the suit was "especially sad and distressing in its callous disregard for the horrific and prolonged global effects" of COVID-19. It added that the star had been paid $20 million, with more coming from back-end participation. But the rub was that the film's box-office performance ranked among the worst for any Marvel release—an outcome, Johansson's camp insisted, assured by the simultaneous release on streaming. A report in the *Wall Street Journal* indicated that Chapek had been approached by Creative Artists Agency cochair Bryan Lourd weeks before the suit was filed about reaching a settlement with his client and heading off a public debacle. His opening proposal was steep—$80 million for Johansson. Chapek brushed Lourd off and delegated the task of negotiating to two senior execs, neither of whom returned CAA's calls or emails.

Johansson's stand earned her superhero status in the talent community. Elizabeth Olsen, who starred in Marvel's Disney+ series *Wanda-Vision*, said in an interview with *Vanity Fair* that Johansson is "so tough." When she heard about the suit, she added, "I was like, 'Good for you, Scarlett.'" A few weeks after the suit, another Marvel release, *Shang-Chi and the Legend of the Ten Rings*, dominated the Labor Day weekend holiday period, grossing a record $90 million in its first four days in theaters. The film did not travel the *Black Widow* path and stream on Disney+ as a Premier Access title, but had instead been released with a forty-five-day exclusive theatrical window. Chapek, during an earnings call with Wall Street analysts, described the release pattern as an "interesting experiment." Star Simu Liu hit back at Chapek on Instagram, noting the film's Asian cast, director, and story DNA. "We are not an experiment," he pointedly wrote. "We are the underdog; the underestimated." Seldom if ever in his decade and a half atop the company had Bob Iger encountered such public backlash. But Iger had long since been kept at the margins, playing out the final months of his storied tenure in a ceremonial role.

As Chapek continued to make unpopular choices in order to prop up Disney+, he had reshaped the org chart to create internal allies. He installed a longtime loyalist, Kareem Daniel, as chairman of the media and entertainment division, charged with making decisions about where to distribute Disney's films, television shows, and sports programming. Chapek said the change would make the company nimbler in creating the content consumers want, delivering it the way they want it—though one former Disney executive interpreted the corporate shuffle as a defensive move that stripped potential internal rivals of the ability to outshine the boss by delivering healthy operating unit profits. Chapek didn't feel threatened by Daniel, whom he had hired as an intern in 2007 from Stanford University's Graduate School of Business. The two worked together in Disney Consumer Products, and later, Daniel would follow Chapek to the CEO's office as his chief of staff. As a kid growing up on the South Side of Chicago, Daniel would spend hours in the comic book store. "A highlight of my career was being a member of the team that worked on the acquisition of Marvel in 2009 and being able to tell my mom about it and better explain what I did for a living," he said.

Daniel joined Chapek and the rest of Disney's senior management team at a virtual investor day on December 10, 2020, aimed at underscoring the company's commitment to Disney+. The three-plus-hour event was produced on the Disney lot, but the restrictions of COVID-19 enabled it to buff and polish the message to a brilliant shine. Green-screen technology and multiple takes meant even the slightest stumble could be airbrushed out. Only a short question-and-answer segment at the end of the event would be conducted live—and even then, via remote video. So while the concept of the event resembled the investor day held in April 2019 to tout Disney+, the effect of the December 2020 event was that of an end-to-end commercial. It smoothed Chapek's sometimes lumpy and nasal delivery of remarks during quarterly earnings calls. More than anything, it showcased Disney's prodigious production pipeline. The Burbank entertainment colossus announced more than one hundred titles—80 percent of which would debut on the streaming service. Every studio chief seemingly rummaged through the Disney vault to dust off popular films and characters ripe for a reboot in a strategy reminiscent of Chapek's earlier direct-to-video days.

Lucasfilm, fresh off the critical success of *The Mandalorian*, offered an early look at a new series drawn from the expansive *Star Wars* universe, *Obi-Wan Kenobi*, in which actor Ewan McGregor would reprise his role as the Jedi master in a series set a decade after the events of *Revenge of the Sith*. Justin Simien, creator of the critically acclaimed and hugely popular Netflix series *Dear White People*, would craft a series built around the smooth-talking gambler and con man turned Rebel hero Lando Calrissian. Outside of the *Star Wars* galaxy, it announced plans to return to another mythical world created by George Lucas, *Willow*.

Walt Disney Television said it would develop series inspired by such Disney family films as *The Mighty Ducks*, *Turner & Hooch*, and *Swiss Family Robinson*. The film studio, meanwhile, continued its live-action remakes of animated classics, this time promising reinterpretations of *The Little Mermaid* and *Pinocchio*, as well as a *101 Dalmatians* prequel, *Cruella*, exploring the villain's early rebellious years in a *Devil Wears Prada*–esque story set in 1970s punk rock London.

Walt Disney Animation Studios creative chief Jennifer Lee said the studio's next animated feature film, *Raya and the Last Dragon*, about an unlikely gang of sworn enemies who unite in a mission to save the

Kingdom of Kumandra, would debut simultaneously in theaters and on Disney+'s paid Premier Access service. The announcement crystallized Disney's film release strategy as the pandemic stretched into its second year, crippling theatrical exhibition. It would continue to support the struggling movie theater chains, whose box-office proceeds were vital to the financial success of Marvel's expensive, effects-driven superhero spectacles, even as it hedged its bets with a $30 video-on-demand offering that would reliably generate revenue.

Pixar promised to jump-start its billion-dollar *Cars* franchise with a series that follows Lightning McQueen and his best friend, Mater, on a cross-country road trip, and announced plans to tell the definitive origin story of Buzz Lightyear in *To Infinity and Beyond*, in an animated prequel to *Toy Story* coming to theaters in 2022. Marvel talked up its first series drawn from its cinematic universe, *WandaVision*—the buzzy, critically lauded homage to TV sitcoms that would prove to be another successful driver of subscriptions, though not in the same league as *Hamilton*—and the forthcoming *The Falcon and the Winter Soldier*, featuring two recognizable superheroes last seen together in the final moments of *Avengers: Endgame*. They were among nearly two dozen series and films drawn from Marvel's muscular roster of four thousand comic book characters, all seemingly poised to leap from ink to the screen.

Confident that its breadth of content would capture a broader global audience and fuel Disney+, the company revised its forecasts, projecting it would attract 230 million to 260 million total subscribers globally by 2024, compared to the initial estimates of 60 million to 90 million. The strong demand emboldened Disney to bump its price to $7.99 a month in the U.S., up from $6.99, and €8.99 in Europe.

Wall Street expressed its approval, driving Disney's stock to a record high the day after the December 10, 2020, investor presentation. "The sheer size and quality of the content tsunami headed to Disney+ was mind-blowing and frightening to any sub-scale company thinking about competing in the scripted entertainment space," wrote entertainment analyst Michael Nathanson.

Case in point was the Christmas Day premiere of Pixar's *Soul*. Activist investor Daniel Loeb had been pressuring Disney to debut more of its movies on Disney+, following on the summer's success of the digital *Hamilton* premiere. The animated film, Pixar's first to feature a Black protagonist, racked up more streaming minutes than *The Office* and the second-season finale of *The Mandalorian*, according to Nielsen. Only another diverted theatrical blockbuster attracted a larger audience: WarnerMedia's *Wonder Woman 1984*, which premiered on the same day in theaters and on HBO Max. One person on the *Soul* creative team described the result of years of effort as satisfying but also something of a letdown. The film had been chosen to screen at the Cannes Film Festival in May and then the New York Film Festival in September, though both dates had gone by the board due to COVID-19. *Soul* had been designed for the big screen, from its sound mix to its blend of colors. "Pixar was built on a blockbuster model, so it's hard to understand how it will work in streaming," the person said. Disney decided to reroute the film to streaming in part to deliver "AWOKs," demographers' shorthand for "adults without kids." *Soul* was a theatrical release internationally, collecting more than $100 million at the box office, mostly in China.

The idea of merging feature film releases with a streaming service had been pioneered by Netflix, which entered 2021 with its market dominance fully intact. With 203.7 million subscribers around the world—twice as many as it had three years earlier—the company had weathered the influx of new competition, though Disney appeared to be the one rival capable of getting into its head. One measure of satisfaction, specifically in regard to Disney, was that the Shonda Rhimes series *Bridgerton* emerged as Netflix's most successful original show ever. Co-CEO Reed Hastings crowed that a bodice-ripping period piece like *Bridgerton* was unlikely to ever be produced by Disney, though he saluted the company for its "incredible execution" and "super-impressive" push into streaming.

AS THE STAR-CROSSED YEAR 2020 ENTERED its final months, HBO Max remained a laggard, nowhere near the flywheel of John Stankey's imaginings. By the end of September, it had mustered about 8.6 million "activations"—meaning, cable subscribers who understood they were eligible to get the streaming app and had actually signed up to use it. Compared with Disney+ and Netflix, it was an also-ran, and only about one-quarter of HBO subscribers were availing themselves of the new streaming service even though it cost them nothing to activate. This reality was quite apparent to Jason Kilar, whose calm veneer and genial guy-in-a-button-down-shirt-and-sneakers energy belied his hard-charging nature as a boss, someone described by employees as a relentless micromanager who didn't tend to respect boundaries. He would send all-staff emails at all hours, including Saturday nights and Sunday mornings. Lieutenants charged with getting HBO Max aloft quickly fell under the microscope. "We would get calls multiple times a day," recalls one senior executive. "He'd want to know, 'What's the matter, why aren't people downloading it? They should know they can get it for free. Who would turn down the chance for a free app with twice as much stuff as they already get?!'"

WarnerMedia's fortunes finally showed signs of turning around by November 2020. Drawing on his relationships at Amazon, some of which date back to his tenure there as an executive, Kilar spearheaded a breakthrough for HBO Max, forging a distribution deal with Amazon Fire TV. The agreement instantly gave the service access to fifty million households. Through a key set of compromises, it also meant that the app would not be fully controlled by Amazon through its Prime Video Channels platform, where many subscription apps gain wide exposure but also surrender valuable data to the tech giant. Stankey, shortly before the launch of HBO Max, had drawn a firm line on where the app would be within Amazon. HBO Now had derived half of its subscribers from the massive funnel of Channels, but to become a truly self-sufficient direct-to-consumer play, HBO Max would need a different arrangement. After the Amazon announcement, the only missing piece in the distribution puzzle was Roku. Combined, Fire and Roku control nearly three-quarters of U.S. streaming households.

Programming on HBO Max was in a threadbare state due to COVID-19, a handicap that Kilar did not deny. "One thing that I wished we had on May 27, which was not there, was an iconic, service-defining series," he said. Even so, he insisted that such a marquee title was not a "*need*-to-have." The intellectual property the company had arrayed under the HBO Max tent—from DC Comics to Looney Tunes to *Friends*—would ultimately make the service indispensable once the consumer messaging got untangled. Along with programming from linear HBO, which released its latest buzzy drama, *The Undoing*, starring Nicole Kidman and Hugh Grant, in late October, Max would have plenty of what Kilar liked to call "handles on the suitcase" for consumers to grab on to. Andy Forssell, a key Kilar deputy as general manager of direct-to-consumer at WarnerMedia, favored the handles metaphor and noted Disney's overflowing luggage rack as fuel for its meteoric rise.

A particularly Instagram-worthy outfit was added to the programming suitcase on the day after Thanksgiving: *The Flight Attendant*. Starring *The Big Bang Theory*'s Kaley Cuoco in the title role, the show was a zesty, international suspense drama with just enough dollops of naughtiness to activate the binge instinct (Cuoco's character, for one thing, is a bed-hopping alcoholic). Yet its upbeat energy and redemption narrative helped it transcend the R-rated boundaries of most HBO fare. That qualified it as, at long last, HBO Max's first genuine original hit, though, in the fine streaming tradition, viewership numbers remained under wraps. The company said the show boosted engagement with HBO Max by more than 30 percent in its first month, never releasing metrics in absolute terms. By the beginning of December, with the Amazon Fire deal kicking in, activations of HBO Max had risen to 12.6 million.

These were encouraging signs, but Kilar was determined to stay proactive. Just like his rival media executives, he was sobered by the mounting rates of coronavirus infection, which were keeping a tight lid on lucrative business lines, chief among them theatrical film. In 2019, Warner Bros. had taken in $4.4 billion at the global box office, with high-profile releases like *Joker* and *It: Chapter Two* minting hundreds of millions more in release windows beyond theaters. By late summer, virus trends showed some improvement and other parts of society (film festivals, colleges, and the NFL) sought a return to some degree of normalcy. Warner Bros. decided to release the Christopher Nolan–directed action movie *Tenet* in theaters, with safety protocols in place. It had postponed the release three times over the course of the year, squandering the buzz from TV commercials that began airing in the spring. Nolan, a cerebral Brit known for resurrecting the *Batman* franchise for Warner Bros. and for stylish brain candy like *Inception* and *Memento*, insisted on a theatrical release. In an op-ed for the *Washington Post*, Nolan made an impassioned plea for theaters to gain broad public support given the "need for collective human engagement." Tom Cruise offered his testimony in the form of a video posted to social media of his going to see *Tenet* in London, in a mask, properly distanced from other patrons, and applauding the spectacle as the end credits rolled. The caption of Cruise's post said it all: "Big Movie. Big Screen. Loved It."

With multiplexes still closed in New York, Los Angeles, and many other parts of the world, however, the results of *Tenet*'s release proved a crashing disappointment. The film grossed nearly $364 million worldwide, but its costs—exacerbated by the release delays—left it $100 million in the red, according to well-placed sources. After encountering resistance from Warner Bros., Nolan had taken his case for a theatrical release directly to John Stankey, and the CEO assented. Stankey and other AT&T executives publicly marveled at what they deemed to be the film's visual mastery and sought to reassure nervous theater owners that they would continue to book titles on the big screen. But critics were largely unmoved. "The stakes, presumably, couldn't be higher—both onscreen and offscreen," wrote Alissa Wilkinson of Vox in her review, "but after watching the movie, I don't understand why I was meant to care." While he positioned his mission as preserving humanity during a once-a-century pandemic, Nolan's insistence on a theatrical release was in another way just the latest ruinous demand by a myopic Hollywood auteur. Seeing the wreckage of *Tenet*, no other studio dared to attempt a major theatrical release, pushing most of their big titles into the second half of 2021 and beyond. The outlook for movie theaters was remarkably bleak approaching the end-of-year holidays, usually a revenue-rich season when Hollywood used to launch billion-dollar properties like *Harry Potter*, *Avatar*, and *Toy Story* into the world.

Sensing the ongoing pandemic shifts and craving a programming flourish that would give HBO Max an "iconic, service-defining" title, Kilar had been in active discussions with Warner Bros. about its upcoming release slate. Accounts differ as to who initiated the talks—the studio or Kilar and his corporate management team—but the spotlight quickly fell on *Wonder Woman 1984*, a follow-up to the studio's breakout from 2018 that reteamed director Patty Jenkins and star Gal Gadot. In late November, WarnerMedia announced that the $200 million sequel would be released simultaneously in theaters and on HBO Max at no extra charge to subscribers. It would stay on the streaming service for a month and then eventually move into other release windows like digital download and rental. Mainly, it would be a draw for consumers who hadn't been persuaded to check out HBO Max. Kilar characterized the move as a one-off and a response to the realities of COVID-19 and also an effort to serve fans. Many of the devoted, he argued in an internal memo, wouldn't choose between theaters and HBO Max. "Super-fans will do both," he maintained in a blog post on Medium explaining the decision. Many moviegoers, of course, could be enticed with the flat-price idea of subscribing to the streaming service and getting a top-tier film release. Disney had employed the exact same strategy with *Soul*, having seen positive subscription results from *Hamilton* over the summer. Netflix, of course, had spent years weaving major feature films into its streaming mix, so the concept was nothing new. Exhibitors, nevertheless, were nervous. Warner Bros. is nearly a century old, with a long history of upholding Hollywood traditions, including the one about theaters getting to play movies first.

If theater owners were antsy in November, they were outright despondent by December. Just two weeks after the *Wonder Woman* announcement, WarnerMedia took an extreme step with implications that Kilar, for all of his tech-sector acumen, could not fully comprehend (or perhaps was indifferent to). The company announced it would release the entire Warner Bros. movie slate for 2021 on HBO Max at the same time as its theatrical release, an explosive move that was dubbed internally "Project Popcorn." The seventeen films included in the venture—among them new *Matrix*, *Suicide Squad*, and *Space Jam* installments; new versions of *Dune* and *Tom & Jerry*; Lin-Manuel Miranda's musical *In the Heights*; and monster mash-up *Godzilla vs. Kong*—would follow the *Wonder Woman* model.

It is not an exaggeration to say that all hell broke loose after the announcement. Part of the reaction was due to the lack of advance notice. Once the plan had been settled, the decision was made by WarnerMedia not to alert talent or producing partners, for fear of a leak. Studio personnel were tasked with divvying up calls to an array of high-level camps, all of which were dumbfounded and blindsided. "It's a telecommunications company that sells phones and they couldn't find a minute to pick up a phone and call anybody?" remarked one high-powered movie agent incredulously. "They're not approaching this with any thought about the human element of this." Two highly effective vaccines for COVID-19 had just been approved by the Food and Drug Administration. Health officials were predicting that their adoption could allow a full reopening of business and society by spring or summer at the latest. Movie theaters were poised for a triumphant comeback—why foreclose on the celebration with a blanket 2021 decision instead of moving more incrementally, as Disney and other studios had been doing? Moreover, why not involve creative and financial partners in the deliberations, as studios typically do with all elements of a release plan, from poster art to release dates?

One of the harshest denouncements of the move came from a long-time favorite son of Warner Bros., who had become the living symbol of a business turned upside down by streaming: *Tenet* director Christopher

Nolan. "Some of our industry's biggest filmmakers and most important movie stars went to bed the night before thinking they were working for the greatest movie studio and woke up to find out they were working for the worst streaming service," Nolan, whose relationship with the studio began in 2002, told the *Hollywood Reporter*. He added, "Warner Bros. had an incredible machine for getting a filmmaker's work out everywhere, both in theaters and in the home, and they are dismantling it as we speak. They don't even understand what they're losing. Their decision makes no economic sense, and even the most casual Wall Street investor can see the difference between disruption and dysfunction."

At Warner Bros., relations with talent—for generations a point of pride for the studio that nurtured singular artists like Stanley Kubrick and Clint Eastwood—were suddenly in jeopardy. Jason Blum, producer of films like *Get Out*, wasn't directly affected by the shift but he sympathized with those caught up in the situation. "If I had gotten that call, I would have been deeply disappointed, and I would have called my lawyer and said, 'Are they allowed to do this?'" Lawyers indeed were summoned. Legendary Entertainment, which co-financed *Godzilla vs. Kong* and *Dune*, threatened to sue. Studio executives pointed to *Tenet*— ironically, the wipeout that demonstrated the instability of theaters in 2020—as proof that they cared deeply for exhibition. Yet they also insisted the goods were perishable. "You can't sit on this amount of content for this long and not begin to put things into the ecosystem," said Carolyn Blackwood, the studio's chief operating officer. "You just can't do it." She said she understood why talent—and their agents—were provoked. "The reps can ask those questions. They should," she said. "No one's trying to hide the ball here. It's actually good news for them. Because the alternative is, those films don't get monetized at all." Warner Bros. didn't create the pandemic, she hastened to add—"We're trying to make lemonade here."

Eventually, Blackwood would help spearhead settlements between WarnerMedia and 170 profit participants, whose rights to back-end revenue from their films vanished when the decision was made to put them on HBO Max. The settlements assumed that each film was a hit—an impossibility in Hollywood—meaning WarnerMedia was paying out hundreds of millions in compensation, on top of forgoing billions in box office. In all, it was an enormous bet on driving significant subscription growth for HBO Max and finally putting it on the map.

"In hindsight, we should have taken the better part of a month to have over 170 conversations" with stakeholders, Kilar conceded during an appearance at Vox Media's Code Conference in September 2021. "We tried to do that in a compressed period of time—less than a week—because of course there was going to be leaks, there was going to be everybody opining on whether we should do this or not do this. And again, change is hard."

Despite all the friction on the content side of the service, HBO Max was finally seeing a smoother path in terms of distribution. Reaching terms with Amazon gave WarnerMedia leverage with Roku, whose customers were agitating for the streaming gatekeeper to add access to the service. The two companies finally reached a deal in mid-December, in time for the Christmas Day release of *Wonder Woman 1984*. By the start of 2021, with a lineup of major movies coming to HBO Max, the service would be available virtually anywhere streaming apps were distributed.

After all the fireworks over its handling of movie releases and a bumpy start to HBO Max's existence, *Wonder Woman 1984* amounted to a whimper. Critics mostly derided the film—not a novel reaction to comic book fare—and audience reaction was mixed and impossible to fully gauge at a time of isolation. Compared with the customary, enthusiasm-building blitz of big-budget movies over the holidays, with red-carpet premieres and lucrative merchandising tie-ins adding to the marketing cacophony, slipping the movie onto a streaming service was a distinct departure from custom. Data about who exactly watched it would remain almost entirely in a vault. The movie pulled in $16.7 million in theaters, with multiplexes in New York, L.A., and Chicago still closed—just one-sixth of the original *Wonder Woman*'s $103.1 million domestic opening. *Wonder Woman 1984* would eventually peter out with $150 million in global ticket sales, well shy of the first film's $823 million global haul. As to its effect on HBO Max, WarnerMedia parent AT&T reported another quarter-to-quarter doubling of the number of paying HBO subscribers who activated their Max accounts. Combined with conventional pay-TV subscriptions, HBO had a U.S. subscriber base of 41.5 million. Nielsen, which had begun to measure streaming through a TV set (meaning mobile is not counted), said *Wonder Woman 1984* drew 2.25 billion minutes of streaming. Given the film's 151-minute running time, the total meant it was viewed an average of 15 million times. A third *Wonder Woman* movie, Warner Bros. announced the week after Christmas, had been put into development. Andy Forssell characterized the distribution of the film as a gift to families "during these very difficult times."

As the 2021 slate started to roll out in theaters and on HBO Max, John Lee Hancock had to shake his head at the final twist of fate that befell his long-nurtured passion project, a thriller called *The Little Things*. The veteran writer-turned-director of films like *The Blind Side* had written the screenplay for the movie in 1993, watching it travel a common road through development hell. A-list directors like Clint Eastwood and Steven Spielberg were briefly attached, and stars came and went from the project. Finally, with Hancock set in the director's chair, a dream cast was assembled, headed by Oscar winners Denzel Washington, Rami Malek, and Jared Leto.

Hancock, who was acquainted with streaming, having directed *The Highwaymen*, a new spin on *Bonnie and Clyde* released by Netflix, knew the *Little Things* release would likely be affected by COVID-19. "Anybody could see that coming, but what I didn't see coming was no conversation about it," he said in an interview with Deadline's Mike Fleming. "What I didn't see coming was a call twenty minutes before the press release, which was how I found out about it." Hancock had resigned himself to the fact that this passion project conceived of before the internet went mainstream would be defined in new ways during Binge Times. The movie business, like TV and music before it, had been thrown into tumult by technology.

Performance metrics would be "anecdotal," Hancock predicted. "I'll hear about it from certain people and expect to have a sense if people are seeing it, or not seeing it. But I don't know, honestly. I have high hopes that lots of people will sign up for HBO Max to watch this and other movies, so I've got my fingers crossed."

The director wouldn't be the only one in Hollywood to be blindsided by AT&T's secretive culture. Three days after a largely flattering profile appeared in the *Wall Street Journal,* in which Kilar defended his decision to upend century-old business practices to build a successful streaming service, Kilar found himself on the outside looking in on a $43 billion deal to spin off WarnerMedia. Mired in debt and under pressure from an activist investor, AT&T announced it would merge its media group with Discovery, whose veteran CEO, David Zaslav, would lead the combined entity. Kilar, who'd received a stock award valued at nearly $50 million for leading WarnerMedia's streaming initiative, would seemingly have no role. Hollywood brimmed with schadenfreude for an executive known for smiling in your face while depositing a time bomb in your lap. One former Time Warner executive put it succinctly: "He's reviled on the inside."

Stankey was equally unpopular, and certainly investors had a tangible reason to not be a fan of his three-year meander through show business. The misadventure with Time Warner, on top of the ill-timed DirecTV acquisition, had cost shareholders $50 billion, a remarkable albatross around the neck of the CEO. In characteristic style, he intimated that his predecessor, Randall Stephenson, was the real culprit. Stephenson, sixty-one, had set the streaming flywheel in motion before stepping down in 2020 and handing the baton to Stankey. He would instead get back to his roots, and those of AT&T: phones. In an epic "toldja" filleting of the "telephonies" from Dallas, writer Richard Rushfield, known for his gimlet-eyed newsletter The Ankler, asked for "a moment of silence" for Stankey and his fellow AT&T execs. "I predicted a few times that the PowerPoint-driven launch of HBO Max would be studied for decades to come as a historic business fiasco," he wrote. "It turns out that I was thinking too narrowly: The Max launch was just one small piece of the wholesale, top-to-bottom, historic business fiasco of The Telephone People's Hollywood Adventure." Punctuating the ignominious end of AT&T's swing-and-miss in entertainment was the yearlong wait until the deal with Discovery would be approved by regulators. Perfect, the vanishing breed of old Time Warner survivors thought, more uncertainty and angst about a new corporate regime. The combined entity had identified $3 billion in synergies—a far greater tally than the AT&T Time Warner deal, which had resulted in the exit of two thousand employees.

Jeffrey Katzenberg's Quibi, meanwhile, would be reanimated even as WarnerMedia and AT&T were changing gears again. As the short-form streaming service wound down its operations in late 2020, Katzenberg and CEO Meg Whitman found a buyer for its library of original content. Roku acquired the rights to the movies and television shows, whose chapter breaks provided the space for advertising. The content would be rebranded as "Roku Originals" and offered free on the Roku Channel, setting the stage for another Silicon Valley player to begin making its own movies and television shows. Shows like *#FreeRayShawn*, a drama about a Black Iraq War veteran who finds himself in a tense standoff with police, garnered Emmy Awards for its stars Laurence Fishburne and Jasmine Cephas Jones but little broad notice.

The deal, which cost Roku "significantly" less than $100 million, according to company executives, was unusual in that it would essentially mean shows' getting another shot to premiere. That's a rare thing in show business, but the second chance came about because Katzenberg's intense effort to generate heat had so utterly failed. The Roku Channel, where the shows would now live, reaches seventy million U.S. households, about ten times the peak number of Quibi subscribers. Sweta Patel, Roku's vice president of engagement growth marketing, said the fact that the Quibi shows had already been available a year before they would debut on Roku did not crop up as an issue in the company's research. "For the vast majority of people, they have not seen this" programming, she said. "There's a small fraction that's seen it."

CHAPTER 21

▶ Amazon on the March

The Culver Studios' long rows of sculpted boxwood hedges stood in for the grand entrance to Rhett Butler and Scarlett O'Hara's Atlanta "big house" in MGM's 1939 Academy Award–winning film *Gone with the Wind*. Eight decades later, the Colonial-style building that now houses Amazon Studios was set to be reunited with its cinematic heritage through Amazon Prime Video's $8.45 billion acquisition of the century-old studio announced in May 2021.

The deal would net MGM's library of four thousand movies, seventeen thousand television episodes, and a trove of franchises that could be reimagined or serialized. In an increasingly crowded streaming marketplace, MGM's well-known cinematic characters, such as James Bond, the Pink Panther, Rocky, and RoboCop, would help Amazon Prime Video rise above the clutter. Ian Fleming's globe-trotting, Martini-drinking, womanizing British secret agent character was the stuff of male fantasy and provided ample fodder for Hollywood's first bona fide film franchise, anchoring twenty-four films over nearly six decades and generating a global box office of $6.9 billion. It was the obvious prize, even though a rights deal hammered out in the 1950s by film producer Albert "Cubby" Broccoli gave his heirs extensive creative control of on-screen portrayals of 007. The deal signaled that Amazon Prime Video might finally fulfill CEO Jeff Bezos's oft-stated desire for a global smash: "I want my *Game of Thrones*."

For years, Hollywood has been perplexed by Amazon's ambitions to break into the movie business, which seemed to be an odd appendage to its core business peddling books and consumer products. It seemed to be playing by a different set of rules than other streaming services. Amazon offered consumers on-demand access to a library of movies and television shows as a perquisite of their Prime membership, which guaranteed packages would show up in two days without an extra shipping charge. To keep pace with Netflix, Amazon began spending liberally to license the streaming rights to movies and popular television shows, paying a reported $240 million in 2011 to 20th Century Fox to bring such films as *Mrs. Doubtfire* and *Butch Cassidy and the Sundance Kid*, and reruns of such popular TV shows as *24*, *The X-Files*, and *Buffy the Vampire Slayer*, to the service. It amassed some forty thousand titles in its race to match Netflix's streaming offer, though it arrived at the same insight as its rival: Amazon Prime Video would need fresh, original content to differentiate its service.

Roy Price, the executive who launched Amazon Studios, was an early advocate for originals. The idea gained the support of Bezos, who saw an opportunity to disrupt the Hollywood development process. Instead of using the top-down process in which network executives in New York or Los Angeles select a handful of projects to develop as pilots and test before a focus group, Amazon would solicit material from everyone and invite its users to serve as judges to evaluate the pitches. The goal was to create a more efficient system that produced fewer expensive flops. In 2010, it put out the call for screenplays and dangled the lure of hundreds of thousands in prizes for the best scripts.

"You're trying to avoid spending eighty million dollars on something people don't want to watch," Price said. "When you have millions of customers, the theory of it is strong. But there are a couple problems with it—the biggest is that people don't want to read a script or watch a long animatic. They don't want to give detailed notes or troubleshoot like that. They're the audience. They want to be entertained!"

The other problem, of course, is that not everyone is a filmmaker or showrunner. Aside from one children's series, *Gortimer Gibbon's Life on Normal Street*, and one pilot developed for TruTV, the effort was a bust. "Expecting to have quality work bubble up through other sources, you're fishing in the wrong part of the pond," Price said. "There are no fish, or at least the kind of fish you want."

Price began traveling to a more familiar fishing hole, Los Angeles, to recruit a team of development executives. The operation set up shop above a Fuddruckers restaurant in Sherman Oaks, where it shared office space with IMDb, an Amazon unit that maintains a database of films and TV shows. As Netflix debuted its first breakthrough hit, the political drama *House of Cards*, in 2013, Amazon announced its own spin on "pilot season."

Customers could watch fourteen projects that were developed as pilots and posted online. This time, it would court two types of viewers, Price recalled. One was the urban, educated, *New York Times*–reading, HBO-watching "Upper West Side" crowd. For those viewers, it developed shows like *Alpha House*, a political satire from *Doonesbury* creator Garry Trudeau, starring John Goodman as a freshman senator. The second target market was the tech-friendly Comic-Con coterie, with shows like *Betas*, about four tech geeks developing a dating app.

Over time, Amazon Studios began to find its aesthetic with a handful of critically acclaimed series that offered a more sophisticated alternative to network television, with *Mozart in the Jungle*, about a flamboyant yet badly behaved conductor of a fictional New York City symphony, and *Transparent*, in which the Pfefferman family patriarch undergoes a gender transition—a story inspired by the father of showrunner Joey Soloway (previously known as Jill). *Transparent* was a breakout success, and in 2015 it became the first streaming series to win a Golden Globe, for both its star, Jeffrey Tambor, and the series.

In January 2015, while still basking in the glow of the industry's acclaim, Amazon acquired its first original movie, Spike Lee's *Chi-Raq*, about violence on the South Side of Chicago. It was the first of a dozen modestly priced indie movies Price planned to acquire in hopes of grabbing the attention of filmmakers and convincing them to take their projects to a company still thought of as an online bookstore. One film picked up at the Sundance Film Festival, *Manchester by the Sea*, starring Casey Affleck as a man who is forced to return home to care for his sixteen-year-old nephew after the death of his brother, would achieve another milestone for Amazon Prime Video. Released in theaters and on the streaming service in 2016, it won Oscars for Affleck and director Kenneth Lonergan, who was awarded best original screenplay—a first for a streaming service.

As Amazon's head of marketing and distribution from 2015 to 2019, Bob Berney helped build out the film strategy, drawing upon his decades of experience in exhibition, distribution, and marketing. "I was able to push the event status of theatrical," said Berney, an Oklahoma native whose gentle reserve belies a zeal for what he champions onscreen. "It was a new business for them, but they really did let me and my team do the job and try it."

The experience of plying his trade in a tech environment proved helpful to Picturehouse, the distribution label he subsequently ran with his wife, Jeanne, Berney said. But it felt like a constant adjustment to adopt the customer focus that preoccupied everyone at Amazon. "We would do things like post a new trailer for a movie on the website a couple of months before it was coming out. You know, just a routine part of how you normally promote," he recalled. "People would write in the comments, 'Why did you put this here if I can't buy it?!' It really opened my eyes. Everything is totally about the consumer experience."

Bezos, who established Amazon's obsessive focus on customers, also understood the importance of generating old-fashioned word of mouth. He was drafted to participate in the Oscar campaign for *Manchester*, hosting a party at his twelve-thousand-square-foot Spanish-style estate in Beverly Hills. He amiably worked the crowd gathered in his vast tented yard, which included such A-listers as Faye Dunaway, Diane Keaton, Matt Damon, Megan Mullally, and Kate Beckinsale. The billionaire had attended the Golden Globes before, even getting lampooned in Jimmy Fallon's opening monologue, but this event elevated his stature in the industry. One veteran filmmaker recognized the opulent bash for what it was—a sign of the billionaire's gathering Hollywood ambitions. "Bezos is the next incarnation of Lew Wasserman," the filmmaker observed to Deadline columnist Peter Bart, in reference to the legendary media mogul who was considered one of the most powerful figures of his time, with influence far beyond Hollywood.

The Amazon founder became increasingly engaged in seizing the opportunities in film and television, doubling the company's spending on Amazon Prime Video from an estimated $2 billion in 2014 to nearly $4.5 billion by 2017. As the investment grew, so too did the pressure on Price and his team to deliver a mainstream hit. They placed a bold bet on *The Man in the High Castle*, spending $72 million to produce and market a series adapted from Philip K. Dick's provocative novel of the same name. It imagines an alternative history of World War II in which Adolph Hitler drops the atomic bomb on Washington and the Axis powers emerge victorious, partitioning North America into the Greater Nazi Reich in the east and the Japanese Pacific States in the west. The series attracted 8 million viewers in the U.S. in its debut season in 2017 and brought in a mere 1.15 million Prime subscribers worldwide, well short of Bezos's *Game of Thrones* aspirations.

At a confrontational meeting in Seattle described in Brad Stone's book *Amazon Unbound*, a frustrated Bezos berated Price for terrible execution and laid out a list of attributes of great storytelling. The twelve characteristics he brainstormed—including the hero's journey, complex world-building, betrayal, and cliffhangers—would hardly surprise even a novice screenwriter. But they served as a checklist for Price and his team, who would provide Bezos with a spreadsheet detailing how each show ticked the boxes (a practice they kept from their creative partners). This formulaic approach hardly insulated Amazon Prime Video from the misfires that followed, which included the forgettable crime series *Too Old to Die Young* and *The Romanoffs*, a meandering anthology series from *Mad Men*'s creator, Matthew Weiner, which Slate critic Willa Paskin wrote "continuously puts its worst, least-interesting foot forward."

These expensive failures eroded Bezos's support for Price, whom he'd once admired for exemplifying the company's "think big" leadership principles, in Stone's account. An exposé by the *Hollywood Reporter*'s editor-at-large Kim Masters sealed Price's fate. She reported that the Amazon Studios chief had repeatedly propositioned Philip K. Dick's daughter, Isa Hackett, on a taxi ride to an Amazon party following a day of promoting *The Man in the High Castle* at Comic-Con. Hackett rejected his overtures, reminding him she was a lesbian with a wife and children. She reported the 2015 incident to Amazon, which conducted an investigation but took no disciplinary action against Price. The report, published a week after the *New York Times*' revelations of sexual misconduct allegations against powerful producer Harvey Weinstein, hastened Price's departure. (Price has maintained that he has an off-kilter sense of humor and that the whole matter resulted from his misinterpreted attempts to make jokes.)

Disney veteran Albert Cheng stepped in as interim chief operating officer of Amazon Studios until Amazon hired NBC Entertainment president Jennifer Salke as head of the studio. Her résumé more closely fit Bezos's mainstream aspirations for the studio: she was an early champion of the blockbuster family drama *This Is Us* and the critically acclaimed sitcom *The Good Place*, and worked with megaproducer Dick Wolf to expand his popular Chicago-based dramas, *Chicago Fire*, *Chicago Med*, and *Chicago PD*. Under her tenure, Amazon Prime Video would see its greatest success with a string of critically acclaimed hits, including *The Marvelous Mrs. Maisel*, an hour-long comedy about an Upper West Side Jewish divorcée who breaks into stand-up comedy in the 1950s; *Fleabag*, an adaptation of Phoebe Waller-Bridge's award-winning play about a young woman coping with life in London; *Tom Clancy's Jack Ryan*, which follows an up-and-coming CIA analyst on a dangerous assignment; and *The Boys*, a series inspired by Garth Ennis and Darick Robertson's graphic novel of the same name, in which a group of vigilantes sets out to take down superheroes who abuse their superpowers. Ironically, all these projects had been developed by Price's team.

"I knew about some of the shows. I obviously had seen *Transparent*; I also had heard about how great this new show *The Marvelous Mrs. Maisel* was going to be," Salke said, noting that some of these shows had broken through in the cultural conversation. "But there were still just a lot of question marks in the industry: 'Who are these people?' 'How does this business work if it's just a benefit of Prime?' And 'How do you measure success, and what is it?'" Salke set out to build a reputation for Amazon Studios as a talent-friendly place with warehouse-sized ambitions.

MIT-and-Harvard-educated Cheng began to impose the sort of analytic rigor the data-driven Bezos craved. He had left Disney's ABC in 2015 for the opportunity to lay his hands on Amazon's first-party data and explore how such a wealth of direct consumer information could guide content and development decisions. As a retailer focused on serving its customers, Amazon Prime Video could identify distinct audience segments and observe what they watched to determine whether there was enough appealing content to keep them entertained. Until his arrival, the entertainment team had been green-lighting pitches the old-fashioned way: based on gut intuition.

Cheng spent two years rooting around in data to glean insights to guide how much of the studio's entertainment resources to devote to particular projects. As is true at Netflix, analytics wouldn't replace a creative executive's judgment about which pitches and showrunners had the potential to make a hit show. But data science could make predictions about a show's success based on historical performance—information that would help frame financial risk.

Under Salke, Amazon Studios focused on global development,

putting into production series from India, Japan, Britain, Germany, Mexico, and elsewhere to fulfill Bezos's vision of Amazon Prime Video as a glittery customer acquisition tool for the Prime subscription service. In markets like Mexico, Prime Video lit up months before Amazon introduced its two-day package delivery. In Brazil, the entertainment service provided one way for Amazon to differentiate its Prime service from domestic competitors like MercadoLibre and B2W Cia.

"It's not hard to figure out how the value of this content works on Amazon. You're driving Prime subscribers as we expand internationally," said Salke. "People are coming in [to Amazon] through the content."

Even as Amazon filled its basket with local-language originals, Salke capitalized on the COVID-afflicted exhibition world to acquire films that otherwise would have premiered on the big screen, among them *Borat Subsequent Moviefilm*, *Coming 2 America*, and *Tom Clancy's Without Remorse*. Whereas Price's mission in the beginning had been to get existing Prime customers to watch more video, thereby helping win their loyalty, Salke used the marquee appeal of these tentpole films to bring in viewers. *Coming 2 America* topped Nielsen's streaming charts and started a relationship with Eddie Murphy that resulted in a three-picture deal. Live sports, including tennis and soccer across Europe and the NFL in the U.S., helped complete the offering and extended the additional promise of advertising revenue.

Amazon Prime Video further cemented its place in the streaming mainstream with its successful bid to acquire MGM. In its heyday, from the 1920s through the early 1950s, the studio produced an uninterrupted string of Best Picture nominees every year for two straight decades. Its roaring studio mascot, Leo the Lion, reigned as king of the Hollywood jungle, and the company's boast that it had "more stars than there are in heaven" was completely justified.

In recent decades MGM had come to resemble a white elephant, a cast-off seemingly always on the block. Billionaire corporate raider Kirk Kerkorian first snagged a substantial stake in MGM in 1969 by outmaneuvering the Bronfman family, eventually merging it with another legendary studio, United Artists. He sold it all in 1986 to cable television magnate Ted Turner for $1.5 billion and bought back the company a year later, minus the library of 2,200 gems, including *The Wizard of Oz*, for $300 million. Next came Italian financier Giancarlo Parretti, who bought MGM/UA for $1.3 billion in 1990, attracted by the United Artists film library, which includes the James Bond, Rocky, and Pink Panther films, and a handful of recent hits, including *A Fish Called Wanda* and *Rain Man*. Parretti threw himself into the Hollywood lifestyle, buying a $9 million Beverly Hills mansion and a Rolls-Royce, even as he ran the studio into the ground. French bank Crédit Lyonnais, which financed the purchase, effectively took over MGM after he defaulted on his loans, and wound up selling it back to Kerkorian six years later for the same price Parretti had paid.

In his third go-round as the steward of MGM, Kerkorian himself tried building a suite of MGM movie channels overseas, but the plan never reached fruition. He struggled for years to sell the company until 2004, when the Sony-led consortium arrived with $5 billion and the prospect of a geyser of cash from DVD sales. Not long after the acquisition, the home video market peaked and plummeted, leaving MGM without the cash to pay off the debt associated with the leveraged buyout of the studio. Kevin Ulrich, CEO of Anchorage Capital Group, bought up loads of the debt for fifty cents on the dollar and became the studio's largest single owner when it emerged from bankruptcy with a court-determined value of $2 billion.

The hedge fund manager had a Parrettian taste for the Hollywood limelight, at one point hiring a public relations firm to secure party invitations, according to the *Wall Street Journal*. The tuxedoed Ulrich could be seen escorting *Vogue*'s stylish director of fashion initiatives, Alexandra Michler, on the red carpet during the 2018 Academy Awards. At United Talent Agency's after-party at Mastro's, he hobnobbed with such celebrities as Taraji P. Henson, Michael Douglas, Sigourney Weaver, Olivia Wilde, Terry Crews, and John Cho.

But MGM's stakeholders—which included Highland Capital

Partners, Davidson Kempner Capital Management, Solus Alternative
Asset Management, and Owl Creek Asset Management—were growing restless, urging Ulrich to seek an exit. They almost prevailed in
2016, when MGM was close to reaching an $8 billion deal with a
Chinese buyer before a government crackdown scuttled talks. Negotiations over a $6 billion deal with Apple collapsed after the board's
ouster of MGM's CEO Gary Barber, though MGM publicly dismissed
those reports as "rumor." Owl Creek's Jeffrey Altman wrote a letter to
the board in 2018 that pressed again for a deal.

Amazon Prime Video's Mike Hopkins had been quietly waiting for
his opportunity, according to a person familiar with the negotiations.
He'd forged close ties with MGM's executive team during his tenure
as Hulu's CEO, as he worked with studio and former NBC Entertainment president Warren Littlefield to develop the platform-defining hit
The Handmaid's Tale. The Emmy Award–winning series, which found a
compelling way to reimagine a mediocre 1990 film adapted from Mar-
garet Atwood's dystopian novel, illustrated the creative team's ability to
polish gems from MGM's dusty vault of intellectual property. It was no
fluke. Littlefield and MGM had successfully created the hit FX series
Fargo, which was inspired by the Coen brothers' crime drama with its
memorably gruesome murder scene involving a wood chipper.

As Hopkins assumed a new role as president of Sony Pictures Television, he stayed in contact with MGM CEO Gary Barber and, after the
studio's executive was ousted, with its chairman, Ulrich. He expected
that the hedge funder would eventually look to sell the once-troubled
asset he'd opportunistically gained control of through bankruptcy.

Tentative deal talks began just weeks before the pandemic forced
MGM to postpone the March 2020 release of the latest James Bond
film, *No Time to Die*. A blockbuster debut would have strengthened
Ulrich's hand at the bargaining table and perhaps helped him fetch a
lofty price. But he had no interest in disposing of the studio as a distressed asset, so talks cooled. By summertime, with the state of exhibition still uncertain, Ulrich was willing to engage once again—though

the $10 billion price tag he sought was too rich, even for Bezos, according to a source close to the deal. He settled for slightly less.

The MGM purchase changed the narrative around the world's richest man, whose Hollywood dabbling was considered by entertainment industry insiders to be nothing more than a hobby. Some billionaires collect art, observed one—Jeff Bezos collects movies. The MGM acquisition, Amazon's second largest after its $13.7 billion purchase of Whole Foods in 2017, recast Amazon Prime Video as something more substantial. It was a potential pillar of the company's business, as important as its retail marketplace, its web services business, and its Alexa voice assistant. Bezos gave the video efforts unusual prominence in the company's final quarterly financial report during his tenure as CEO, in April 2021. (He would pass the reins to Andy Jassy over the summer while remaining involved in the company as executive chairman.) He revealed that more than 175 million Prime members had streamed shows and movies over the previous year, with overall streaming rising more than 70 percent year over year. "Two of our kids are now ten and fifteen years old," he said, alluding to Prime Video and Amazon Web Services, "and after years of being nurtured, they're growing up fast and coming into their own."

CHAPTER 22

► *Paciencia y Fe*

Lin-Manuel Miranda grabbed the microphone from Robert De Niro and jumped around the stage like an unleashed labradoodle. "Well, what's up, *In the Heights* opening night?!" he joyously shouted. The crowd in the United Palace roared its approval. Moviegoing, one of the oldest rituals in American cultural life, had officially returned after the depths and deprivations of the coronavirus pandemic.

The atmosphere in the theater turned celebratory, even giddy, a mood uncannily matched by the high-spirited film itself. The premiere of *In the Heights* was kicking off the twentieth annual Tribeca Film Festival, the first festival in North America to feature in-person screenings since COVID-19 hit in early 2020. "Before COVID," Tribeca cofounder De Niro said before the lights went down, "the simple act of going out to a movie theater was something that you would take for granted. Now we remember that it's a special event."

Unlike many movie premieres, where those affiliated with the film take bows and then get whisked away without even catching the screening, *In the Heights* was a can't-miss affair. Miranda recalled that before he shot to global fame by creating *Hamilton* (and "before [he] had any money"), he helped fund the restoration of the United Palace, which was built in 1930 as one of five Loew's "Wonder Theatres." The theater takes up a full city block in New York's Washington Heights, the very neighborhood that is the namesake, subject, and shooting location for the film. Miranda still lives there, where he was born and raised. Hundreds of residents lined Upper Broadway on the sultry late-spring evening of the gala, snapping pics with cell phones and taking in the pageantry that almost never came to their own block. On a plaza next to the theater, Warner Bros. had rolled out a yellow carpet and erected a photo-friendly version of the kinds of shops that actually sat just a few hundred feet past the security gates. The simulacrum came complete with an ersatz bodega.

A dozen bursts of applause greeted the film's spectacular dance sequences. Due to COVID safety protocols, only a few hundred fully vaccinated guests were allowed inside the theater, which seats 3,300. They occupied every other row, but their reaction resonated beyond the attendance figures. Streaming was never mentioned in any of the official remarks, but the poster art for the film included the standard pitch—"See it in theaters / also on HBO Max"—in small type. Not even two hours after its world premiere, the film would become available to stream, a stark departure from longtime industry norms. Even though the film's director, Jon M. Chu, was among dozens of other stakeholders who had been compensated by WarnerMedia after it decided to implement Project Popcorn, he still viewed *In the Heights* as a big-screen experience. "ALERT!! Box Office matters," Chu tweeted on the day of the premiere. "Show up. Buy a ticket for a friend, a school, co-workers, total strangers . . . whoever needs to see it. Each ticket is a vote for more movies that showcase the incredible Latina/Latino talent & stories that are still out there. Make it a fact."

The party after the screening, held at an open-air, riverside venue called the Hudson, felt like the Before Times. Hugs, kisses, and handshakes were freely exchanged. Crowds formed packed lines for rum cocktails and platters of Cuban food. Spontaneous salsa dances broke out, including a joyous one featuring Miranda and Olga Merediz, who originated the role of Abuela Claudia onstage and played her in the film.

Jason Kilar, who had announced he planned to continue in the CEO role at WarnerMedia until the close of the Discovery merger, didn't dance, but he came pretty close. Beaming a bright smile, he said the premiere was his fourth time seeing the film. Showing the fanboy zeal he often brought to the job, as well as to social media, he explained the behind-the-scenes technology used to create a dizzying dance sequence that featured the side of a building tilting to create a ballroom. A poignant song sung by Merediz, whose character is caught between life and death but embraces *paciencia y fe* (patience and faith), "never hit [him] as hard as it did tonight," Kilar said.

The exec gave a bear hug to Chu, whose *Crazy Rich Asians* had been a watershed hit for Warner Bros. before Kilar's time, in 2018. A media CEO attending the party who spoke to Chu said he had asked him earlier in the evening what he thought about the film's being on HBO Max. "No comment," the director replied. While the party mood was ebullient, several attendees expressed doubt about the commercial prospects for *In the Heights*. It featured Jimmy Smits, Miranda, Marc Anthony, and other recognizable names in its ensemble cast, but none was a proven box-office draw. All-Latino casts remained a rare sight in the film business. Even though a 2019 study had shown that 24 percent of those who attend movies once a month are Latino, only 4 percent of films released in recent years had a single Latino character among the leads. "People will probably come out for it in New York and L.A., but I do wonder about the rest of the country," one exhibition executive said. Another exec not working at Warner Bros. agreed: "It plays through the roof, but I wonder if people will turn out. It's not *Hamilton*."

As the party continued past midnight, *In the Heights* began streaming on HBO Max. It wasn't the first film to stream "day and date" with its theatrical opening, but the timing of the premiere made the digital availability seem especially abrupt.

As the film hit streaming, its box office fell short of projections. It finished with a wan $11.5 million in its opening weekend, despite rapturous reviews and overall momentum at the box office in prior weeks. It wasn't that COVID-anxious audiences were avoiding theaters—though perhaps eighteen- to twenty-four-year-olds, who tend to be the most avid moviegoers, had returned to the multiplex first. The week's top-grossing film, *A Quiet Place Part II*, brought in $11.7 million to push the film past the $100 million mark, making it the first blockbuster since the pandemic. Disney's *Cruella* rang up $6.7 million in domestic box-office sales, bringing in a total of $56 million—not including the revenue from those who opted to watch the Cruella de Vil origin story at home at a $30 Premier Access premium for Disney+ subscribers. How much had HBO Max sapped from box-office revenue, and was the trade-off worth it? It would be difficult to say, even once the numbers had been tallied. Other day-and-date Warner Bros. releases, such as *Godzilla vs. Kong* and *The Conjuring: The Devil Made Me Do It*, had fared well theatrically even as they also goosed HBO Max subscriber numbers. Warner Bros. had an industry-leading 35 percent market share heading into the release of *In the Heights*. But were those movies resonating like they usually would? Patty Jenkins, director of *Wonder Woman* and its HBO Max–streamed sequel, offered a barbed assessment of the 2021 marketplace in an appearance at industry conference CinemaCon. "All of the films that streaming services are putting out, I'm sorry, they look like fake movies to me," she said, saying the decision to move forward with day-and-date on *Wonder Woman 1984* had been a "very, very, very difficult" one. "I don't hear about them, I don't read about them. It's not working as a model for establishing legendary greatness."

Jenkins wasn't alone. One lingering effect of Project Popcorn was the reputational harm to the studio, even after financial settlements were reached with talent. AT&T and Kilar had taken most of the blame for the poorly communicated message to the creative community, but the ill will lingered. In a rare on-the-record comment to the *Los Angeles Times*, CAA cochairman Bryan Lourd said of Warner Bros. studio chief Toby Emmerich, "There's the Toby that I know that is super artist friendly and built a career on relationships, and then there's the Toby that's had to work for people that made him deliver just the opposite of artist-friendly news." Asked if he thought the studio had repaired the damage to its talent relationships, Lourd offered a blunt reply: "No, I don't."

Among the guests at the *In the Heights* premiere was a longtime executive at Discovery. After twenty-two years at the company, having seen it rise from a straitlaced purveyor of nature documentaries to a global powerhouse known more for snackable reality series like *Flip or Flop* and *90 Day Fiancée*, he expressed an optimism about the merger that bordered on the Pollyannaish. "The IP is in amazing shape—Warner Bros. is just killing it, HBO is killing it," he said. "We just have to fix the corporate culture. People need to know that they can work together. It's really early for that but I think it will be great once we get everybody together."

At the valet, about to climb into a black Escalade, he spotted an executive from WarnerMedia and offered an even more fulsome version of the same pep talk. "It's going to be amazing," he said. "We're not going to be another version of the guys from Dallas. It's going to be great." It was a full-throated repudiation of the Bell Heads, who had believed they understood the film and TV business better than media veterans.

The mere presence of the Discovery exec, part of a concerted effort to speed the merger with WarnerMedia through the regulatory approval merger process, illustrated how unsettled the media landscape had become as streaming mania continued unabated. The big were getting bigger, and another wave of mergers and acquisitions seemed inevitable, following AT&T's acquisition of Time Warner, Disney's grab for most of 21st Century Fox, and Discovery's takeover of Scripps Interactive, all in the span of a few months in 2017 and 2018. The collective value of those mergers was several hundred billion dollars, and they had resulted in tens of thousands of layoffs, a remarkable thinning of the entertainment herd that suggested the media titans were preparing for lean days ahead as streaming eclipsed the old, lucrative world of pay TV.

Viacom and CBS reunited at the end of 2019, after more than a decade apart, and poured their collective entertainment resources into Paramount+, a rebranded and expanded version of CBS All Access that launched in March 2021. Cable stalwart Discovery had launched a direct-to-consumer service, Discovery+, just before embarking on secret merger talks with WarnerMedia. Around the same time, NBCUniversal paid about $1 billion to make stand-alone streaming service WWE Network (home of pro wrestling bouts) a part of Peacock.

NBCUniversal was seen as having much bigger plans. While it had taken a sedate approach to streaming, compared with its peers, its traditional businesses were taking on water. The company, which had gone toe-to-toe with Disney over the Fox assets as well as a controlling stake in Sky, did not immediately come forward with a counteroffer for WarnerMedia, as many industry insiders anticipated. As Comcast set Peacock's international rollout, it decided to form a joint venture with ViacomCBS on a combined offering in Europe, to be dubbed SkyShowtime.

More domestic maneuvering seemed all but assured. Billionaire John Malone, Discovery's chairman, is a wily dealmaker who had once assembled a massive portfolio of cable assets before cashing out in an eye-popping $48 billion sale to—who else?—AT&T in 1999. He also helped mastermind the Discovery-WarnerMedia combination, knowing Comcast CEO Brian Roberts had his eyes on the same prize. "My comment to Brian was that this is the pickle out of the jar," Malone told CNBC. "If the regulatory environment permitted, down the road, all kinds of relationships could be contemplated between this enterprise that we're creating and Brian's enterprise. I think there are many opportunities for this enterprise to work with NBCUniversal to develop successful businesses."

It was possible the new Warner Bros. Discovery would bundle HBO Max and Discovery+, much as Disney had packaged its trio of streaming services. HBO Max had finally launched a cheaper, ad-supported tier, a $10-a-month version with four minutes of commercials per hour airing everywhere on the platform except on HBO's shows. Warner Bros.' day-and-date movies, like *In the Heights*, were reserved for subscribers to the premium, ad-free service. Advertising benefits, which had been vaguely teased by AT&T ever since executives had first proposed buying Time Warner back in 2016, were central to the new vision. Discovery CEO David Zaslav was an ad man to his core and had climbed the industry ladder by selling ads for the Olympics and other events during a lengthy run at NBC. He had never lost his showman's zeal. On the morning the WarnerMedia deal was announced, Zaslav prompted more than a few eye-rolls by praising the Warner brothers by name—Harry, Albert, Sam, and Jack. He spoke of taking an office on the Warner lot and spending more time in L.A., where he had just bought the Bel Air estate once owned by Paramount chief Robert Evans, who nurtured classics like *The Godfather* and *Chinatown*. When the name of the combined entity was formalized as Warner Bros. Discovery, its logo included a starstruck tagline endorsed by Zaslav, "The stuff that dreams are made of," derived from the studio's 1941 release *The Maltese Falcon*. Like many "original" Hollywood creations, the line is actually a paraphrase of one from Shakespeare's *The Tempest*.

Of the five new players in streaming we had tracked the most closely, the most unambiguous winner was Disney. Its $14-a-month streaming bundle, with Hulu, Disney+, and ESPN+, had been a resounding success, as judged by the individual growth of each of its components. While most media rivals lacked comparable assets, Apple was clearly positioning itself as a twenty-first-century aggregator, a digital version of yesteryear's cable company. The tech giant's vast portfolio of services, spanning cloud storage, music, apps, news, video games, and television, was arranged in bundles in 2020. Because of the opacity of the company's accounting, it was hard to untangle the performance of individual services, but Apple said in March 2021 it had amassed a grand total of 660 million subscribers across its portfolio of services.

Apple had looked at MGM but concluded that it didn't need to build a library. Its endgame was different from being able to offer subscribers a new spin on *Legally Blonde*, according to several sources with direct knowledge of its strategy. The Apple TV+ service was merely a leaping-off point to a broader collection of entertainment services accessed through its platform, such as Netflix, Disney+, and Prime Video. Like Amazon or Roku, it was out to enable streaming in a more comprehensive way than just propping up its own subscription service—and, of course, collect a fee as the distributor.

At the *In the Heights* after-party, Evan Shapiro, a former cable and streaming executive who collaborated with Lin-Manuel Miranda on Miranda's *Freestyle Love Supreme* TV show, took a moment to muse about the changing media landscape over Cuban food and cocktails. In recent years, teaching classes for NYU and other universities, Shapiro had maintained what he dubbed the "Media Universe Map." The document, which he billed as a more comprehensive version of one that the website Recode had popularized, showed a range of media, telecom, tech, video game, and other companies, depicted as multicolored planets whose market value dictated their size.

While the map was frequently updated, "almost none of these deals work!" Shapiro marveled. "Of course, the initial reaction to any deal is that the buyer overpaid. But even accounting for that, the vast majority of mergers do not pan out. And yet, it's all people can talk about." Streaming, he agreed, had made the race for more scale more frantic than ever. His alma mater, AMC Networks, a cable programming outfit where he ran IFC and Sundance TV, was bucking the mass-entertainment tide and instead opting for a niche strategy. Its streaming portfolio, with targeted services like Shudder for horror fans and Acorn TV for adherents of British drama, was expected to reach a combined twenty-five million subscribers by 2025. Being a niche player "is a nice place to be, and not by accident," AMC Networks CEO Josh Sapan said a few months before announcing his exit after a twenty-six-year run. The company "did envision a time when there would be a number of very large, worldwide, big-box" streaming services, "and [AMC] would have specialized services." The aim, he added, was to have a portfolio marked by "very deep" subscriber loyalty. Having viewed what the company was offering, they would determine that "all of it spoke to them." Before 2021 was out, Sapan and his number two, Ed Carroll, would depart

AMC after a combined sixty years with the company. The appointment of former Showtime chief Matt Blank as interim CEO fueled speculation that the company was prime to finally cash in its value in a surging mergers-and-acquisitions market.

Consumers were having a difficult time feeling the kind of "very deep" connection Sapan described. As galvanizing as the *In the Heights* premiere may have been, its ebullience felt dampened by the environment of movie theaters as they were convulsed by change. The total of forty thousand movie screens, which swelled in the 1990s and 2000s as Hollywood offered a constant supply of mass spectacle, would undoubtedly shrink. The economics had dramatically changed for both distributors and exhibitors. The very theater chains that had refused to play movies like Netflix's *The Irishman* in 2019, amid a standoff over the length of its exclusive theatrical run, were ready to welcome streaming fare, even with dramatically shorter windows. Netflix and the number three U.S. exhibitor, Cinemark, set a deal for the Zack Snyder zombie action movie *Army of the Dead*, which played exclusively for a week in all 331 Cinemark theaters in the U.S., as well as a few other circuits, before hitting streaming a week later. Apple had placed large bets on films like Martin Scorsese's reteaming with Leonardo DiCaprio and Robert De Niro, *Killers of the Flower Moon*. Warner Bros., Disney, and other studios were splitting their efforts between theatrical and streaming. In 2022, as it stepped away from Project Popcorn, Warner Bros. was planning to have about half of its slate of twenty films go direct to streaming. The other half would enjoy a forty-five-day run in theaters, about half the length of the traditional one. Because most of the performance of streaming is shrouded in mystery, though, Hollywood would have less and less of a sense of what was working. A theatrical misfire like *In the Heights* could be deemed a success depending on how many HBO Max sign-ups it prompted.

Pay TV was another major question mark, but its trajectory would likely decline gradually rather than drop off a cliff, with aging viewers refusing to surrender the remote control. The long, gradual fade recalls that of AOL, perhaps the ultimate example of a customer base's remaining loyal despite dramatic changes in the broader landscape. Even though the onetime kingpin of the dial-up age found itself overtaken by broadband and purveyors of open-internet alternatives to its walled-garden offerings, a loyal base of users never jumped ship. Even as recently as May 2021, there were 1.5 million paying customers of AOL, though they weren't getting dial-up internet for their money, but rather identity-theft protection and technical support.

Bundling has long been predicted as the next evolution of streaming, if only to lift the overwhelming burden of too many choices. Given the dozens of platforms where streaming apps can be accessed and the amount of toggling and searching that is required, the hope is that the billions invested in streaming will create a more satisfying user experience. Netflix in 2021 began phasing in a "Play Something" button to help users paralyzed by the sheer volume of options. Other, newer streaming entrants have appeared with new tools aimed at helping customers find the stuff they want. Struum, a startup run by several former Disney digital executives and backed by former Disney CEO Michael Eisner, offers a package of streaming channels under a ClassPass model. Subscribers pay a fixed monthly fee and receive a number of "credits," which they use to broadly sample TV shows and movies across a collection of entertainment services. CEO Lauren DeVillier said the company was, by design, setting out to be an aggregator. Research shows that some customers like channel surfing, but at least one-third of streaming viewers are looking for programming in their areas of passion. Struum gathers a few dozen services and about forty thousand pieces of programming, presenting them in a searchable package. "It is the access to all of that content, the ability to discover what they're passionate about and the value of that bundle of having right now over sixty services to pick from and to be able to watch the content that you want to watch," DeVillier said.

Billions of dollars into their streaming investments, media players were finding themselves more constrained than ever. In some ways, it was folly to think they could simply green-light a streaming service like it was just the latest theme park attraction or action movie. One Netflix executive said AT&T's entry into streaming didn't seem feasible from the moment the company closed its acquisition of Time Warner. "As soon as we looked at how much debt they had from doing the deal, we knew that they would never really be able to commit to the budgets they would need," the executive said. "The math just didn't work."

Solving equations would not get any easier as legacy assets felt more strain. The traditional pay-TV bundle would continue to unravel. Movie theaters would limp along under government-imposed capacity constraints and lingering consumer fears about returning to a crowded, darkened place with a group of strangers. Perhaps, as Netflix's Ted Sarandos asserts, consumer habits have permanently changed and going to the movies will be an occasional social event—like going to the theater.

As streaming rises in popularity, it's likely these new services will not produce anywhere near the revenue of the old businesses they're sidelining. Consider the fate of the music industry, which was the first to experience digital disruption in the form of piracy, which resulted in a wave of consolidation and layoffs as the industry struggled to survive. The music business has rebounded from its dark nadir in Napster's heyday, with recorded music sales growing for the sixth consecutive year, thanks to the popularity of streaming services like Spotify. But global revenues of $21.6 billion for 2020 are a fraction of the unadjusted $39 billion it collected at its peak in 1999, when consumers still went to record stores to buy CDs. Artists can continue to mint millions, but they do it by running successful tours and social media empires, not by selling records.

"It's definitely the right answer for these legacy media companies to go all in on this—if they have enough scale and if they can convince themselves they can be competitive," said one former media company CEO. "But that doesn't mean that it's more profitable than their businesses used to be."

Streaming would demand a culture shift within traditional U.S.

media companies, requiring executives to focus on building relationships with the consumer, not their business partners (pay-TV companies or theater circuits). And it would require extensive data analysis to determine how best to design a service that would be successful against, say, Charter Spectrum in Tulsa, Oklahoma. "That sort of hand-to-hand stuff, those sorts of tactics, are really hard to imbue in an organization that's essentially a wholesale organization," the executive said.

Across the field of new streaming hopefuls and the incumbents, we witnessed firsthand how difficult it is for legacy companies to leave their past behind. "To me, it was always super clear that everything was going to be streamed," Roku founder and CEO Anthony Wood said, with an offhandedness that was almost unsettling. "The cable bundle was going to break. It was all going to go away. It was just a question of when. And some people also got that. A lot of people in the industry, it surprised me how much they just didn't believe it."

By the summer of 2021, one of the executives who dragged Warner-Media through its wrenching transition found himself suddenly displaced, a virtual tourist on his own backlot. One morning in July, Kilar conducted a VIP tour for a studio executive visiting from Europe. They peeked in on Soundstage 23, which held a massive pirate ship set where director Taika Waititi was shooting the HBO Max original series *Our Flag Means Death*. Kilar laughed when he recalled next popping into the *La La Land* coffee shop where Emma Stone's Mia character underwent a transformation from server to star. "This is a really special business," Kilar gushed. "We get to move the world through story, and that is— God, is that a privilege. Not many people get to do it."

Weeks earlier, Kilar had made comments in the same vein to the *Wall Street Journal*, posing for photos amid the palm trees and sun-splashed soundstages. In one of the more remarkable sandbaggings anyone in Hollywood could recall, the lengthy *WSJ* profile—fully sanctioned by top AT&T brass—published just a day before Kilar got the news that he was soon to be out of a job. AT&T was spinning off WarnerMedia into a merger with Discovery. The maneuver would leave the digital pathbreaker and mastermind of Project Popcorn as little more than a caretaker who would look after the company until the merger closed.

Kilar declined to address his uncertain job status, promising to share his thoughts about the turn of events down the line. But he acknowledged that his penchant for wandering the lot and conducting one-on-one meetings on foot recalled the habits of another disruptor before him: Steve Jobs, forever a deity for any rising tech evangelist. The Apple cofounder would convene meetings while walking the Infinite Loop road that ringed his company's corporate headquarters in Cupertino.

In Silicon Valley, the provocative change agent gets immortalized. In Hollywood, it gets the hook.

▶ Epilogue

The biggest show on television in the fall of 2021 did not air on a broadcast network. It wasn't featured on an emerging digital service like Disney+ or HBO Max. No, the global phenomenon known as *Squid Game*, a dystopian, hyperviolent survival drama from South Korea, could really have been launched by only one company: Netflix. A quarter century after its founding, the streaming leader was still defying skeptics and reasserting itself as the alpha and omega of a field it had created and defined.

Squid Game vividly signaled the future of streaming, which meant that the goalposts would continue to move for Netflix's growing array of rivals. Just days after its release, the series hit number one in ninety countries, transcending language and cultural barriers even more convincingly than predecessors like *Casa de Papel, Dark,* and *Lupin. Squid Game* appeared destined to become the most popular Netflix original title ever, surpassing *Bridgerton,* which the company said had been watched in eighty-two million households in its first month. An investment in subtitling and dubbing movies and series in more than thirty languages (far more than any competitor) enabled Netflix shows to cross-pollinate. In the U.S., where Netflix subscriptions had plateaued, titles like *Squid Game* offered a welcome boost to engagement. Viewing of non-English-language Netflix programming surged 71 percent in the U.S. from 2019 to 2021, according to data the company shared with *Vulture.*

The imperialist Hollywood model of exporting domestic titles was starting to seem hopelessly dated. In 2020, South Korean film *Parasite* (not a Netflix production) set global box-office records and also became the first foreign-language film to win an Oscar for Best Picture. Viewers, it seemed, had begun to seek out genuine stories that also pushed narrative and geographic boundaries. "The platform certainly is global, but the reason why these shows play outside of their territory is the goal is hyper-authenticity," Netflix co-CEO Ted Sarandos said in an interview. "So, the teams that are making a show for us in Germany, their mandate is that it's got to be massively impactful in Germany, because if it isn't, plenty of Germans want to watch *Ozark*. The more authentically German it is, the more authentically human it is."

One of *Squid Game*'s U.S. admirers, Amazon founder and executive chairman Jeff Bezos, was surprisingly gushy, given his hypercompetitive nature. "Reed Hastings and Ted Sarandos and the team at Netflix get it right so often," he raved on Twitter. "Their internationalization strategy isn't easy, and they're making it work. Impressive and inspiring. (And I can't wait to watch the show.)"

His rhapsody likely turned up the heat on the Prime Video executive team, which had yet to launch a comparable success despite prodding from Bezos and a vast war chest. The tweet also prompted a round of dizzy speculation: Was it a signal that Amazon might be looking to do the unthinkable and make a bid for Netflix? With a market value of $1.7 trillion, Amazon is more than five times the size of Netflix, making a purchase of the streaming giant financially possible. "Something's up," producer Franklin Leonard replied to Bezos, who quickly wrote back, "No, just simple admiration."

A merger involving two of the members of the fabled FAANG quintet (as Facebook, Apple, Amazon, Netflix, and Google are known on Wall Street) appeared highly unlikely for a few reasons: Already, Amazon was under considerable regulatory scrutiny for the far smaller acquisition of MGM and for its general business practices given its massive scale. Strategically, Amazon was more focused on endeavors like selling advertising and, outside the realm of entertainment, providing same-day shipping.

Nevertheless, the fact that Bezos set so many tongues wagging emphasized how thoroughly streaming had disrupted the media industry. History suggests that evolution will only accelerate. With wealth being created at a stunning pace (in 2021, Bezos himself was dislodged by Tesla founder Elon Musk as the world's richest person) and recent favorable economic conditions, the next mega-merger could well involve participants previously unimagined.

Just as it had been in 2013, when Netflix redefined the medium of television by dropping *House of Cards*, the challenge rivals faced was not merely a matter of talent relations or taste. It was a question of resources. Apple TV+ had begun looking for global titles, bankrolling its first Korean-language project, *Dr. Brain*, a sci-fi thriller based on a popular webtoon, in 2021. Despite making headway with *Ted Lasso*, however, Apple's streaming motivations were fuzzy. Streaming remained an ingredient in service bundles, no more or less important a commodity on a corporate level than cloud storage, arcade games, music, or fitness offerings. Warner-Media started rolling out HBO Max outside the U.S. in mid-2021, but legacy HBO distribution arrangements would keep it from launching in the UK, Germany, and Italy until 2025. Comcast opted to form a joint streaming venture in Europe with ViacomCBS, using Peacock's tech infrastructure, an acknowledgment of the financial strain of going it alone.

Disney had been the one rival to ever truly unsettle Netflix, at least internally. In its first two years, Disney+ had expanded to more than fifty countries and racked up more than 120 million subscribers. Analysts expect it to surpass Netflix in total subscribers as soon as 2024. The value of those lofty subscriber numbers, though, is likely to remain the subject of debate. Disney runs the traditional playbook expertly, but it is still primarily an exporter. It only began commissioning projects developed outside the U.S. in 2021—though it anticipates a steady increase, with fifty international projects planned by 2024. More than one-third of its subscriber tally came from Disney+ being offered as a cheap add-on for subscribers to Hotstar, the streaming service popular across South Asia. Average revenue per user, a common metric used to evaluate streaming services, hovered at around $4 for Disney+, less than half of Netflix's average, though more scale does enable subscription prices to keep rising.

As Bob Iger prepared to wrap his nearly five-decade-long media career, stepping down in December 2021, Disney's longtime CEO feared the regime of his successor, Bob Chapek, had become too entranced by data. Creative excellence, augmented by digitally harvested insights, would best serve the company's streaming ambitions, Iger told executives and the board of directors, according to the *Hollywood Reporter*. Movies like *Coco*, *Black Panther*, and *Shang-Chi and the Legend of the Ten Rings* would never have broken out as hits had research alone guided decisions, Iger insisted. At Disney and other companies, though, the perpetual-motion machinery of traditional media would be difficult to modulate. One top executive after another had stepped forward to forecast Netflix's downfall, predicting the tech interloper would no longer be able to beat Hollywood at its own game. So far, this prophecy has yet to be fulfilled.

Reed Hastings, for his part, said Netflix is "fired up" by Disney's strong start. "It's going to be great for the world" for the two companies to compete, the co-CEO said during a 2021 earnings interview. Still, he described the company he had cofounded in 1997 as an "insurgent," rebelling against convention. He argued that Disney's key market advantage, its century-old, family-friendly brand, also binds it in a pair of golden handcuffs. Disney controls Hulu and could stock it with edgier fare to goose subscriber growth—the decision to make Hulu the streaming home for FX's adult dramas was supposed to scratch that particular itch—but such a push could be self-defeating. Comcast still owns 33 percent of Hulu and can compel Disney to buy its stake at fair market value as soon as 2024, creating a valid reason not to prioritize Hulu. That helps explain why *Squid Game*, *Bridgerton*, *Too Hot to Handle*, and countless other global smashes are the kind of programming, Hastings predicted with a satisfied grin, "that I don't think you're going to see on Disney anytime soon."

◗ Acknowledgments

This book had a much narrower scope when our proposal for it, fortuitously, landed in the inbox of Daniel Greenberg, our good shepherd at Levine, Greenberg & Rostan. He immediately seized on its potential, and then took our black-and-white 4:3 idea and showed us how it could be rendered in full CinemaScope. We are forever grateful for his vision, guidance, and friendship.

The home Daniel found for the book, William Morrow, turned out to be ideal. Our sage, shrewd, and companionable editor, Mauro DiPreto, retained every bit of his original enthusiasm for the project even as the coronavirus pandemic blew it—and publishing, and civilization—sideways. We benefited at every step from his equanimity and wisdom. *Grazie mille*, Mauro! Our sincere thanks also go to Morrow's Vedika Khanna for keeping the many editorial elements on track, and to Aja Pollock, our sharp-eyed copy editor, whose thoroughness and flair for culture high and not-so-high are an exceedingly rare combination.

Reporting this book was a complex undertaking even before the pandemic. In 2018, our year of collaborating at Deadline, we got to work closely with some of the most impeccably sourced journalists covering Hollywood, most notably the site's co-editors, Mike Fleming and Nellie Andreeva. As Dade continued his Deadline adventure and the book took flight, he received only encouragement and accommodation from Mike, Nellie, publisher Stacie Farish, and many other colleagues. Deadline front-liners Patrick Hipes, Denise Petski, Erik Pedersen, Jill Goldsmith, Peter White, Greg Evans, Dominic Patten, Pete Hammond,

Tom Tapp, Andreas Weisman, and many others have enriched this project (whether they are aware of it or not) and been welcome collaborators, sounding boards, and fellow travelers. Dawn headed off to the land of billionaires, Forbes, where she gained access to some of the most powerful players in media—and received unflagging support from her editors, Randall Lane, Rob LaFranco, Laura Mandaro, Luisa Kroll, and Michael Noer. She also wishes to acknowledge her colleagues, Madeline Berg, Ariel Shapiro, Chloe Sorvino, Kristin Stoller, and others, who offered encouragement and listened patiently to random anecdotes gathered over the course of this reporting project, as well as Forbes's director of research, Sue Radlauer, for her generous help in unearthing hard-to-find contact information and clips.

We appreciate the many people affiliated with the companies we focus on in these pages. Countless individuals assisted us along the way, by making conversation and connections. Among them: Peter Bart, Eric Becker, Nathaniel Brown, Keith Cocozza, Jeff Cusson, Missy Davy, Sheila Feren, Karen Hobson, Erik Hodge, David Jefferson, Jeff Klein, Jim Lanzone, Chris Legentil, Michael Mand, Beth McClinton, Candice McDonough, Jonathan Miller, Christian Muirhead, Seth Oster, Paul Pflug, Mark Robichaux, Matt Sazama, Evan Shapiro, Brandon Shaw, Marie Sheehy, Cory Shields, Richard Siklos, Lisa Stein, Michael Thornton, Brent Weinstein, Alan Wolk, Lauren Zalaznick, and Mel Zukerman.

Last but certainly not least, Dade extends his love to his family. Stella, Margot, and Finley provided boundless encouragement and served as the possibly best longitudinal focus group on streaming ever convened. Emily offered both contemporary analysis and reminiscences about the three-network days, experienced via a wood-paneled TV set on Cobblestone Drive. Carol and Phil Hayes set me on the path, I love you both. And from the first noodlings in Maine many years ago, Alla Broeksmit and her family supported this undertaking in ways large and small.

Dawn also wishes to express her love and gratitude to Dan, Alex, Maddie, and JoAnn. Thank you for your unwavering support over the two-plus-year process of researching and writing this book and for sharing your own insights on the streaming revolution, as viewed from the perspective of three generations. Thanks to my dear friends who listened to long streaming-related monologues while riding, running, lifting, or simply attempting to enjoy a meal. I appreciate your endless encouragement. Thanks, too, to Kim Landon, who prepared me for this journey nearly four decades ago and continues to cheer me on.

▶ Notes

Not much typically escapes from streaming's mythical "black box," the broadly applied term for the vault of analytics at the burgeoning industry's core. Fortunately, in the case of this book, two and a half years of research and reporting yielded a significant degree of insight into the marketplace and the corporations and personalities who shape streaming. Across the country, virtually and in person, in Los Angeles; New York; Silicon Valley; Washington, D.C.; Miami; Denver; and elsewhere, we conducted more than two hundred interviews with current and former executives, technologists, producers, consultants, agents, and many more. We selectively drew from our own pieces for Deadline and *Forbes*, which are cited below along with other source material. Our goal was not to aggregate our old reports, but rather to build a stand-alone narrative. As such, we took pains to draw a clear line between our daily coverage and specific conversations and in-person opportunities intended for this book.

The major players in our drama, by and large, welcomed us in, though it was a constantly evolving and always-sensitive conversation. Disney proved to be a wholly unique situation, becoming a virtually impenetrable fortress for all journalists (and even many of its business partners) once COVID-19 hit in early 2020. With their company hanging in the balance and a new executive at the helm, Disney opted to put on a brave face and keep mum rather than discuss the myriad challenges confronting its businesses. For a time, publicists stopped responding to emails, phone calls, and texts after initially making numerous pledges to connect us with top executives. Apple also denied our repeated requests for conversations with senior management. In the cases of Apple and Disney, as well as the entire field, we gleaned information by attending company events and speaking with creative and business partners as well as a number of long-tenured former executives.

Binge Times draws upon the insightful work of our media peers, including Joe Flint, Ben Mullin, Edmund Lee, Brooks Barnes, Nicole Sperling, Meg James, Ryan Faughnder, Lucas Shaw, Cynthia Littleton, and Josef Adalian. Along with a field of emerging voices too numerous to mention by name, we aggressively covered a story that was developing even as we wrote. A burgeoning conversation on Twitter among a number of consultants, executives, and assorted pundits also stimulated our thoughts. A range of senior entertainment industry executives and connected insiders spoke to us on condition of anonymity so they could speak freely about behind-the-scenes events without fear of alienating their employers or business partners. We agreed to honor those requests.

PREFACE

Netflix chief content officer Ted Sarandos is quoted from a *Vanity Fair* New Establishment Summit interview in 2018; Amazon CEO Jeff Bezos is quoted from the Code Conference in 2016; Steven Friedlander's quote is from his Facebook post.

"By the Waters of Babylon," by Steven Vincent Benét, was first published on July 31, 1937, in the *Saturday Evening Post* as "The Place of the Gods." Manny Farber's "White Elephant Art vs. Termite Art" was published in *Film Culture* 27, Winter 1962–63.

INTRODUCTION: THE RECKONING

Jane Rosenthal and John Stankey were interviewed by the authors. Material from the *Game of Thrones*, *Morning Show*, and *Irishman* premieres is from the authors' firsthand account. The chapter draws from Brendan Klinkenberg, "Apple's Beats 1 Radio Is Censoring Music," BuzzFeed, June 30, 2015, and Maria Elena Fernandez, "*The Morning Show* Was a Challenge Kerry Ehrin Couldn't Resist," *New York*, November 1, 2019. Thierry Frémaux's comments were made in an interview with *Le Film Français*, as reported in Rhonda Richford, "Cannes Artistic Director Explains Netflix Competition Ban," *Hollywood Reporter*, March 23, 2018.

CHAPTER 1: THE DISCOVERY OF TELEVISION AMONG THE BEES

David Blair, Thomas Kessler, Mark Cuban, Rob Glaser, Jonathan Taplin, and Ira Rubenstein were interviewed by the authors. This chapter also draws from material in John Battelle, "WAX or the Discovery of Television Among the Bees," *Wired*, February 2, 1993; John Markoff, "Cult Film Is a First on Internet," *New York Times*, May 24, 1993; Kara Swisher and Evan Ramstad, "Yahoo to Announce Acquisition of Broadcast.com for $5.7 Billion," *Wall Street Journal*, April 1, 1999; "Blockbuster Acquires Movielink," Bloomberg News, August 9, 2007; and John Kisseloff's *The Box: An Oral History of Television, 1929–1961* (Golden, CO: ReAnimus Press, 2013).

In addition to Kisseloff, another excellent resource that informed this chapter is historian Erik Barnouw's *Tube of Plenty: The Evolution of American Television*, 2nd rev. ed. (New York and Oxford: Oxford University Press, 1990).

CHAPTER 2: HOLLYWOOD'S NEW CENTER OF GRAVITY

Marc Randolph, Patty McCord, and Joe Amodei were interviewed by the authors. Arthur Miller is quoted in Jean Stein's oral history *West of Eden: An American Place* (New York: Random House, 2016), which also contains details about Jack Warner's estate. The chapter relies on an article by Scott Markus, "Los Angeles Ghosts—the Spirit of Hollywood's First Sex Symbol Rudolph Valentino" on AmericanGhost Walks.com; Joe Flint, "Netflix's Reed Hastings Deems Remote Work 'a Pure Negative,'" *Wall Street Journal*, September 7, 2020; Brooks Barnes, "'The Town Hall of Hollywood.' Welcome to the Netflix Lobby," *New York Times*, July 14, 2019; Marc Randolph, *That Will Never Work* (New York: Little, Brown and Company, 2019); Dawn Chmielewski, "How Reed Hastings Rewrote the Hollywood Script," *Forbes*, September 7, 2020; Reed Hastings and Erin Meyer, *No Rules Rules: Netflix and the Culture of Reinvention* (New York: Penguin Press, 2020); Stephen Armstrong, "Has TV Gone Too Far?" *Times* (London), January 15, 2017; Vivian Giang, "She Created Netflix's Culture and It Ultimately Got Her Fired," *Fast Company*, February 17, 2016; Shalini Ramachandran and Joe Flint, "At Netflix, Radical Transparency and Blunt Firings Unsettle the Ranks," *Wall Street Journal*, October 25, 2018; Patty McCord, *Powerful: Building a Culture of Freedom and Responsibility* (Silicon Guild, 2017); and Susan Adams, "The Alchemist," *Forbes*, May 27, 2002.

Additional material from Ted Sarandos comes from his appearance on the *SmartLess* podcast, April 5, 2021. Other quotes and background come from a keynote conversation featuring Sarandos during SeriesFest, a TV festival in Denver attended by the authors in June 2019. Some additional Marc Randolph material comes from his presentation at UK public event series 5x15 on October 2, 2019, https://youtu.be/l-2rS0BhukE.

CHAPTER 3: NETFLIX LIVES UP TO ITS NAME

Ted Sarandos, Neil Hunt, Anthony Wood, Chris Albrecht, Cindy Holland, Steve Swasey, and Roy Price were interviewed by the authors. The chapter also derives material from Randolph's *That Will Never Work*; Eliot Van Buskirk, "How the Netflix Prize Was Won," *Wired*, September 22, 2009; Richard Barton's interview by Dawn Chmielewski for "How Netflix's Reed Hastings Rewrote the Hollywood Script"; Austin Carr, "Inside Netflix's Project Griffin: The Forgotten History of Roku Under Reed Hastings," *Fast Company*, January 23, 2013; Brian Stelter, "Netflix to Pay Nearly $1 Billion to Add Films to On-Demand Service," *New York Times*, August 10, 2010; Hastings's comments on Qwikster are drawn from Hastings and Meyer, *No Rules Rules*; Dorothy Pomerantz, "Did Disney Just Save Netflix?," *Forbes*, December 5, 2012; Jim Lanzone interviewed by Dawn Chmielewski for "How Netflix's Reed Hastings Rewrote the Hollywood Script"; Dawn Chmielewski, "Ted Sarandos Upends Hollywood with Netflix Revolution," *Los*

Angeles Times, August 25, 2013; Christina Radish, "Steven Van Zandt Talks 'Lily-hammer,' Netflix's Original Programming, Living and Working in Norway, and What He Hopes Viewers Get from Watching the Show," Collider, December 12, 2013; Reed Hastings keynote at the Consumer Electronics Show, January 6, 2016.

CHAPTER 4: THE RED WEDDING

Accounts of the antitrust trial in Washington are based on the authors' coverage there as well as reports of the Trump administration's motivations for pursuing the lawsuit, among them Jane Mayer's "The Making of the Fox News White House," *New Yorker*, March 4, 2019. Deadline coverage by the authors includes "AT&T–Time Warner Merger Approved," June 12, 2018.

Jonathan Miller and Chris Albrecht were interviewed by the authors. The chapter also draws material from Edmund Lee and John Koblin, "HBO Must Get Bigger and Broader, Says Its New Overseer," *New York Times*, July 8, 2018; Nancy Hass, "And the Award for the Next HBO Goes to . . . ," *GQ*, January 29, 2013; and Jeff Bewkes's interview with Julia Boorstin, CNBC's *Power Lunch*, January 6, 2011. Randall Stephenson's appearance at the Goldman Sachs Communacopia conference in New York was on September 12, 2018. Maclain Way and Chapman Way comments are from their appearance at *Vanity Fair*'s New Establishment Summit, Los Angeles, October 9, 2018.

CHAPTER 5: "THE STATUS QUO, WE KNEW, WAS NOT SUSTAINABLE"

Kevin Mayer, Albert Cheng, Anne Sweeney, Joe Ambeault, Denise Denson, Andy Bird, and Bob Bowman were interviewed by the authors.

The chapter draws from Claudia Eller, Kim Christensen, and Dawn Chmielewski, "Disney Pins Its Digital Future on Pixar Deal," *Los Angeles Times*, January 25, 2006; Bob Iger, *The Ride of a Lifetime* (New York: Random House, 2019); Dawn Chmielewski, "Steve Jobs Brought His Magic to Disney," *Los Angeles Times*, October 6, 2011; Dade Hayes, "The Anatomy of a Comeback," *Globe and Mail*, May 5, 2017; Eliot Van Buskirk, "Cable Departs from Hulu Model with 'TV Everywhere,'" *Wired*, June 26, 2009; and Todd Spangler, "How Critical Is TV Everywhere?" *Multichannel News*, October 17, 2011. Richard Greenfield interview with Phillip Dampier, "Cable's TV Everywhere Online Viewing Loaded Down by Endless Ads That Often Exceed Traditional TV," Stop the Cap!, July 10, 2014; James B. Stewart, *DisneyWar* (New York: Simon & Schuster, 2005).

Iger comments are taken from *The Bill Simmons Podcast*, February 9, 2020, as well as from an interview with David Farber for CNBC's *Squawk on the Street*, April 12, 2019. Iger's address at the National Cable Television Association was quoted in articles including Kenneth Li, "Disney Warns on Restraints to Web Viewing," *Financial Times*, April 2, 2009.

CHAPTER 6: LIVE FROM CUPERTINO

Details of the Apple event are the authors' firsthand account. The chapter also draws upon Dawn Chmielewski, "Apple Brings Out Oprah to Tout Apple TV+ Streaming TV but Leaves Viewers Guessing," *Forbes*, March 25, 2019; Jessica E. Lessin and Amir Efrati, "Apple's TV Push Stalls as Partners Hesitate," Information, July 30, 2014; Jimmy Iovine interview with Ben Sisario, "Jimmy Iovine Knows Music and Tech. Here's Why He's Worried," *New York Times*, December 30, 2019; Tim Cook remarks, Apple Keynote Event, March 25, 2019; Mark Lawson, "Apple TV+: Less a Rival to Netflix, More a Smug Religious Cult," *Guardian*, March 25, 2019; Josef Adalian, "We Learned a Lot About Apple TV+ Today, but Not How Much It'll Cost," *New York*, March 25, 2019; Elahe Izadi, "Bono Is Sorry U2's Album Automatically Showed Up on Your iTunes," *Washington Post*, October 15, 2014.

CHAPTER 7: COOKING UP "QUICK BITES"

Jeffrey Katzenberg interview with Dawn Chmielewski, "Coronavirus Lockdown Will Boost Meg Whitman's and Jeff Katzenberg's New Mobile Streaming Service Quibi," *Forbes*, April 3, 2020; Katzenberg interview with Andrew Wallenstein, "Inside Jeffrey Katzenberg's Plan to Revolutionize Media on Mobile Screens," *Variety*, July 19, 2017; Dawn Chmielewski interview with Meg Whitman, "Coronavirus Lockdown Will Boost Meg Whitman's and Jeff Katzenberg's New Mobile Streaming Service Quibi"; Meg Whitman with Joan O'C. Hamilton, *The Power of Many* (New York: Crown Publishers, 2010), 22; Jason Blum interview with authors, October 16, 2020; Cody Heller interview with authors, July 8, 2020; Tegan Jones, "Dummy Is the Hilariously Filthy and Raw Show We Need Right Now," Gizmodo, April 21, 2020; Jeffrey Katzenberg interview with Bill Snyder, "Jeffrey Katzenberg: How Failure Makes a Better Leader," *Stanford Business*, March 13, 2018; Benjamin Mullin, "Jeffrey Katzenberg and Meg Whitman Struggle with Their Startup—and Each Other," *Wall Street Journal*, June 14, 2020; Jeffrey Katzenberg and Meg Whitman keynote, Consumer Electronics Show, January 8, 2020; Dawn Chmielewski interview with Zach Wechter, "Meg Whitman, Jeffrey Katzenberg Raise $400 Million Second Funding Round as Quibi Prepares to Launch," *Forbes*, January 8, 2020; Van Toffler interview with the authors, March 12, 2020.

CHAPTER 8: THE KID WITH THE CARTOONS

Matt Strauss, Bonnie Hammer, and Steve Burke were interviewed by the authors. The chapter also draws upon Brian Roberts's remarks at Morgan Stanley's Technology, Media & Telecom conference in San Francisco, February 26, 2019; E. B. White, "Around the Corner," *New Yorker*, November 14, 1936; Iger, *Ride of a Lifetime*; Warren Buffett interview with Tim Arango and Bill Carter, "A Little Less

Drama at NBC," *New York Times*, January 26, 2011; Shalini Ramachandran and Keach Hagey, "Two Titans' Rocky Relationship Stands Between Comcast and Fox," *Wall Street Journal*, June 21, 2018.

CHAPTER 9: LONG GAME

John Skipper, Joe and Anthony Russo, Jimmy Pitaro, Scott Rosenberg, and Nick Khan were interviewed by the authors. The chapter also relies on Amanda D. Lotz's *We Now Disrupt This Broadcast* (Cambridge, MA: MIT Press, 2018).

CHAPTER 10: THE BIRTH OF CLOWNCO

Mike Hopkins, Jean-Briac Perrette, Jason Kilar, and Randy Freer were interviewed by the authors. The chapter also draws upon Maureen Kilar, "Enough Is Too Much," *Penn-Franklin News*, January 8, 1979; Chuck Salter, "Can Hulu Save Traditional TV?," *Fast Company*, November 1, 2009; Jason Kilar, "The Future of TV," Hulu.com blog post, February 3, 2011.

CHAPTER 11: THE FLYWHEEL

Chris Spadaccini was interviewed by the authors; Tim Wu, *The Master Switch* (New York: Random House, 2010); John Stankey remarks from the AT&T investor day on November 29, 2018, a transcript of which appears on AT&T's investor relations website, investors.att.com; and the 2018 *Vanity Fair* New Establishment Summit, October 9, 2018.

CHAPTER 12: TOUCHED BY TINKER BELL'S WAND

Kevin Mayer, Randy Freer, and Nick van Dyk were interviewed by the authors. Bob Iger, Ricky Strauss, Michael Paull, and Christine McCarthy remarks made at the Walt Disney Co. investor day, April 11, 2019. The chapter also draws material from Whitman and Hamilton, *Power of Many*, and Erich Schwartzel and Joe Flint, "Can Kevin Mayer Deliver the Future of Disney?," *Wall Street Journal*, November 9, 2019.

CHAPTER 13: "I LOVE THAT SHOW AND I THINK YOU WILL TOO"

Lucian Grainge, Ted Cohen, Richard Plepler, and Lee Eisenberg were interviewed by the authors; Tim Cook is quoted from Apple's September 10, 2019, product launch; Eddy Cue's remarks are from an interview with Stuart McGurk, "Can Apple Hack It in Hollywood? We Talk to the Man Behind Apple TV+," *GQ*, July 1, 2019.

CHAPTER 14: QUIBI VADIS?

Interviews with Jeffrey Katzenberg and Meg Whitman; Dawn Chmielewski, "Coronavirus Lockdown Will Boost Meg Whitman's and Jeff Katzenberg's New

Mobile Streaming Service Quibi"; Jason Blum spoke with the authors and Grace Watkins posted remarks to Twitter. Our account also was informed by Spencer Kornhaber, "Quibi Is a Vast Wasteland," *Atlantic*, April 11, 2020; Kate Knibbs, "Laughing at Quibi Is Way More Fun Than Watching Quibi," *Wired*, July 15, 2020; Benjamin Mullin and Sahil Patel, "Quibi, Jeffrey Katzenberg's On-the-Go Streaming Bet, Adjusts to Life on the Couch," *Wall Street Journal*, May 4, 2020; Nicole Sperling, "Jeffrey Katzenberg Blames Pandemic for Quibi's Rough Start," *New York Times*, May 11, 2020.

CHAPTER 15: "IF YOU WANT TO GRAB PEOPLE'S ATTENTION, YOU HAVE TO TEASE"

Bonnie Hammer and Matt Strauss were interviewed by the authors; Steve Burke remarks are from the January 16, 2020, NBCUniversal Peacock investor presentation.

CHAPTER 16: THE IQ TEST

Details and quotes from the WarnerMedia investor day are from the authors' firsthand account. Kevin Reilly, Bob Greenblatt, and Jeremy Legg were also interviewed by the authors. Sarah Aubrey remarks are from a panel moderated by Dade Hayes at the National Association of Broadcasters Show in Las Vegas in April 2019. Select material also came from Jeff Beer, "HBO Max Is a Branding Disaster, and This Ad Proves It," *Fast Company*, April 28, 2020.

CHAPTER 17: NETFLIX BETS ON ITSELF

Chris Silbermann, Cindy Holland, Andy Yeatman, and Jim Lanzone were interviewed by the authors; Reed Hastings was interviewed by Dawn Chmielewski for "How Netflix's Reed Hastings Rewrote the Hollywood Script"; Ted Sarandos's remarks are from the 2018 *Vanity Fair* New Establishment Summit.

CHAPTER 18: LIFTOFF

Kevin Mayer, Jason Cloth, Bob Greenblatt, Jeremy Legg, Kevin Reilly, and Jason Kilar were interviewed by the authors. Descriptions of the virtual *Love Life* premiere are the authors' firsthand account. Michael Paull comments about preparing for launch are from Julia Alexander, "Overload and Day One Crashing Are Things the Disney+ Team Is Thinking 'Very Much' About," Verge, August 26, 2019; James Poniewozik, "Review: Apple's 'Morning Show'? Wait for the Upgrade," *New York Times*, October 31, 2019; Troy Patterson, "'Dickinson,' from Apple TV+, Is Deeply Weird and Dazzles Gradually," *New Yorker*, October 31, 2019; Hailee Steinfeld remarks are from the Tribeca TV Festival premiere, September 14, 2019, attended by Dade Hayes; Tony Goncalves interview with

Nilay Patel and Julia Alexander, "The Head of HBO Max on Launching Without Roku, Adding 4K HDR, and the Snyder Cut," Verge, June 2, 2020; John Ridley, "Op-Ed: Hey, HBO, 'Gone with the Wind' Romanticizes the Horrors of Slavery. Take It Off Your Platform for Now," *Los Angeles Times*, June 8, 2020; Brooks Barnes, "Disney Is New to Streaming but Its Marketing Is Unmatched," *New York Times*, October 27, 2019.

CHAPTER 19: IN SPACE, NO ONE CAN HEAR YOU STREAM
Cindy Holland, Joe and Anthony Russo, and Bob and Jeanne Berney were interviewed by the authors. The chapter also draws material from Anthony Kaufman, "Netflix Folds Red Envelope, Exits Theatrical Acquisition and Production Biz," IndieWire, July 23, 2008; Dade Hayes, "Scott Stuber and Ron Howard Talk Pay Models, Theatrical, Green Light Process," Deadline, November 9, 2019.

CHAPTER 20: TO EVERYTHING (CHURN, CHURN, CHURN)
Jason Kilar, Jason Blum, and Carolyn Blackwood were interviewed by the authors. Sweta Patel was interviewed by Dade Hayes for "Quibi Shows Returning as Roku Originals on May 20 as Streaming Provider Begins New Programming Chapter," Deadline, May 13, 2021. The chapter also relies on Mike Fleming, "John Lee Hancock on a 30-Year Odyssey Making 'The Little Things' with Denzel Washington, Rami Malek & Jared Leto, and the Abrupt HBO Max Pandemic Pivot," Deadline, December 22, 2020; Dade Hayes, "HBO Max Year One: WarnerMedia Direct-to-Consumer Chief Andy Forssell on Finding Streaming Mojo, Warner Bros Day-and-Date Takeaways, AVOD Plan & More," Deadline, May 3, 2021; John Meyers, "Disney's Bob Iger Resigns from Newsom Task Force as Tensions Mount over Theme Park Closures," *Los Angeles Times*, October 1, 2020; Christopher Palmeri, "Disney's Kareem Daniel Rises from Intern to Streaming Czar," Bloomberg, October 12, 2020; Chapek comments during his appearance at Indiana University on March 3, 2021, were taken from a video of the event on YouTube, "A livestream interview with IU alumnus and Disney CEO Bob Chapek," https://youtu.be/k8kL_kMwmt0.

CHAPTER 21: AMAZON ON THE MARCH
Mike Hopkins, Jenifer Salke, and Roy Price were interviewed by the authors. The chapter also draws upon Dawn Chmielewski and David Jeans, "Why Amazon Is Paying More for MGM Than Disney Did for Star Wars and Marvel," *Forbes*, May 26, 2021; Peter Bart, "Jeff Bezos Is Taking Aim at Hollywood," Deadline, December 9, 2016; and Jeff Bezos comments in Amazon's April 29, 2021, quarterly earnings release.

CHAPTER 22: *PACIENCIA Y FE*
Details of the premiere of *In the Heights* and interviews with the principals are the authors' firsthand accounts and from Dade Hayes, "*In the Heights* Moves the Masses at Tribeca Festival Premiere," Deadline, June 9, 2021. Josh Sapan, Lauren DeVillier, and Jason Kilar were interviewed by the authors.

▶ Index